TAMPERING with ASYLUM

A Universal Humanitarian Problem

Father Frank Brennan SJ AO, a Jesuit priest and lawyer, is the Associate Director of Uniya, the Jesuit Social Justice Centre in Sydney, and an Adjunct Fellow of the Research School of Asian and Pacific Studies at the Australian National University. His books on Aboriginal issues include *The Wik Debate*, *One Land One Nation*, *Sharing the Country*, and *Land Rights Queensland Style*. His books on civil liberties are *Too Much Order with Too Little Law* and *Legislating Liberty*.

He received the Order of Australia (AO) for services to Aboriginal Australians, particularly as an advocate in the areas of law, social justice and reconciliation. In 1996 he and Pat Dobson shared the inaugural ACFOA Human Rights Award. In 1997 he was Rapporteur at the Australian Reconciliation Convention.

In 2002 he returned from 18 months in East Timor where he was the Director of the Jesuit Refugee Service. He was awarded the Humanitarian Overseas Service Medal for his work in East Timor and was a recipient of the Australian Centenary Medal in 2003 for his services to refugees and for human rights work in the Asia Pacific region.

Other books by the author

Too Much Order with Too Little Law
Land Rights Queensland Style
Sharing the Country
One Land, One Nation
Legislating Liberty
The Wik Debate

TAMPER ING
A Universal Humanitarian Problem
with ASYLUM

FRANK BRENNAN

UQP

First published 2003 by University of Queensland Press
Box 6042, St Lucia, Queensland 4067 Australia

www.uqp.uq.edu.au

Typeset by University of Queensland Press
Printed in Australia by McPherson's Printing Group

Distributed in the USA and Canada by
International Specialized Book Services, Inc.,
5824 N.E. Hassalo Street, Portland, Oregon 97213–3640

 Sponsored by the Queensland Office
of Arts and Cultural Development.

Queensland
Government
Arts Queensland

Cataloguing in Publication Data
National Library of Australia

Brennan, Frank, 1954–   .
    Tampering with asylum: a universal humanitarian problem.

    1. Political refugees — Government policy — Australia.
    2. Refugees — Government policy — Moral and ethical
    aspects — Australia 3. Asylum, Right of — Australia.
    4. Detention of persons — Australia. 5. Australia —
    Emigration and immigration — Government policy. I. Title

325.210994

ISBN 0 7022 3416 8

Contents

Preface

In 2001 I was directing the Jesuit Refugee Service in East Timor, which was assisting with the return of tens of thousands of East Timorese from the squalid camps on the Indonesian side of the border. Some of these people were refugees; others were militia leaders and their families; others were still drawing salaries from the Indonesian government, having been civil servants in East Timor prior to 1999; and others were simply timid villagers uncertain about the future in the new East Timor. There was no urgency to have these people leave the camps. There was no immediate requirement that they be classified as refugees or economic migrants. They were simply the latest example of that flow of humanity across national borders whenever there is conflict or disaster. The Indonesians had their own political and economic reasons for tolerating the ongoing presence of these people. Those on the East Timor side of the border who were building the new East Timor wanted those in the camps to know that they were welcome to return and that they would be safe. The only exception was those who perpetrated serious crimes during the bloody conflict of 1999 in the lead-up to the popular consultation at which the East Timorese voted overwhelmingly for independence.

On Monday morning, 27 August 2001, I awoke in Dili to the sound of the BBC World Service News. A Norwegian, Captain Arne Rinnan, was telling the unlikely tale that Australian authorities had asked him to pick up a boatload of persons in distress on the high seas and that the Australian authorities were now denying him permission to land his human cargo in Australia. They were even denying him permission to enter Australian territorial waters. At my regular round of meetings around Dili that day, United Nations workers from every corner of the globe were asking me what my country was up to. Australia had such a fine reputation for its humanitarian intervention in East Timor, driving the pace for UN peacekeeping and making up the shortfall in the interim with the leadership of INTERFET. Here now was the same government, the same nation, refusing humanitarian aid to a boatload of asylum seekers.

Soon after my return to Australia in January 2002, I made my first visit to the Woomera Immigration Reception and Processing Centre, six hours drive from Adelaide, on the outskirts of the small town owned and run by the Defence Department. Afghan asylum seekers had sewn their lips in protest at the government's decision to suspend the processing of their asylum claims, despite their ongoing detention in the middle of the desert, in light of the changing political situation in Afghanistan. From there I went to Canberra. In my wanderings around the corridors of Parliament House I met with Mr Bill Heffernan, a member of the Howard government, who explained the government strategy starkly and simply. Having been a local councillor and being a lifetime farmer, he described to me the moral dilemma that confronts you during a major bushfire. You have to build a firebreak. You have to choose someone's property as the firebreak. In destroying their property, you will save the neighbourhood. 'It's not pretty. These are hard moral decisions. But you have to do it.' The government's boast a year later was that the firebreak seemed to have worked, at least for the moment. The boats had stopped coming. The borders were secure and Australia could choose those refugees to whom it wished to offer places under its generous offshore refugee selection program.

For a year I visited centres such as Woomera, Port Hedland and Baxter every month, each time coming away emotionally drained by the contact with desperate men, women and children behind the razor wire. Every two months I went to Parliament House in Canberra and met with the political architects of this policy, thinking that there must be a better way than rhetorical stand-offs in the media. The politicians were as convinced of their decency in implementing the policy as was I in decrying it. In the wake of the events of 11 September 2001 and the inevitable security concerns about border protection, politicians warned that if there were further changes, they were likely to be even less favourable to people arriving in boats without a visa.

Wrestling with the moral and political difficulties, I have been inspired by the resolute hope in the midst of the despair of the detained asylum seekers. At Woomera for many months I would meet with a group of Palestinians whose refugee claims had been rejected. They were awaiting removal to the Gaza Strip. Not surprisingly, the Australian government was having great difficulty in moving them. In the end, one of the Palestinians, Akram Ouda Mohammad Al Masri, decided to challenge the legality of his detention in the Federal Court. His case was then listed before Justice Merkel. I felt obligated to inform the Palestinians that the judge was Jewish with a fine reputation for upholding human rights. Akram won his case and was released from detention. The next time I returned to Woomera, the three remaining Palestinians decided that they would also like to take a case to court. Their first question to me, with a smile, was, 'Do you think we could get the Jewish judge?' In the middle of the Australian desert, some of the most complex conflicts seem resolvable. There is hope when persons are treated with dignity and respect under the rule of law regardless of the history and the politics.

Unlike some refugee advocates, I am happy publicly to acknowledge the very difficult challenges that confront governments in this field. A person who turns up uninvited on a boat, having transited various countries, and then having destroyed all travel documents and forms of identification, must expect, post–September 11, to be detained until identity and security issues can be resolved. Not everyone who crosses a border uninvited and claiming asylum is a refugee. Many such persons when released into the community do not present themselves for removal when their refugee claim has been rejected. Governments running an orderly migration program are entitled to insist on measures to facilitate their removal.

Unlike many of the government personnel involved in this field, I want to insist on some non-negotiable parameters for dealing with these difficult issues. Even though someone is not proved to be a refugee, there may still be compelling reasons for allowing that person to remain at least temporarily until the troubles in the home country have subsided. Though it may be convenient for a government to keep people in detention for months while their asylum claims are being processed, the deprivation of liberty and the harm, especially to children, is disproportionate to the convenience. Having wrestled with the moral issues for a year, I sympathise with Minister Philip Ruddock and his colleagues who are anxious to keep the borders secure and the country safe. I empathise with the asylum seekers who have spent years in detention in remote desert locations before most of them have then been recognised as refugees. They rightly invoke our protection obligations, having fled the same terror we fear, condemning the terrorist as much as any of us do.

The majority of Australians have supported the government policy. Many others have felt more than a little queasy about the way the government has treated the asylum seekers. Even some of those uneasy about the policy are now content that the crisis has passed, the firebreak is in place, and Australia is now well positioned to run an orderly migration and refugee program with secure borders post–September 11. I am far from convinced that this is the case. This firebreak requires ongoing action and maintenance. It demands ongoing, excessively brutal treatment of those who turn up on our shores without a visa. It is important that the key components of any permanent firebreak are decent, workable and affordable.

No one can be sure that the crisis has passed. The arrival of the *Tampa* was an event waiting 25 years to happen. We Australians have had four waves of boat people since the end of the Vietnam War. The *Tampa* returned to Australian waters putting an end to the fourth wave. There is sure to be another wave when trouble erupts somewhere in the world and fleeing people with the resources and the courage become so desperate that they will risk the perilous journeys without visas, even as far as Australia. When a place like Afghanistan or Iraq erupts, the human dispersal is similar to the effect of a stone being thrown into a pond — asylum seekers, like the water, spread everywhere. Asylum seekers turn up in countries near and far. Some asylum seekers who have spent years living in an adjacent country (like Iran) also take fright and flee further afield. Now there is a lull. It is timely to review what has happened and to put in place a border protection regime which is more sustainable because it works decently and because it is not like a sledge hammer being used to crack a small nut.

There would, of course, be no point in even a Jesuit writing a book that simply moralises with a wringing of the hands, regretting events past and hoping that there is no recurrence, or which moralises with a washing of the hands, hoping the political dilemmas will resolve themselves. Liberal principles, transparency and openness in government, the Australian pride that we comply with best international practice when it comes to the care of refugees, and the Howard government's constant invocation of the 'fair go for all' are still important to us. We can learn from the past mistakes of four waves of boat people and put in place arrangements that protect borders as well as the rights and dignity of asylum seekers. It is time for Australia once again to become a good neighbour and a responsible international citizen pulling its weight and contributing collaboratively to international solutions to these vexed issues rather than going it alone with solutions that other countries could not, would not or should not want to emulate. Australia is in a good position to lead the way with more workable, more compassionate trials because we do receive such a small number of onshore asylum seekers.

Yes, the boats have stopped coming for the moment. No matter what we do, no matter how oppressive we are, one day they will come again. Nothing we do on our high seas or in our Woomeras or on outlying Pacific islands will ever match the enormity of the atrocities committed by the Taliban or Saddam Hussein or whoever is the latest tyrant prepared to terrorise minorities in his own country. Now is the time to secure our borders decently. We must accept that the borders even of an island continent nation can be made impregnable only at too high a price. Everyone pays: the asylum seekers, the hired disrupters offshore, the navy deck hands on the high seas, the detention officers in the desert and on the Pacific islands, and the Australians who want to sing honestly and with conviction, 'We've boundless plains to share'.

There are many long-term refugee advocates and legal and political academics in this field. Their expertise is often sidelined because their positions are so well known and unyielding. I am a visitor to detention centres and an interlocutor with government. I will be well pleased if this book has some appeal both to the refugee advocate who appreciates more readily the government perspective and to the government public servant who gains a more dispassionate insight into the concerns of the refugee advocate. Taking democracy seriously, I will be even more delighted if some members of the public after such a vitriolic public debate have reason to question some of their presuppositions, thereby contributing to a better political resolution of the real complexities of the asylum issue. Living in a democracy, I cherish the hope that I can look the detained Iranian mother and her seven-year-old son in the eye, knowing that we have scrutinised their claim and treated them in a fair and decent manner, all things considered and whatever the result of their claim. I dedicate this book to them and to others who have shared their fate on our shores. For ten years we have wronged them in Australia.

Now is the time to try and get it right not just for Australia but for the international community which respects the sovereignty of the nation state and the rights of the asylum seeker. Except for place and time of birth, any of us could be a refugee, and any of us with initiative could be an asylum seeker knocking at the door of a first-world country uninvited, undocumented and unconvinced that protection was available to us and our family elsewhere en route. The golden rule simply dictates that we design a system which we would consider fair whether we be a first-world taxpayer, a boat person or a refugee languishing in a faraway camp oblivious of any queue, slumped on a pile of humanity trapped between borders.

After the 2002 Christmas fires in the gulag of Australian detention centres, one detainee who offered to assist police with their inquiries was given a guarantee by senior immigration officials in Canberra. He would not have to return to a detention centre. He was moved to a motel for nine days and provided information to the police. The guarantee from Canberra was then withdrawn. He had no legal remedy and no political leverage. I thought the treatment he received was un-Australian. But on reflection, I concluded in the wake of the *Tampa* incident that the treatment was very Australian. Asylum seekers who have arrived in Australia without visas have been used by government as a means to an end. Their detention has been used to transmit a double signal, warning other asylum seekers to take a detour to any other country but ours and luring those voters who appreciate a government prepared to take a tough stand against the one who is 'other'. It is time for the nation once again to respect the dignity and basic rights of those who come to our shores seeking asylum.

Walking through Sydney Airport one day, Walid, one of the Palestinian asylum seekers whom I had known in Woomera, greeted me. At first I did not recognise him. He had been granted a temporary protection visa (TPV). He was wearing new clothes and his bearing was confident and graceful. In Woomera, in the desert dust, detainees do not have or wear good clothes. They are often downcast and despairing. I then met Geoff Clark, Chairman of ATSIC, and asked if he would have time to meet Walid. He greeted him with the words, 'You and I have the same minister.' Philip Ruddock has been Minister for Immigration and Minister for Indigenous Affairs. At that moment, I realised that he was minister for everyone who is 'other' in contemporary Australia. Clark explained to Walid, 'I have told our minister, "I don't mind you making tough laws for boat people *provided* you make them retrospective".' Then pointing at me, he said, 'This is the trouble in this country. This mob, they're all boat people. But now they think they can run the show.' Six months later I received a phone call from an Aboriginal community asking how it might be possible for them to retain the services of an Afghan asylum seeker whose temporary visa was about to expire. If we stopped tampering with asylum and granted protection decently to those on our shores who deserve that protection, we might contribute to a more reconciled society in this land. By extending a welcome to the deserving other, we might all belong.

Frank Brennan SJ
Canberra

Acknowledgments

I thank the many asylum seekers who have shared their stories and their anxieties with me during this last year while they have languished in the Australian detention centres, and those TPV (temporary protection visa) holders who have shown such strength and resilience while they have shared their journeys with me. I mention especially the Brisbane Tiger XI and their manager Camilla Cowley, and the unaccompanied minors in Adelaide whose passion for education and a better life is boundless. I pay tribute to the many volunteer lawyers who kept watch at the Woomera Legal Outpost. I also thank the Jesuit Refugee Service in Australia, the United States, the United Kingdom, Germany and Brussels for their assistance. As ever, I am grateful to the Research School of Social Sciences at the Australian National University and to Fr John Eddy SJ, the Director of the Australian Institute of Jesuit Studies, who assisted with an historical context and a contemporary passion for justice for refugees. I thank the Department of Immigration and Multicultural and Indigenous Affairs (DIMIA) officers who have been cooperative in my visits to detention centres and Canberra, and their predecessor Harold Grant whose insights are exceeded only by his memories. I have been ably assisted by historian Ann-Mari Jordens, my researcher Anna-Louise van Gelder and the staff at Uniya, the Jesuit Social Justice Centre. Rosie Fitzgibbon and Felicity Shea at the University of Queensland Press have gracefully steered the book to publication. I am grateful to Philip Ruddock whose door was always open, though I doubt that we have changed each other's minds to any degree. This highlights the problem and the need for this book.

Acronyms

ADF	Australian Defence Force
AFP	Australian Federal Police
APP	Advance Passenger Processing
APS	Australian Protective Services
BID	Bail for Immigration Detention (UK)
CAT	Convention Against Torture
DED	Deferred enforced departure (US)
DFAT	Department of Foreign Affairs and Trade
DIMIA	Department of Immigration and Multicultural and Indigenous Affairs
ECHR	European Convention for the Protection of Human Rights and Fundamental Freedoms
ECRE	European Council on Refugees and Exiles
ELR	'Exceptional leave to remain' (UK)
ETA	Electronic travel authority
HECS	Higher Education Contribution Scheme
ICCPR	International Covenant on Civil and Political Rights
IDAG	Immigration Detention Advisory Group
INS	Immigration and Naturalization Service (US)
IOM	International Organisation for Migration
IRO	International Refugee Organisation
JAS	Justice for Asylum Seekers

NASS	National Asylum Support Services (UK)
RRT	Refugee Review Tribunal
SAS	Special Air Service
SIEV	Suspected illegal entry vessel
TPS	Temporary protected status (US)
TPV	Temporary protection visa
UNHCR	United Nations High Commissioner for Refugees

Introduction

Since 1788 Australia has been built on migration. At the end of World War II, Arthur Calwell led the Chifley government, the Parliament and the nation into accepting the need for large-scale migration, though under the rubric of a White Australia policy. Happy to receive migrants who might be selected by government on the basis of race and work skills, Australia was wary about opening its doors to uninvited refugees of all races who might be seeking asylum. Australia had not got off to a good start when Europe was first considering the plight of Jewish refugees fleeing Germany back in the 1930s. At a 1938 conference in Switzerland, T. W. White, the Australian delegate, misjudged his present and future audience when he said that it would 'no doubt be appreciated that as we have no racial problem we are not desirous of importing one'.[1]

When the Universal Declaration of Human Rights was being drafted after World War II, Australia was one of the countries that was very testy about recognising any general 'right of asylum' for refugees. Australia conceded that a person had the right to live in their country; they had a right to leave their country; they had a right not to be returned to their country if they were in another country and if they feared persecution on return to their own country. But, Australia believed, people did not have the right to enter another country without invitation, having exercised the right to leave their own country, even if they feared persecution. In 1948 the drafters of the universal declaration proposed that a person have the right to be 'granted asylum'. Australia was one of the strong opponents, being prepared to acknowledge only the individual's right 'to seek and enjoy asylum', because such a right would not include the right to enter another country and it would not create a duty for a country to permit entry by the asylum seeker.

During the preparations for the 1948 discussions, Tasman Heyes, Secretary of the Department of Immigration wrote:

> If it is intended to mean that any person or body of persons who may suffer persecution in a particular country shall have the right to enter another country irrespective of their suitability as settlers in the second country this would not be acceptable to Australia as it would be tantamount to the abandonment of the right which every sovereign state possesses to determine the composition of its own population, and who shall be admitted to its territories.[2]

Australia was on the winning side and was able to live with Article 14 of the Declaration of Human Rights — that 'Everyone has the right to seek and to enjoy in other countries asylum from persecution.' You could ask for asylum. You were not guaranteed a favourable answer, but if you received an invitation to enter, you then had the right to enjoy your asylum. The matter returned to the United Nations' agenda with the drafting of the International Covenant on Civil and Political Rights. The Australian government's 1955 Brief in preparation for the General Assembly pointed out that the Department of Immigration thought 'any limitation of the right to exclude undesirable immigrants or visitors unacceptable'. In 1960 the Russians proposed a general right of asylum. Australia maintained its resistance. No right of asylum was included in the covenant.

With 11 million displaced non-Germans in Europe at the end of the War, the International Refugee Organisation (IRO) had been established in 1946 to facilitate repatriation and resettlement. Australia was a willing participant because it wanted to complement its British migrants with an increasing number of other European migrants. Australia would have preferred to take only British migrants, but the British government was not willing to lose too many skilled workers, given the need to rebuild after the Blitz. Having visited the camps for displaced persons in Germany, Calwell cabled Chifley with the advice that 'this by far most speedy and economical method of securing best type of migrants required for Australia's economic rehabilitation from non-British sources in shortest possible time'.[3] The main problem was organising and paying for the shipping of new migrants. The IRO was already committed to shipping displaced Europeans to South America. The Australians convinced the IRO that they could transport migrants to Australia if Australia were to pay the additional 10 pounds required to carry a person to Australia rather than South America. Calwell signed an agreement to take 12,000 refugees a year. Within two years there would be 19 IRO ships working the Naples–Australia route. Calwell then met with Viscount Addison, the Secretary of State for Dominion Affairs, and pleaded with him for open-ended migration from Britain. He insisted that 'migration had to be taken into the realms of high political endeavour' because there were '1,200 million Asiatics within 24 hours flying time of Australia' and 'the survival of Australia and Great Britain would depend to a large extent upon the success which attended their efforts in securing the maximum number of people available to build up economically and defensively, the Australian Continent'.[4] Calwell always doubted the capacity of European refugees to assimilate. With the imperative to populate or perish, the Australian government in time was happy to accept European refugees who, given their two-year work commitment, were more easily placed than British migrants. These Europeans were accepted primarily as migrant workers who would build the nation, not as refugees in need of protection. From the very beginning, Australian politicians have led the public into welcoming the screened refugee and the invited stranger on the basis that such a welcome was in the national interest. There was no case made for welcoming the unscreened refugee or uninvited stranger. That test would come when the first boatloads of Vietnamese refugees started arriving after the fall of Saigon in 1975.

After World War II, Australia was an attractive destination for European refugees because, unlike the United States, we did not insist on their having a sponsor who would provide housing and a job. Unlike Canada, we allowed the refugees to bring their families, though the men would have to give a guarantee that they would work up to two years away from their families on projects such as the Snowy Mountains Scheme. Within six years, over 170,000 IRO refugees had arrived by boat in Australia under government sponsorship. Another 11,000 had come largely with the assistance of local Jewish agencies.[5] By 1950 the RSL was prepared to endorse the government proposal that displaced Germans also be eligible for migration to Australia.

When the IRO wound up its activities in 1951, it was replaced by two organisations — UNHCR (United Nations High Commissioner for Refugees) and the Provisional Intergovernmental Committee for the Movement of Migrants from Europe which later became ICEM and is now IOM (International Organisation for Migration). The UNHCR acts under the authority of the General Assembly of the United Nations and is charged with providing for the protection of refugees. Countries are free to join IOM if they have 'a demonstrated interest in the principle of free movement of persons' and if they are prepared to make financial contributions to the administration of the organisation. IOM has always been under strong US influence. It is available, at a fee, to provide services to countries wanting assistance with the organised transfer of, or assistance to, migrants or refugees. Australia was a founding member of IOM. The Whitlam government terminated membership in 1973 and the Hawke government renewed membership in 1985. Australia is now a very active Member State and a regular client of IOM, which provides assistance with Australian migration concerns, especially in Indonesia with asylum seekers in transit and in Nauru with asylum seekers awaiting the processing of their claims under the 'Pacific Solution'.

Since World War II more than six million people have come to Australia as new settlers. More than 600,000 of these people have come as refugees or displaced persons in need of humanitarian assistance. A quarter of Australia's 19 million people were born overseas. Less than 2 per cent can claim indigenous heritage. Australia offers permanent residence to about 100,000 new migrants each year. More than 30,000 persons a year permanently depart Australia. The Howard government has rejigged the migration program so that the bigger stream is now the 'Skill' stream (60,700 persons) and the 'Family' stream (43,200) is now the smaller stream. The most negative effect of this rejigging is that recent migrants find it more difficult to sponsor other family members to join them in Australia. The most positive effect is that migration is now more in tune with business. The government claims that the

'Skill' stream adds $500 million a year to the Commonwealth budget, offsetting the cost of other migration initiatives.

In addition to the regular 'non-humanitarian' migration program, the government also runs a humanitarian program that provides up to 12,000 places a year for persons in need. Four thousand places go to refugees who have not yet entered Australia. Most of them are refugees in camps in countries of first asylum and have been referred by the UNHCR. If they are accepted, the government pays their travel costs and the cost of medical examinations. Each year, up to 420 of these 4,000 refugees are women at risk. The other 8,000 places are allocated to persons under the Special Humanitarian Program, which offers permanent residence to persons who have fled their home country having experienced substantial discrimination amounting to a gross violation of human rights. To enter Australia under this program, the person must demonstrate some connection with Australia, and be formally proposed by an Australian permanent resident or organisation responsible for providing accommodation and for financing travel and medical examinations. In recent years, any onshore asylum seeker who successfully applies for protection takes one of the places in the humanitarian program, whether they are given a temporary or a permanent protection visa.

Most asylum seekers come to Australia lawfully by plane. They arrive with a valid visa. At some time during their stay in Australia, they apply for asylum. Most of them remain in the community while their claim is being processed. Even those taken into detention are then eligible for release into the community on a bridging visa, usually on the payment of a bond, provided they are not a risk to the community and provided there is little chance of their absconding. Of those asylum seekers who come to Australia unlawfully, the majority in most years come by plane and they do not cause much upset in the Australian media. Occasionally, a wave of boat people arrives. These people arouse a sense of fear and apprehension in the Australian community. Politicians feel that they must respond to the phenomenon of boat people. There have been four waves: first, the Vietnamese after the end of the Vietnam War; second, the Cambodians and the Chinese from 1989; third, the Vietnamese and the Chinese between 1994 and 1998; and, most recently, the Afghans, the Iraqis and the Iranians in 2000–2001.

With each wave, the spirit of the 1951 Refugees Convention has been further tested and the loopholes exploited by governments attempting to close their borders.

Australia now has a distinctive approach to asylum seekers who seek to reach Australia for protection. The approach includes:

- 'upstream disruption' in Indonesia whereby Australia pays and trains Indonesian authorities to disrupt the activities of persons trying to set sail from Indonesia to Australia
- high-risk brinkmanship between Australian navy personnel and boat people on the high seas
- mandatory detention of persons arriving without a visa
- the detention and processing in the Pacific of asylum seekers who reach Australian territorial waters but who fail to reach the Australian mainland, with no guarantee that those who are refugees will be permitted to reside in Australia
- attempts to limit appeals to the courts
- the granting of a restrictive three-year visa to successful onshore asylum seekers if they arrived without a visa.

This approach needs to be scrutinised against the practices of other countries that are also experimenting with ways of reducing the number of onshore asylum applications. It needs to be seen against the background of the international arrangements put in place for the protection of refugees.

When the Convention Relating to the Status of Refugees was adopted in 1951 and entered into force in 1954, it was common ground among the agreeing parties that refugees would not be forcibly returned to their home country of persecution once they had entered the territory of a nation state. There was no guaranteed right that a refugee could enter the territory of another nation state. It was only once they had managed to enter that the receiving country's international obligations came into play. Since 1951 the world has changed in many ways. International travel is much easier. The Berlin Wall has come down. Many of the conflicts that produce refugees are now internal conflicts that have not previously engaged the interest or the commitment of the international community. People smugglers ply their trade.

Post–September 11, even countries that are generous to refugees are concerned about the protection of their borders.

With computerisation and better communications, it is now possible for countries to set up a comprehensive visa regime so that virtually no one is permitted to enter without a visa and everyone who enters is documented. By identifying countries that are likely to produce refugees and then subjecting their visa applicants to increased scrutiny, first-world countries are able to set up a virtual, offshore border. If someone were to be seeking asylum by lawfully entering a country, that person would have to misrepresent the real purpose of their visit to that country. Obviously no one would be granted a visa to enter a country as a visitor or student if he or she were to state at the time of their application that they wished to seek asylum. Those seeking asylum on shore in a country are now doing so having entered the country unlawfully or having entered the country without making a full disclosure about their real purpose for travel. The only exception is the case of the person who does enter a country for the purpose of visiting friends, studying, touring or doing business but then, in the course of the visit, discovers that there are grounds for seeking asylum because the situation back home has changed.

Though countries that are signatories to the Convention on Refugees do have to process onshore asylum seekers, many of them have refined the techniques in recent years for ensuring that as few as possible of such people reach their shores. Persons coming from 'safe third countries' are deemed to be 'secondary movers' and are returned to the third country from which they came, the argument being that they were assured protection in that country and they have moved on simply to obtain a more beneficial migration outcome. Persons arriving at land borders or airports without adequate documentation are deemed not to have entered the country, and many of them who make asylum claims are then placed in an expedited process for the determination of their claims on the basis that their claim is manifestly unfounded. Persons seeking access by aeroplane encounter government airport liaison officers at key transit ports en route, who inspect their documents and then ensure that they do not board the plane should their documentation be inadequate. If anyone gets through the loops, the airlines are fined; so the airlines have an increased incentive for ensuring that every passenger is authorised to enter the country. Australia has led the field in some of these developments, especially with the comprehensive visa regime. For example, persons working for the United Nations in East Timor were required to have transit visas for travel through Darwin even if they were staying for only a few hours.

In recent years Australian immigration officials have been satisfied that the only unmanageable issue of border entry has been the arrival of unauthorised boat people, who have come in waves and who have instilled media-generated fear in the hearts and minds of Australian voters. Because of the limitations of the 1951 Refugee Convention and because of the ad hoc responses by governments and opposition parties to boat people over the years, it was only a matter of time before the *Tampa* came onto the Australian political horizon. Once it did, Australia decided to break from the pack and be a little bolder in going it alone, trying to find answers to border security in the light of contemporary secondary movement patterns.

Other countries, including Europe and the United States, have also been tampering with asylum, trying to stem the flow of unauthorised arrivals that come by sea, air or overland. Everyone is agreed that it is best to contribute to the resolution or avoidance of conflicts that produce a flow of asylum seekers in the first place. They are also agreed that it is imperative to assist those countries of first asylum which, being adjacent to the countries producing the flows, are usually as poor and as under-resourced as the source countries. The problem is that the country of first asylum is often not much more stable or secure than the source country. Or the country of first asylum is not necessarily spared the presence of some of the warring factions from the source country.

It is no surprise that some asylum seekers look further afield for protection, especially when the conflict has dragged on for years and they are unable to get on with their lives either back home or in the country of first asylum. The fact that an extended family is prepared to contribute their life savings so that a people smuggler can deliver one family member to a country with secure protection might not be evidence of secondary movement and the desire for a migration outcome by an economic migrant. It may well be evidence that the person arriving on the boat is a genuine refugee who had no option but to pay the people smuggler the price for the cheapest destination offering guaranteed protection. Sometimes it is just too neat to describe the further movement as secondary movement in search of a migration outcome. By the time they arrive in a country like Australia, they are identified as queue jumpers seeking to displace the more needy refugees offshore in camps, and as queue jumpers who could never have satisfied the criteria for admission under the regular migration program. They may well be refugees who thought they had no other realistic option for obtaining true protection.

Like many other countries, Australia is committed to:

- protection of its borders and heightened security in the light of September 11
- assisting bona fide refugees who seek protection
- assisting the UNHCR and those countries that are the chief countries of first asylum.

Like many other western governments, the Australian government, no matter which party is in power, is anxious to:

- reduce the number of persons arriving on shore without a visa
- avoid becoming a country of first asylum
- reduce secondary movement and 'forum shopping' by asylum seekers
- maintain control of its migration program
- honour its international obligations at least to the same extent as other similar countries.

Australia is distinctive in the following ways:

- Australia is an island nation continent sharing no land borders, and because of its geographic isolation it is rarely a transit stop for persons en route to another destination.
- Given its geo-political situation, Australia to date has not been surrounded by neighbouring nation states that produce refugees, with the result that most refugees who arrive in Australia are presumed to have had the option of seeking protection at a place closer to their home country.
- Australia has Indonesia, Papua New Guinea and the Pacific island countries as neighbours and a far-distant offshore territory (Christ-

mas Island), thereby having an enhanced capacity for cheque-book solutions shifting its border protection and protection for asylum seekers offshore.

- Australia is a net migration country and so is in a good position to assist the international community with those refugees who are in need of permanent resettlement in a third country.
- Australia is one of ten countries that pledge an annual quota of refugees that it will accept for resettlement, assisting the UNHCR in its planning.
- Australia does not have a bill of rights and so the government and Parliament are more free to encroach on the basic human rights of asylum seekers than those countries that do have a bill of rights, now including the United Kingdom, Canada and the United States. The government can be more certain of being able to exclude their asylum, border and detention decisions from scrutiny by the courts.
- Australian is a federation and so the Commonwealth government has difficulty in delivering services to persons in detention centres in remote places unless they have the agreement and cooperation of the state governments.
- Australia receives a small number of onshore asylum applications each year when compared with countries such as the United Kingdom, the United States, Canada and Germany.
- Until recently there has been strong bipartisan support in the parliament for the mandatory detention of all asylum seekers who arrive without a visa, pending the recognition of their refugee status or their removal from Australia.

Australians are very sensitive to the unauthorised arrival of persons by boat. Each of the four significant waves of boat people since the end of the Vietnam War has prompted new laws and tighter policies about asylum seekers. Many Australians see no need for desperate people to force their way through the back door without an invitation when there is a front door through which the per-capita quota of refugees and humanitarian cases entering each year is greater than in most other countries. Though Australia is one of only ten countries that offer to take an annual quota of refugees from UNHCR for resettlement, there are more than 70 countries that receive refugees each year. Australia ranks 38th in the number of refugees received per capita of population — just behind countries such as Kazakhstan and Syria.

There will be future waves of boat people who will come if there is a situation of gross desperation in their home country and an opportunity to move on from a country of first asylum where there is no guaranteed protection. As we prepare for these waves, it is timely to consider how the Australian system might be rendered more decent and more workable. It is helpful to look at how other equivalent countries have also been tampering with asylum, attempting to isolate their countries from increased flows of asylum seekers.

Australian governments of each political persuasion have continued to claim that the great majority of those who come to Australia by boat are making secondary movements. On the grounds of efficiency and fairness, they then argue that it is proper to treat all boat people as if they are secondary movers, therefore being entitled to place them in detention. The current Immigration Minister, Philip Ruddock, who has been responsible for the immigration portfolio for over a decade, in Opposition and in government, is always careful to argue that detention is not punitive nor is it meant to be a deterrent.

The immorality and inequity in world burden-sharing resulting from our present 'slam the back door' policy is highlighted by a simple thought experiment. Imagine that every country signed the Refugee Convention and then adopted the Australian policy. No refugee would be able to flee from persecution to protection without being placed in detention. If they wanted to avoid long-term detention while their claim was being processed, they would have to remain in their country of persecution and join the mythical queue for a protection visa. If anyone dared to cross a border without a visa while fleeing persecution, they would immediately be held in detention (probably for a year or so) to await a determination of their claim. All refugees in the world would be condemned to remain subject to persecution or to proceed straight to open-ended, judicially unreviewable detention. The purpose of the Refugee Convention would be completely thwarted.

The myopic argument runs that we Australians are entitled to use a sledge hammer to crack this small nut because we are prepared to take 12,000 applicants a year through the front door provided they wait their turn in the queue back in the country of persecution or first asylum. The argument overlooks the fact that 8,000 of the 12,000 successful applicants each year are brought to the head of the queue because they have Australian contacts. If other countries used our sledge hammer tactic, tens of thousands of asylum seekers would wait in detention or in places where there was no adequate protection.

If detention is to remain a cornerstone of Australian border protection and front-door immigration entry, there is a need for alternative arrangements to render the present detention policy more humane and effective. Although Minister Ruddock continually restates that 'detention is not punitive nor meant as a deterrent', this is not necessarily the case. Given the modesty of the problem confronting Australia, we would do well to ensure compliance with the standards set by other countries who receive far more asylum seekers than we ever have.

I ask three simple questions:

- Given that we have the advantage of geographic isolation, why don't we try to be just a little more decent rather than less decent than other countries with the same living standards when it comes to our treatment of those who arrive (with or without a visa) invoking our protection obligations?
- If that is judged too naive, why don't we aim to be just as decent as those who receive ten times more asylum seekers than we do?
- If that is too much to ask (given the fear-driven mandate of the 2001 election and the continued popularity of the government policy), why don't we limit our indecency to our treatment of adults, ensuring that never again are children put in the line of batons and tear gas in the name of border protection, as they were at Woomera during Easter 2002?

It is time to put to a simple test the Australian regime of upstream disruption in Indonesia, the interdiction by our Navy on the high seas, the detention from arrival to acceptance as a refugee, the granting of a temporary protection visa, and the Pacific Solution. Given that there is an ongoing international problem with the reception and processing of asylum seekers, are we handling the matter as decently as others handle it? Or are we using some of our distinctive characteristics to do indecent things that other countries could never contemplate even if they had the capacity? Though we are all living through an era of some

experimentation with asylum practices, Australia has exploited its isolation and minimal onshore asylum problem to devise solutions which,
if adopted by other countries, would set up a gulag of refugee detention
centres in poor countries around the globe. Philip Ruddock once
described the task in familiar terms of doing good and fighting evil:

> The good is extending our compassion and welcome to refugees who have
> no other option. The fight against evil is against the exploitation by people
> smugglers of people desirous of a better life and the resultant abuse and
> distortions of the system that has been set up to support refugees. Only if
> we join together to do both will we restore to the neediest of refugees that
> quintessentially Australian right — the fair go.[6]

This book offers an assessment of the fair go and suggestions as to
how we might more readily and more quickly restore a fair go to the
neediest of refugees, including those who come by boat uninvited to
our shores.

In the next few years the European Union is undertaking a harmonisation of its laws and policies relating to asylum. Some of the European
discussion provides a useful perspective for assessing the contemporary Australian approach. Often refugee advocates will draw comparisons with countries such as Sweden and Canada. These are countries
that have better records in the reception and processing of asylum
seekers. Recent Australian governments and the Australian voting
public have had little interest in keeping company with the countries
of best practice. Given Australia's satisfaction in retiring at least temporarily from being a leader in the field, it is more useful to draw comparisons with those western countries that have greater problems to
confront than Australia but which have maintained a greater commitment to due process and liberty for asylum seekers. This book offers an
assessment and proposes reforms of Australian practices, following
the path of asylum seekers from upstream disruption in Indonesia to
detention in the Pacific or in the Australian desert and through to temporary protection in Australia. The most useful comparisons are with
the United Kingdom, Germany and the United States, because these
three countries receive the largest number of individual asylum applications of all countries in the world. In 2001 they received 92,000,
88,300 and 83,200 applications respectively. Australia received
12,400 applications.[7] In 2001 the main countries producing asylum

applicants fleeing to the industrialised world were Afghanistan and Iraq, as reflected in the nationalities most represented in Australian detention centres at this time. In so far as we continue to fall short of the measures adopted by the United Kingdom, Germany and the United States, we are failing to pull our weight in the world and we are failing to give all comers a fair go. Trailing behind countries like Canada and Sweden, Australia is not a country of best practice. At all costs we must avoid any Australian practices that will further undermine the rights and dignity of asylum seekers worldwide, especially when practices such as mandatory detention of unvisaed asylum seekers are engaged in without any proven benefit to the nation.

CHAPTER 1

The 1951 Convention on Refugees and the moral complexities of today

The 1951 Convention Relating to the Status of Refugees is the main legal document that sets down how nation states are to protect refugees. It was drafted with one eye on Europe's refugee crises at the end of World War II. The other eye was on the risk of mass population flows from the third world to the first world. Australia participated in the drafting of the Convention and was a signatory when the Convention entered into force on 22 April 1954. The Convention defined a refugee as a person who:

> owing to well-founded fear of being persecuted for reasons of race, religion, nationality, membership of a particular social group or political opinion, is outside the country of his nationality and is unable or, owing to such fear, is unwilling to avail himself of the protection of that country; or who, not having a nationality and being outside the country of his former habitual residence as a result of such events, is unable or, owing to such fear, is unwilling to return to it.[1]

The primary obligation of contracting states to the Convention is not to 'expel or return (*refouler*) a refugee in any manner whatsoever to the frontiers of territories where his life or freedom would be threatened on account of his race, religion, nationality, membership of a particular social group or political opinion'.[2] The Convention envisages that many refugees in flight will have to enter another country seeking protection without having complied with the migration laws of the country where they are seeking asylum. It prohibits the contracting states from imposing penalties 'on account of their illegal entry or presence, on refugees who, coming directly from a territory where their life or freedom was threatened, enter or are present in their territory without authorisation, provided they present themselves without delay to the authorities and show good cause for their illegal entry or presence'.[3]

International travel in 1954 was not what it is today. Australia happily participated in the formulation of the Convention, maintaining its White Australia policy, presuming that there would never be a need to admit non-white refugees to Australian shores, and initially stating reservations that ensured that refugees would not take Australian jobs.[4] Prior to 1973, Australia was committed only to recognising refugees made such by events in Europe before 1951. There had never been an influx of refugees arriving in Australia uninvited. In 1956 the Federal Cabinet, in preparation for the Melbourne Olympics, for the first time considered the prospect of non-Europeans in Australia claiming asylum. Cabinet decided on a softly, softly approach. Any Asian refugees would not be granted permanent residence but they would be given 'certificates of exemption, renewable if and when necessary'. When the Dutch relinquished West Papua to Indonesia in 1963, Australia for the first time confronted the reality of a land border with territory that could produce a steady refugee flow. Sir Garfield Barwick, Minister for Foreign Affairs, told parliament, 'If any requests are received under the heading of political asylum, they will be entertained and decided on their political merits from a very high humanitarian point of view in accordance with traditional British principles.'[5] He told his departmental officers that they 'should not be too infected with the British notion of being a home for the oppressed'.[6] Six months later Barwick had to call in the Indonesian Ambassador and let him know that there were just too many Papuans presenting themselves at the border of Australia's colony and trust territory complaining of ill-treatment by Indonesian officials. Barwick's policy was to return them to Indonesia, but he warned:

If the numbers and circumstances of the people seeking political asylum evoked humanitarian considerations, public opinion in Australia would react sharply and the Australian government could not take a rigid or seemingly harsh line. It was therefore important that the apprehension of the West Papuans should not be aroused.[7]

In 1967 the international community added a protocol to the Convention broadening its application beyond the European post-war situation. Australia agreed at this time to recognise refugees beyond Europe. Australia was still not minded to sign the protocol, which contained no limit on time or place for the situations producing refugees, 'because she was unhappy about allowing to stay within her borders, as the Protocol might well have required her to do, any number of Papuans or West Irianese who might take small boats from the southern coast of Papua to the Torres Strait Islands and claim they were refugees seeking asylum; as, indeed, a few West Irianese did some years later'.[8] The Whitlam government acceded to the protocol in 1973 but with the rider that 'The Government of Australia will not extend the provisions of the Protocol to Papua/New Guinea'. From the beginning we Australians were adamant that we would not have the international community pressuring us in the unlikely event that there was ever to be a significant influx of boat people coming uninvited from our nearest neighbouring country seeking asylum. In our isolation, we could never contemplate ourselves being a country of first asylum. The seeds of the *Tampa* crisis (see Chapter 2) are readily discernible in the initial compromises made by the international community in the negotiation of the Convention on Refugees finalised in 1951. The loopholes in the Convention were sure to cause problems even for an isolated country such as Australia.

It was not until 1980 that there was any reference in Australian legislation to the Convention on Refugees and its key terms. The granting of refugee status was never seen to be a matter for the courts. A government minister, being advised by his or her public servants, would decide to grant a person a right of residence in Australia because they were accepted as a refugee. There were very few onshore applications for permanent residence or continued temporary residence on the basis that the person was a refugee. Australia accepted many refugees from overseas but they were not given any special migration status.

When the first wave of boat people arrived after the Vietnam War, their future status was a matter in the hands of the politicians, spared from any scrutiny by the courts and without any comprehensive legislative scheme setting out procedures for their reception and assessment. There were no precedents and the policy about boat people would be made on the run as each wave arrived. As Nancy Viviani said, 'The story of Australia's policy towards the entry of Indochinese has elements of both pride and shame, of fair treatment alongside bias and arbitrary dealing with the lives of families and individuals, of bureaucratic ineptitude and probity and of ministerial stupidity and inspiration.'9 All these elements have been at play in the Australian parliament and in the Australian community as we have come to terms with four waves of boat people whose presence has evoked fear, loathing, welcome and anticipation in the Australian community. With each wave, the law and policy have become more restrictive.

Politics, like life, is full of competing needs and conflicting principles. When an uninvited asylum seeker from a poor, unstable country turns up on the border of a rich democratic country that respects the rule of law, people of good will vehemently disagree about how best to strike the balance in treating the asylum seeker. When asylum seekers from as far away as Afghanistan and Iraq started arriving on the Australian shores by boat, most Australians endorsed the government's tough response in 2001. The government was very clear in its policy and practice:

- giving a preference to refugees who came through the front door having been invited and with visas in hand
- deterring boat people from coming
- detaining those who successfully ran the gauntlet, and limiting access to the courts for review of their refugee decisions
- restricting the uninvited refugee's right to remain permanently in the country
- removing future boat people to Pacific countries for processing and detention, with no guarantee that they would be permitted to reside in Australia even if family members were already living lawfully in Australia.

A vocal minority of citizens thought the government's response was mean-spirited and unfair. The government and its supporters thought the response was generous, measured and realistic, especially in the light of the events of 11 September 2001.

During the last ten years there has been a common pattern in government responses to asylum seekers in Australia, regardless of which party was in power. In that time, every Minister for Immigration whether from the Left of the Labor Party or from the centre of the Liberal Party has caused controversy and upset with every major legislative change he has made. Surveying the situation in other first-world countries such as the United States, the United Kingdom and Germany, and studying the present European exercise to harmonise asylum law and policy, the reader can appreciate that a plaintive recitation of the UN conventions and human rights instruments does not actually get us far in resolving the modern problems and predicaments — though everyone gives notional assent to all of them.

In Australia the boats have stopped coming for the time being. This is a public moment for everyone to step back from the policy-making on the run and from the vitriolic exchanges on the airwaves. We must assess whether our tampering with asylum in these last two years has been a guide or a distraction to a more decent and more workable asylum policy for first-world countries whose citizens are anxious about their own security post–September 11 and whose borders are more assailable given the services of people smugglers. One of the good things about living in a stable democracy is that we are able with our fellow citizens to provide assistance to some other human beings who are in situations of heart-wrenching need. One of the things about being human is that the person on our doorstep (even if uninvited) evokes the desire to be of assistance more than does the person on the other side of the world. The person on the other side of the world may be in even greater need. With international cooperation and a targeted commitment of resources, it may be possible to render more assistance to one or other, or to both. The moral calculus is difficult.

For those turning up uninvited, no country has yet found the right balance between detention for removal and liberty for processing of claims, nor between judicial supervision of the decision-making process and unfettered executive action that is quick, fair and efficient. No country has yet found a way to discriminate fairly between two types of people who arrive uninvited at the border:

- the asylum seeker who had no option but to engage a people smuggler, transiting through various countries to find the first available place where the family might feel secure, find protection, and be guaranteed that they will not be sent back home to face persecution;
- the asylum seeker who had protection available to self and family in a country closer to home, but who cleverly took the opportunity of flight from persecution to look further afield and seek a migration outcome in a country where life would be much better for the family.

Understandably governments want to clamp down on the so-called secondary movement of the second type of asylum seeker. Refugee advocates do not want that clamp-down to result in punitive action against the first type of asylum seeker.

The political compromises forged at the time of the 1951 Refugee Convention and the moral certainties in refugee discourse before the end of the Cold War and before September 11 no longer provide the answers. In Australia, there have been ten years of mistrust between governments of each political persuasion and refugee advocates. Courts have often been caught in the middle of the crossfire. This could be a good time for some positive, internationally cooperative reconstruction of the asylum system. It could also be a time when hard-fought gains protecting the rights and dignity of asylum seekers are lost in the name of national security and border protection.

The moral basis for the nation state is its capacity to provide the conditions for the citizen to enjoy those things necessary for a good life. The state is able efficiently to protect the dignity and freedom of the citizen. The state can uphold the human rights of the citizen and others in the state's territory. It can guarantee the law-abiding citizen a place of belonging. The citizens of a democratic nation state with laws respecting the human rights of all its citizens are not likely to see any case for other states or citizens of other states interfering in their domestic affairs. They are entitled to insist upon their sovereignty. Non-interference will be guaranteed in international relations only to the extent that there is reciprocity of respect, even for those nation states which are not democratic or which do not give full recognition to the human rights of their citizens. Interference in the affairs of another state in the name of protecting the human rights of abused citizens will be possible only if that other state has previously agreed to some international arrangement authorising outside intervention. Sovereign nation states agreeing to implement and to be scrutinised according to international human rights standards are still the best means of protecting persons throughout the world.

Any nation state wanting to maintain its sovereignty and anxious to uphold the international order of a United Nations consisting of nation states will need to play its part in assisting those persons who flee from the territory of their nation state having been persecuted by their own government. If these persons were not to be given protection by other nation states, they would have no self-interested reason to respect or uphold the sovereignty of other nation states and there would be a real difficulty in upholding the moral legitimacy of sovereign nation states. Providing protection for refugees is a responsibility to be shared by all sovereign nation states if the collective sovereignty of nation states is to continue with some moral basis.

The special case for the international obligation to protect the refugee has been made out by accepting the need to acknowledge the sovereignty of the nation state. International acknowledgement of this sovereignty could not be given unless there was some fall-back mechanism for providing protection to those persons singled out and persecuted by the government of the nation state on account of their religion, race, nationality, political belief or membership of a particular social group.

Those fleeing persecution by their own government cannot be expected to return home until it is safe to do so. Many of those who flee across borders will seek and find protection in the country next door. Others will need to go further afield to find that protection. Whenever there is a major crisis, the victims will scatter to the four winds and refugees can be expected to turn up in countries near and far. In the fifty years since the Convention was finalised, international travel has changed. Those fleeing persecution may now have more options available to them. This creates the new problem of secondary movement. Though governments ought to have no objection to refugees who are fleeing directly from persecution, they have understandable concerns about those refugees who see their moment of flight as an opportunity to seek a more beneficial migration outcome for themselves and their families. Given the widening gap between the first and the third world, it is not surprising that some people fleeing persecution will look further afield for more secure protection together with more hopeful economic and educational opportunities. Having the status of a refugee has never been accepted as a passport to the migration country of one's choice. Then again, the international community has never been so callous or short-sighted as to say that during a mass influx one has access only to the country next door in seeking protection even if you have family, friends or community members living in a more distant country.

The responsible nation state that is pulling its weight will not only open its borders to the refugees from the adjoining countries but will expect some flow over from major conflicts wherever they might occur. It is no surprise that Afghan and Iraqi refugees have turned up on the doorstep of all first-world countries in recent times. With the ease of international travel and the services of people smugglers, it has become very difficult to draw the distinction between refugees who are coming directly from a territory where their life or freedom has been

Australian, 8 May 2002.
Reproduced with Peter Nicholson's permission.

threatened and those refugees who, having fled, have already been accorded protection, but have now taken an onward journey seeking a more beneficial migration outcome. First-world governments say they cannot tolerate the latter because they would then be jeopardising their own migration programs and weakening their borders every time there was a refugee-producing situation in the world no matter how close or how far it occurred from their own shores. This problem is not solved by drawing careful legal distinctions, because one person's preferred migration outcome is simply another person's first port of call where they thought there was a realistic prospect of getting protection for themselves and their families.

The problem cannot be solved by refugee advocates pretending that it does not exist or hoping that it will simply go away. Neither can it be solved by governments pretending that all persons who arrive on their shores without a visa are secondary movers. When mass movements occur during a conflict, it is necessary for governments to cooperate, ensuring that adequate protection can be given to persons closer to their home country before then closing off the secondary movement route except by means of legal migration. When countries of first asylum are stretched and unstable, other countries must be prepared to receive those who travel further seeking protection.

The global village, with the widening gap between rich and poor countries and between democratic and tyrannical countries, is very different from the world of 1951. First-world countries now have to put up legal barriers to mass population flows across their borders. In the past, the tyranny of distance was enough to keep such flows well at bay. To do this responsibly, the international community must continue to work cooperatively, providing protection in countries which otherwise would become transit countries through which the refugees would travel seeking protection ultimately on the shores and borders of the first-world. If this does not happen, poor transit countries will imitate wealthy, remote countries and close their borders to fleeing asylum seekers.

With declining birth rates, most first-world countries now need migrants if only to help them maintain their national living standards and to provide services and care for the aging population. Any first-world country that is a net migration country should include some offshore refugees in their annual migration intake. The UNHCR is the peak international body that assists refugees in need of resettlement. Obviously it is in everyone's interests if refugees can safely be returned home. If they cannot be, the next most convenient option is that they be integrated into the local community where they have landed on their journey, having fled and having sought protection in the first available country. The UNHCR identifies eight criteria for refugees who may need to be resettled in third countries, including first-world countries far distant from their conflict zone. They are refugees with special ongoing protection needs, survivors of violence and torture, refugees with certain medical needs, women at risk, refugees whose families members are already resident in another country, children and adolescents, elderly refugees, and others who for various reasons have no prospects of local integration. At the moment there are ten countries including Australia which guarantee the UNHCR 75,000 resettlement places a year. Other countries also accept persons for resettlement on the recommendation of the UNHCR but they do not give the UNHCR an advance quota. Countries that provide a quota of spaces then make their own selection of refugees from those screened by the UNHCR and matching the criteria. As well as accepting some offshore refugees for resettlement, first-world countries should also provide assistance to those less wealthy countries that carry more of the burden of refugee protection on account of their proximity to refugee-producing countries.

All countries, regardless of their wealth, stability or migration needs, need to process the asylum claims of those persons in their territory who claim to be fleeing persecution back in their own country. It is an absolute obligation on all countries who have signed the convention that they not send back (*refoule*) bona fide refugees in their territory. Countries such as the United States have continued to process their onshore asylum claims while at the same time maintaining their offshore annual refugee quota. The United States guarantees the UNHCR that it will take 70,000 offshore refugees a year regardless of the number of onshore asylum seekers it processes, that usually being about 60,000 a year. Australia used to take the same approach. Now Australia has decided to tie its onshore caseload to its offshore quota such that for every person who gets recognised as a refugee in need of protection onshore there is one less place for refugees offshore. This way, the government has been able to argue that, by getting tough on asylum seekers trying to reach Australia without a visa, it is able to make more places available to the refugees in greatest need, identified by UNHCR and Australian field offices around the globe. This nexus of the offshore and onshore components has allowed the government to appear firm but fair, seeking a maximum outcome for the refugees in greatest need. This is a moral calculus completely of the government's own construction. Many onshore refugees are eligible only for a three-year visa, but they still take the places of offshore refugees who would be granted permanent residence. Would not the Australian government be even more warm-hearted and decent if it both maintained its offshore commitment and processed all onshore asylum applicants? If the number of onshore applicants grew disproportionately, there might then be a case for reviewing the offshore quota. It must be conceded that there are many Australians who think we are being warm-hearted and decent enough if we take a fixed number of refugees a year regardless of whether they be offshore or onshore, giving first place to those who happen to be onshore.

In a democracy, governments should craft a migration and refugee program that is acceptable to the people. Often the people can be led by their community and political leaders to accept that it is in the national interest to be more welcoming rather than less, more generous rather than less. Especially since the destruction of the World Trade Centre, citizens in democracies are suspicious about newcomers to their societies. There is a need for increased security. Anyone arriving without a visa, without identity documents, and in the hands of a people smuggler must expect to be subject to heightened scrutiny. Each country still needs to do its part in providing protection for the refugees of the world. Our elected leaders do not help refugees or the polity when they stigmatise persons as unlawful non-citizens when they may indeed be refugees. They may even be refugees in flight entitled to seek entry. In a 2002 Federal Court decision, Justice Merkel had the opportunity to observe the unhelpfulness of some of the public political language used in these situations. He said:

> The Refugees Convention is a part of conventional international law that has been given legislative effect in Australia. It has always been funda-

mental to the operation of the Refugees Convention that many applicants for refugee status will, of necessity, have left their countries of nationality unlawfully and therefore, of necessity, will have entered the country in which they seek asylum unlawfully. Jews seeking refuge from war-torn Europe, Tutsis seeking refuge from Rwanda, Kurds seeking refuge from Iraq, Hazaras seeking refuge from the Taliban in Afghanistan and many others may also be called 'unlawful non-citizens' in the countries in which they seek asylum. Such a description, however, conceals, rather than reveals, their *lawful* entitlement under conventional international law since the early 1950s (which has been enacted into Australian law) to claim refugee status as persons who are 'unlawfully' in the country in which the asylum application is made.[10]

In the ideal world there might not be any national borders. Such a world is presently unimaginable, let alone achievable. Where contiguous nation states have relationships with each other, there may be the ready crossing of borders at times of crisis and disaster. What about the moral obligation towards those who are not refugees but who are still fleeing some disaster such as civil war, drought or flood? There are always situations of persons visiting a nation state who though not refugees would be facing humanitarian disaster if they were forcibly returned home immediately. The nation state needs to be able to accommodate such people. In a democracy, many citizens would be anxious that their government make provision for such humanitarian cases. One of the advantages of living in a stable democracy respectful of the rights of all should be the communal capacity to extend humanitarian assistance to all persons in the territory for as long as the assistance is required. This is not to deny that it is difficult to gauge the extent to which a government needs to extend such humanitarian assistance.

These moral reflections highlight the complexity confronting any government wanting to exercise responsibly the sovereign right of determining who comes and goes in the community of the nation state, and under what conditions. Net migration countries have a little more latitude to respond to the humanitarian challenges, as do wealthy countries, and as do democratic countries with a sound human rights ethos. Then again, democratic countries seized by fear of outsiders, wealthy countries wanting to maintain their distance from the poor and net migration countries wanting to use migration for business and skills development may become more isolationist and less humanitarian.

There is a need for considered moral discourse between government and the governed, avoiding the high moral ground and political rhetoric. There must be respectful dialogue so that the sovereign right to decide who comes, who stays and in what circumstances might be discussed and exercised. This requires considerations not only of the national interest but also of the contribution which the nation should make to the protection of persons, including those persecuted by their own governments or by other agents whose persecutory actions are endorsed by or beyond the control of government.

CHAPTER 2

Four waves, Tampa and a firebreak

All first-world countries are wrestling to achieve the right balance between the right of sovereign border protection and the humanitarian obligations that confront any nation playing its part in the world. Having lived through the Australian bushfire of the last two years, we are well placed to sit on the verandah and look back, contemplating whether we have the balance right. What does it now take to be a 'warm-hearted, decent international citizen', not a soft touch to be trampled upon but a good neighbour who plays her part?

Nowadays all warm-hearted, decent international citizens are anxious to maintain the integrity of their borders, and are willing to spend vast amounts of money on controlling access across borders. Enjoying the benefit of being an island nation continent and using the most up-to-date technology, Australia has designed a comprehensive visa system such that everyone who enters Australia lawfully comes as a citizen of Australia or New Zealand or else with a visa or an electronic travel authority (ETA). The ETA is available to the passport holders of 33 listed countries, provided they are staying in Australia for less than three months for tourism, a family visit or business. Airlines receive infringement notices each time they carry someone to Australia without adequate documentation. There are about 5,000 violations a year and airlines must pay $5,000 for each infringement. Qantas alone is liable for about 1,000 infringements a year. The airlines now engage the services of liaison officers from the Immigration Department at Bangkok and Singapore. There are fewer than 30 stowaways on ships arriving in Australia each year. In ten years there have been only 252 people who have come as unauthorised boat arrivals in the Torres Strait between Australia and Papua New Guinea. Only 40 of those went through the process of applying for asylum in Australia. The other 212 were turned around because they had no credible claim to refugee status. Usually there are more unauthorised arrivals by air than by sea in Australia. The four significant waves of boat people in the last 30 years have heightened the concerns of government and the public that Australian borders are not secure.

At the immediate end of the Vietnam War the Whitlam government was not sympathetic to receiving large numbers of Vietnamese refugees. The Whitlam government had abolished the last vestiges of the White Australia policy. Having amalgamated the Immigration Department with the Department of Labour, Whitlam did not want to encourage refugee flows that would put the labour market out of kilter. The minister, Clyde Cameron, was a great protector of trade union interests. He later wrote that 'unemployment had already risen to a very high level and my job was to foster migration policies that would not make the unemployment position any worse'. The migrant intake was to be reduced to a post–World War II low of 50,000 in 1975–76. Cameron was therefore delighted with Whitlam's intervention to stop Don Willessee's request for a relaxation of the conditions of entry for Vietnamese asylum seekers. Cameron reported the infamous conversation when Whitlam erupted at Willessee: 'I'm not having hundreds of f- - -ing Vietnamese Balts coming into this country with their religious and political hatreds against us!'[1] When elected to government at the end of 1975, the Coalition quickly moved to re-establish a Department of Immigration and Ethnic Affairs.

The first wave of 2,077 Indochinese boat people came to Australia in 54 boats between 1976 and 1981. In that time, Australia was to resettle another 56,000 Indochinese through regular migration channels. The first boatload of asylum seekers arrived in Darwin Harbour on 28 July 1976. The five Vietnamese had made the 6,500-kilometre journey in a small boat. At the end of that year another two boats arrived carrying 106 people who were screened for health reasons and then flown to the Wacol migrant hostel outside Brisbane. When the third Vietnamese boat of the first wave arrived, there was some media agitation about the threatened invasion by boat people. One Melbourne newspaper reported that 'today's trickle of unannounced visitors to our lonely northern coastline could well become a tide of human flotsam'. The paper asked how the nation would respond to 'the coming invasion of its far north by hundreds, thousands and even tens of thousands of Asian refugees'.[2] The invasion never occurred.

In 1978 the Communist government in Vietnam outlawed private business ventures. Tens of thousands, mainly ethnic Chinese, then fled by boat. The outflow of Vietnamese boat people throughout the region gave rise to great moral dilemmas in the implementation of government policies. Countries such as Malaysia would periodically declare that their camps were full and they could take no more boat people. They would even threaten to shoot new arrivals on sight. Alternatively, they would provide them with food, fuel and repairs so they could set off for another country. Meanwhile Vietnamese officials were profiting by charging the boat people high departure fees.

Camps were filling around Southeast Asia. There was no let-up in the departures from Vietnam. In the end there was a negotiated agreement involving Vietnam, the countries of first asylum such as Thailand and Malaysia, and the resettlement countries, chiefly the United States, Canada and Australia. In 1982 the Australian government announced that the Vietnamese government had agreed to an Orderly Departure Program. Australian immigration ministers Michael MacKellar and Ian Macphee were able to set up procedures for the reception of Vietnamese from camps in Southeast Asia as well as those coming directly from Vietnam under a special migration program. With careful management, they were able to have the public accept up to 15,000 Vietnamese refugees a year when the annual migrant intake was as low as 70,000.

In 1978 the government set up a Determination of Refugee Status (DORS) Committee which would determine onshore refugee claims. A UNHCR representative joined this committee of public servants from the key departments. The committee made only recommendations to the minister. If it rejected an application, it could still recommend that the applicant be given temporary or permanent residence 'on humanitarian or strong compassionate grounds'. In the early 1980s the committee considered fewer than 200 applications a year, with less than a one-third approval rating.

In 1982 the government decided that even offshore cases would be decided on a case by case basis. It would no longer accept the UNHCR's blanket determination that anyone from Indochina was a refugee. It was now seven years since the end of the Vietnam War and it was more likely that some of those departing Vietnam were economic migrants unimpressed by their economic prospects under a communist regime rather than refugees who were fleeing in fear of persecution. At the same time the government set up a Special Humanitarian Program to complement the offshore refugee program. In the first year, there were 20,216 offshore refugees and 1,701 applicants approved for migration to Australia under the Special Humanitarian Program. Within eight years there were only 1,537 under the offshore refugee category and 10,411 under the Special Humanitarian Program. Onshore, it was also possible for persons to gain residence on humanitarian or compassionate grounds. Initially it was assumed that there would be only a few hundred of such onshore cases a year. That all changed when the courts got involved.

In 1985 the High Court by the narrowest of margins (3 to 2) decided that ministerial decisions rejecting the grant or extension of an entry permit on the grounds that the applicant was not a refugee were reviewable by the courts.[3] Also the failed applicant would be entitled to a written statement of reasons for the minister's rejection. From now on, refugee status was to be a matter of law rather than unreviewable ministerial discretion. Judges as well as ministers were to have a say. On the same reasoning, it was only a matter of time before the courts started reviewing ministerial or bureaucratic decisions rejecting people's humanitarian claims. Neither parliament nor the government had foreseen such court intervention.

When the Vietnamese camps throughout Southeast Asia were still full a decade after the first large-scale departures from Vietnam, the key governments drew up a comprehensive plan of action which provided mandatory return of those screened out of the refugee process. Those who arrived in the Hong Kong camps after June 1988 were told that they would not be assured resettlement and that they would be subjected to individual status determination. March 1989 was the cut-off date for guaranteed resettlement in all camps throughout Asia. By the end of the post–Vietnam War migration, Australia had accepted 177,000 Vietnamese of whom only about 2,000 came to Australia un-invited by boat. Despite the public apprehension about people turning up in boats, the first wave of boat people on our shores was miniscule compared with the waves of human movement around the region. The public disquiet was enough to warrant Australia's active participation in initiatives to empty the Vietnamese camps and to return those who were not refugees back to Vietnam.

The first groups of Vietnamese boat people were not held in deten-tion. They were allowed to remain in Australia. Vietnamese refugees fled to many countries throughout the region. No boats turned up on Australian shores between 1981 and November 1989. The Vietnamese refugee flow was a classic illustration of the Cold War paradigm. Fol-lowing a local war in which the warring parties were backed by the su-perpowers, those who fled the conflict were offered asylum by those countries that shared their political allegiance in the international bal-ance of power. Malcolm Fraser, who was prime minister at the time, of-fered this assessment in 2002: 'The Government believed that there was an ethical obligation to provide a safe haven for many of those whom we had supported in what had become a most misguided con-flict.' Taking seriously the will of the people and the role of political leadership in a democracy, he concluded, 'If any of the political parties had tried to make politics over the resettlement of the Indo-Chinese in the seventies and eighties, Australians would have found it difficult to support the policy. The political parties were united in the policy and Australians accepted the policy as right for the nation.'[4]

The second wave of boat people commenced with the arrival of a Cambodian boat at Pender Bay near Broome on 25 November 1989. After their one-month voyage, the 26 Cambodians who had come via Singapore and Indonesia saw land. Three of them came ashore looking for water. They met a couple of local Aborigines who then alerted the Coastwatch. This wave over the next six years comprised about 2,000 arrivals mainly from China and Cambodia. This time the boat people were not our allies fleeing from aggressors who had been our enemies. Australia had invested much in the Cambodian peace process and insisted that persecution had ended in the new Cambodia under United Nations auspices. Gareth Evans was one of the chief architects of the Cambodian arrangements and was adamant that those leaving Cambodia by boat were more likely to be economic migrants than refugees. The arrangements became known as the Evans peace plan. Though Prime Minister Bob Hawke had wept at the sight of the repression in Tiananmen Square that year, his compassion for the Chinese students resident in Australia was tempered by the realisation, impressed upon him by Immigration Department officials, that allowing the students to stay in Australia carried the added undertaking of permitting their immediate family members to join them. There could be a blowout in the careful management of the migration program and a growing perception in China that migration to the first world of Australia was an easy option.

On 9 December 1989, just after the arrival of the first boatload of Cambodians, the High Court of Australia delivered a refugee decision that was a real slap in the face to the government.[5] A Chinese stowaway, Chan Yee Kin, who had entered Australia illegally in August 1980 had fought an unrelenting legal battle against the government, claiming that he was a refugee and therefore entitled to remain in Australia. The High Court was scathing about the decision-making process of the minister's delegate, deciding that 'the conclusion reached by the delegate on the basis of the findings made by him was so unreasonable as to amount to an improper exercise of the power to determine refugee status'. The delegate's decision was 'so unreasonable that no reasonable person could have come to it'.[6] Chan's application for refugee status had to be reconsidered by the minister's delegate. Chief Justice Mason in the course of his judgment observed that he did not find the UNHCR *Handbook on Procedures and Criteria for Determining Refugee Status* especially useful. He thought it 'more a practical guide for the use of those who are required to determine whether or not a person is a refugee' than a 'document purporting to interpret the meaning of the relevant parts of the Convention'.[7] This was not good news for the Immigration Department officials, who until now had been able to decide these matters without lawyers getting too involved. There was every chance that lawyers would be bringing applications of boat people to court claiming that the bureaucrats following the handbook and political directions were not attuned to the finer points of law that might now be spelt out in detail even by the highest court in the land.

On the very day of this High Court decision, boat people from the Pender Bay group engaged lawyers to assist them in their refugee claims. Even when they were moved from Sydney to Darwin, there were lawyers to assist and visit them. The minister, Gerry Hand, was furious. He was pleased to discover BHP's abandoned single men's quarters in Port Hedland on the Western Australian coast. Being equidistant from Perth and Darwin, Port Hedland was not likely to be very accessible to lawyers and the other community groups labelled by government as 'do-gooders'. In 1991 the government opened Australia's first immigration reception and processing centre tailor-made for the mandatory detention of illegals. At this time, there was no government rationale for detention, such as deterrence or ensuring that people were available for removal. The government was primarily focused on trying to get these asylum seekers away from the lawyers so that their public description as economic migrants would stick without causing any hemorrhaging of the Evans peace plan. The High Court was ultimately to rule that the detention of these persons was unlawful prior to the introduction of new legislation on 5 May 1992. The Australian parliament was adamant that these were unmeritorious persons. Parliament legislated to limit the damages for the unlawful detention to $1 per day. On the same day, it was revealed that Leo McLeay, the Speaker of the Parliament, was paid $65,000 damages for a fall on a Parliament House bicycle.

The government's main problem at this time was not boat people. In 1989 there had been only one boat carrying 26 people. There were 1,148 onshore applications for protection. In 1990 there were two boats carrying 198 people. Because of the post-Tiananmen situation, the onshore protection applications increased to 11,335. In 1991 there were six boats with 213 people on board and 13,045 onshore applications. These onshore applicants could go all the way to the High Court challenging the assessments made of their refugee status. Even more worrying for the government, which was trying to keep a lid on onshore migration applications, was the willingness of the courts to second-guess whether there were 'strong compassionate or humanitarian grounds' for a person to be allowed to stay in Australia. By 1991 the

Reproduced with Alan Moir's permission.

Immigration Department concluded that it 'had virtually only one cri-
terion left to it'. Applicants had only to show 'that if they were forced to
leave Australia, they would face a situation that would invoke strong
feelings of pity or compassion in the ordinary member of the Australian
public'.[8] Virtually anyone who was onshore and who had their refugee
claim rejected could then go to the courts and claim permanent
residence on humanitarian grounds.

Just as the boat arrived at Pender Bay in November 1989, at the start
of the second wave, the parliament abolished the means for onshore
applicants to obtain residence on compassionate and humanitarian
grounds. People would be judged to be refugees or they would be dependent on the discretion of the minister, who could decide the application without any review by a court and without any need to refer to
criteria such as compassionate and humanitarian grounds. That discretion of the minister would be exercised only after the applicant had
been rejected as a refugee. This has led to the contorted outcome that
anyone wanting to remain in Australian on humanitarian or compassionate grounds would first have to apply for refugee status even if
everyone knew that they were not refugees. The absurdity of this law
and policy was revealed in 2002 when the government insisted that all
East Timorese whose status was awaiting determination after the

change of regime in East Timor in 1999 would first have to be assessed as refugees. Only then could the minister consider whether any of them should be permitted to stay on humanitarian grounds.

Once the second wave had started, the Hawke Labor government decided that it was time to get tough on 'illegals'. Hawke had no sympathy for the Cambodians. On 6 June 1990 Jana Wendt interviewed him on Channel 9's *A Current Affair*:

> Wendt: We woke up this morning to read that we're asking the Cambodian Government to take back some of the Cambodian boat people who came to our shores. Why are we doing that?
>
> PM: For the obvious reason. I mean, we have a compassionate humanitarian policy which will stand comparison with any other country in the world. But we're not here with an open-door policy saying anyone who wants to come to Australia can come. These people are not political refugees.
>
> Wendt: How can you be sure of that, Mr Hawke?
>
> PM: Simply there is not a regime now in Cambodia which is exercising terror, political terror, upon its population.
>
> Wendt: What do you make then of these hundreds of people —
>
> PM: What we make —
>
> Wendt: — Who get on their tin boats and travel across —
>
> PM: What we make of it is that there is obviously a combination of economic refugeeism, if you like. People saying they don't like a particular regime or they don't like their economic circumstances, therefore they're going to up, pull up stumps, get in a boat and lob in Australia. Well, that's not on.
>
> Wendt: And risk their lives to do it?
>
> PM: Their lives is not, I mean, we have an orderly migration program. We're not going to allow people just to jump that queue by saying we'll jump into a boat, here we are, bugger the people who've been around the world. We have a ratio of more than 10 to 1 of people who want to come to this country compared to the numbers that we take in.
>
> Wendt: And you personally have no qualms about that?
>
> PM: Not only no qualms about it, but I will be forceful in ensuring that that is what's followed.

The government dispatched an interdepartmental group of senior officers to Phnom Penh for 'discussions with authorities there on the orderly return of Cambodian displaced persons and boat people'. The minister, Gerry Hand, implemented the decision that boat people would be held in loose detention with limited access to community groups anxious for their welfare. Then they gained access to lawyers. This was the last thing the government wanted. Government officials were adamant that these Cambodians were economic migrants and they did not want them having access to individual refugee assessments, or assistance from lawyers who did not share the government's confidence that the Evans peace plan had precluded the possibility of any refugees being produced in Cambodia. Bob Hawke maintained his opposition to the 220 Cambodian boat people, warning:

> Do not let any people, or any group of people in the world think that because Australia has that proud record, that all they've got to do is to break the rules, jump the queue, lob here and Bob's your uncle. Bob is not your uncle on this issue, other than in accordance with the appropriate rules. We will continue to be one of the most humanitarian countries in the world. But it is not an open-door policy.[9]

Responding to the second wave of boat people and the blow-out of Chinese onshore applicants, the Australian government decided on a three-pronged approach: imposing mandatory detention for all persons arriving without lawful authority under Australia's migration laws; establishing a Refugee Review Tribunal to determine asylum claims, with reduced access to the courts; and giving the minister sole discretion to determine humanitarian cases, with no review by the courts. In 1992 the High Court ruled that the detention of aliens without a court order and without court supervision was constitutional provided the detention was for a migration purpose and was not punitive or designed as a deterrent. The government needed to show that they were detaining persons to assist with the processing of their migration claims. A court would need to be convinced that the government was not detaining persons as punishment or to send a message deterring others from attempting unlawful entry. Only in these circumstances could the government continue the detention without any court order.

In this way, the court set the broad constitutional limits for government acting unilaterally to detain persons under the immigration power, without recourse to the courts. Those limits are less restrictive than the European Convention on Human Rights. Under the European Convention, deprivation of liberty in migration cases is authorised only for 'the lawful arrest or detention of a person to prevent his effecting an unauthorised entry into the country or of a person against whom action is being taken with a view to deportation or extradition'.[10] Once people have effected an unlawful entry they cannot be detained for a substantial period except on a court order or while awaiting deportation. Long-term detention without judicial order or supervision simply for the purpose of processing asylum claims when there is no proven security risk or risk of absconding is just not an option in Europe. Here in Australia, where we have no bill of rights, the High Court has recognised that government and parliament have a broader discretion to detain. In the 1992 decision the High Court found that migration detention laws would be valid:

> if the detention which they require and authorise is limited to what is reasonably capable of being seen as necessary for the purposes of deportation or necessary to enable an application for an entry permit to be made and considered. On the other hand, if the detention which those sections require and authorise is not so limited, the authority which they purportedly confer upon the Executive cannot properly be seen as an incident of the executive powers to exclude, admit and deport an alien. In that event, they will be of a punitive nature and contravene Chapter III's insistence that the judicial power of the Commonwealth be vested exclusively in the courts which it designates.[11]

It is these observations of the High Court which explain the tenor of Mr Ruddock's oft-repeated remark that 'Detention is not arbitrary. It is humane and is not designed to be punitive.'[12] The government has no problem in justifying initial detention of an unlawful entrant in order to satisfy health and security concerns. Neither is there a problem with detaining someone who is awaiting removal from Australia having been found not to be a refugee. The government's problem has been in establishing that ongoing detention is necessary to enable the government to process a refugee claim more fairly and more quickly. There has just not been the evidence that detention helps the processing of claims. There is now evidence that detention actually hinders quick and fair decision making. In these circumstances, detention takes on a punitive appearance. Also government continues to insist that its raft of measures, including mandatory detention, helps to deter people from attempting unlawful entry. These ministerial comments about deterrence and the non-punitive intent of the detention are related to the constitutional doubts about the validity of legislation authorising administrative detention of persons without access to the courts. When detention is neither relevant nor incidental to the processing of applications for an entry permit, and when the detention is neither relevant nor incidental to removal or deportation in the foreseeable future, there is a legal problem.

There can be no doubt that Mr Ruddock's ministerial predecessors Messrs Hand and Bolkus were keen to make an example of the Cambodian boat people in the second wave. They did not want more Cambodians risking the journey. Their senior departmental staff were urging that the Cambodians not be allowed to remain lest this send the wrong signal. They wanted them kept in secure detention so as to send the right signal back to Cambodia. Under no circumstances did the department want these Cambodians to be allowed to remain in Australia on humanitarian grounds. In December 1989 the Australian embassy in Hanoi informed Canberra that 'only the repatriation to Cambodia of those who had reached Australia would be a strong enough disincentive to further departures'. On 18 January 1990 a cable was sent from the Australian embassy in Bangkok warning that more boat people could be preparing to set sail and that 'the decision of those who are already in Australia will obviously be of significant influence to any potential flow'.[13] At this time the Evans peace plan was being formulated and was attempting to repatriate 300,000 Cambodians from Thailand. It was in all the politicians' interests that the handful of boat people turning up in Australia be found to be economic migrants. In short, if those turning up in Australia were refugees, there was no way the peace plan could work. A 'sensitive' Department of Foreign Affairs and Trade (DFAT) cable of June 1990 reported that Neal Blewett, the Trade Minister, had told an Indonesian minister that Australia had already informed Hun Sen, Prime Minister of Cambodia, that 'the boat people were going to be treated as illegal immigrants and repatriated'.[14] No wonder the politicians did not want lawyers and judges getting involved in these cases on the Australian mainland.

Ministers Hand and Bolkus had been happy to talk about the need for deterrence. Even the Immigration Department's senior officers were prepared to tell parliament, 'Deterrence also provides part of the

rationale for detention, but it is only one component in efforts to discourage unauthorised arrivals.'[15] No boats came between 1981 and
1989 when there was no policy of mandatory detention. Some boats did
come in a second wave after a policy of mandatory detention was put in
place. Nancy Viviani concluded in 1996 that 'senior immigration officials want to keep detention even if it does not work because detention
is a public demonstration that the Department has Australia's borders
"under control" — even though it does not in terms of the number of
onshore illegal immigrants'.[16]

The third wave of 2,000 boat people arrived between 1994 and
1998. (As with the previous two waves, the number of unauthorised arrivals by plane continued to exceed the number of unauthorised arrivals by boat. Unauthorised air arrivals have never excited the same
commotion with the Australian government or people as have boat arrivals.) These Vietnamese and Chinese boat people were the last victims of the Comprehensive Plan of Action which proposed the
compulsory repatriation back to Vietnam of those left in the camps
around Asia. Those coming from China came from Beihei province in
the South, having originally been resettled there after the end of the
Vietnam War. The Australian government decided on a detailed legislative response that put these people beyond the reach of Australia's
protection obligations. China was deemed to be a 'safe third country'
and all persons subject to the Comprehensive Plan of Action were
excluded from the possibility of bringing onshore asylum claims in
Australia.

The fourth and biggest wave of boat people in modern Australian
history could not so readily be categorised as non-refugees or as refugees who had their claims determined elsewhere. In late 1999 boat
people started arriving from Afghanistan, Iraq and Iran via Indonesia.
Australia's relations with Indonesia were tense in light of the East
Timor conflict. Australia had taken the high moral ground and Prime
Minister Howard had allowed himself to be quoted as if Australia was
the United States' deputy sheriff in the region. No doubt there were
some officials in Jakarta interested to see how the morally pure international citizen Australia might deal with some extra boatloads of asylum seekers who found their way from Indonesia to Australia.
Arresting the flow would then require some astute diplomacy, with

many items on the table including the mopping up of the East Timor fall-out. It would be difficult for Indonesia if Australia were to be too insistent on international intervention in bringing Indonesian military officers to trial for human rights violations in East Timor. From mid-1999 until mid-2001, 8,300 boat people arrived in Australia, twice as many as the total since 1989 and more than the total number of boat people who had arrived since the end of the Vietnam War. Of even greater psychological significance in the political debate, this was the first time that the number of unauthorised boat arrivals far exceeded the number of unauthorised air arrivals over a sustained period. The government accurately read and fed the public perception that we were a nation besieged by an avalanche of boat people who had to be stopped. A line had to be drawn.

In late August 2001 a large Norwegian container vessel MV *Tampa* was steaming from Perth to Singapore on the high seas when the captain, Arne Rinnan, received a call from the Rescue Coordination Centre of the Australian Maritime Safety Authority that a ship was in distress on the high seas. Under the guidance of an Australian Coastwatch plane, the captain sailed for about four hours to pick up 433 people from a wooden, overcrowded boat, *Palapa 1*, which was within the Indonesian maritime rescue zone. Though far from the Australian mainland, the *Palapa* was only about 75 nautical miles from Christmas Island, an Australian territory in the Indian Ocean closer to Indonesia than to the Western Australian coastline. The captain intended to proceed to the Indonesian port of Merak about 250 nautical miles distant to discharge his human cargo. He then intended to complete his voyage to Singapore with a cargo of largely empty containers. His ship usually carried a crew of 27, so it was not designed or licensed to carry hundreds of people long distances. The ship was licensed to carry only 40 persons. Once all of the boat people were on board, five of the new passengers came up to the bridge to speak with the captain. According to Arne Rinnan, 'They were in an aggravated mood and they said that if we did not head to Christmas Island then they would go crazy or start jumping overboard.'[17] Rinnan decided that the most responsible decision he could make as a captain concerned for the safety of his ship, his crew and his new passengers was to change course and head for Christmas Island, the nearest harbour, discharging the 433 at the closest landfall. Very soon the Australian authorities were on the radio denying him permission to enter Australian territorial waters. By daybreak on Monday 27 August Rinnan thought that 'some politics [had] got into the picture'. That afternoon Prime Minister John Howard told the Australian parliament, 'We have indicated to the captain that permission to land in Australia will not be granted to this vessel ... Australia has sought on all occasions to balance against the undoubted right of this country to decide who comes here and in what circumstances, a right that any other sovereign nation has, our humanitarian obligations as a warm-hearted, decent international citizen.'[18] At the diplomatic level, Australia then informed Norway that the conveying of a distress call by the Australian authorities 'does not carry with it any obligation to allow the persons rescued into Australian territory'. Despite, or because of, the threats made to the captain by the passengers on the bridge, Australia expected the *Tampa* to take to the high seas with 460 persons aboard and 40 life jackets, returning the rescued persons 'either to their point of departure or to the original intended destination of the *Tampa*'.[19]

On 29 August 2001 the *Tampa* entered into Australian territorial waters approaching Christmas Island. The prime minister told parliament that the captain had decided on this course of action because a spokesman for the asylum seekers 'had indicated that they would begin jumping overboard if medical assistance was not provided quickly'.[20] Captain Rinnan gave a different reason for his decision: 'We weren't seaworthy to sail to Indonesia. There were life jackets for only 40 people. The sanitary conditions were terrible.'[21] The SAS came aboard and took over the *Tampa*. An Australian Defence Force doctor was given 43 minutes to make a medical assessment of the 433 asylum seekers. He reported, 'Four persons required IV (2 urgent including 1 woman 8 months pregnant).' Captain Rinnan was surprised at the prompt medical assessment, because his crew had already identified ten people who were barely conscious lying in the sun on the deck of the ship. The prime minister then made a finely timed ministerial statement to parliament insisting that 'nobody — and I repeat nobody — has presented as being in need of urgent medical assistance as would require their removal to the Australian mainland or to Christmas Island'.[22] One hundred and thirty-one fortunate asylum seekers were

Reproduced with Alan Moir's permission.

granted immediate asylum by the New Zealand government. The rest, having been transported to Nauru, awaited processing under the evolving Pacific Solution.

The Australian government set about implementing a detailed legislative response to this latest wave of boat arrivals. The government was determined that none of the people on the *Tampa* would ever be permitted to settle in Australia. John Howard was keen to send 'a message to people smugglers and others around the world that, whilst this is a humanitarian, decent country, we are not a soft touch and we are not a nation whose sovereign rights in relation to who comes here are going to be trampled on'.[23] The government presumes that the message was rightly transmitted and heard, because the boats stopped coming. Others who heard the message were not convinced of the transmitter's humanitarian decency.

Prior to the fourth wave of boat people there was only one year when the number of unauthorised arrivals by boat exceeded the number by air. That changed in 1999 with the arrival of 86 boats. For two years in a row there were more than 4,000 boat people arriving each year and there was no sign of a let-up. When the *Tampa* received the rescue call, the Australian government had good intelligence that there were another 2,500 people already waiting in Indonesia to make the journey.

Having decided that most, if not all, of this fourth wave of boat people were secondary movers seeking a migration outcome, the government decided that it was time to get very tough. Policy makers usually speak of 'push factors' and 'pull factors' with refugees. Push factors are those reasons that push them out of their own country. Pull factors are those reasons that attract them to the country where they seek asylum. The government conceded that the push factors usually outweighed the pull factors when people fled their homelands with no assurance of future residence. With this wave of boat people, the push factors included the harshness of the Saddam Hussein regime in Iraq and the oppressiveness of the Taliban in Afghanistan. It is push factors that dictate that people flee their homeland, but the pull factors may attract refugees to extend their journey to a more remote but more desirable location. As far as possible, the Australian government wanted to reduce the pull factors, even being prepared to be punitive and justifying this approach by claiming that those arriving by boat were not seeking protection, and that they could have obtained the minimal protection guaranteed by the Refugees Convention at other points on their journey. They were attracted to come further afield, the government said, because if they arrived in Australia they knew they would be guaranteed resettlement in Australia if they proved they were refugees.

The government faced three problems. Or to put it another way, there were three distinct advantages that asylum seekers and people smugglers saw in making the perilous journey by boat to Australia.

- First, if you made it to Australia, there was a good chance that the Australian authorities would find that you were a refugee. The Immigration Minister, Philip Ruddock, was fond of quoting the statistic that 84 per cent of boat people were being found to be refugees whereas only 14 per cent of the contingent from the same countries of flight and who presented at the UNHCR office in Indonesia were found to be refugees. Ever since its election in 1996, the Howard government had wanted to reduce the involvement of the courts in reviewing refugee cases, as it thought that the judges were being too soft on applicants and were being too cavalier in their willingness to expand the categories for refugee status under the convention.

- Second, if you were found to be a refugee after you have landed in

Australia, you were guaranteed residence in Australia. If you had waited in a camp in Pakistan or in a transit city such as Jakarta awaiting a UNHCR determination, you not only had less chance of being found to be a refugee, you also had no guarantee of being re-settled in a country where you would feel secure, let alone one in which you could avail yourself of the benefits of life in a first-world, democratic country.

* Third, if you were granted permanent residence in Australia, you would over time be able to bring your family to join you and they would be able to travel safely and legally by commercial aircraft.

From the government perspective, those coming by boat were jump-ing the queue in the sense that the government already had a commit-ment to accept an annual quota of proven refugees from camps and transit centres throughout the world. The government was unwilling to reward those who took the initiative of coming by boat without a visa. The Howard government had gone to the electorate with a policy every bit as punitive as that of the previous Labor governments. In fact, it wanted to go even further in closing the back door for unlawful arrivals so that it might maintain strict control of the invitations issued through the front door. Though the Labor government, with the full support of the Coalition parties in opposition, had implemented a regime of man-datory detention for all persons who arrived without a visa, there was another blip on the graph in 1994–95 with the arrival of 1,071 boat people. In previous years there had been fewer than 200 boat people a year. It happened that the election of the Howard government in March 1996 coincided with an exponential increase in the number of boats arriving. Whereas only eight boats a year had arrived on average from 1989 until the election of the Howard government, 39 boats a year on average came from March 1996 until the *Tampa* was denied permis-sion to land in August 2001.

Prior to the election of the Howard government, there had been fewer than 2,000 boat arrivals during this third wave, about 400 a year. The Howard government was treated to the spectacle of 11,500 boat arrivals, about 2,000 a year. Even more troubling for the government was that, with the troubles in Iraq, Afghanistan and Iran, the word was clearly out that Australia provided a good escape route via Malaysia and Indonesia. In the two years before the *Tampa* incident there were more than 4,000 boat arrivals a year. Twice as many boats arrived in the second three-year term of the Howard government than in the previous ten years. All previous efforts to offset the push factors by turning the pull factors into 'push away' factors had failed. The government maintained its commitment to the offshore refugee component. It tied the onshore component to the offshore component such that each one approved onshore meant one less place for those offshore. The government thought that it was in a strong moral position as well as a strong political position to send a clear message to boat people.

The strategy was:

- to cooperate with the Indonesian authorities in the upstream disruption of boats
- to positively deter boats attempting to enter Australian territorial waters
- to keep people in remote detention centres away from lawyers and 'do-gooders', reducing the access to the courts for those on shore
- to confine the definition of refugee status
- to process people offshore, as far as possible, so that they would not have any guarantee of resettlement in Australia even if they were proved to be refugees
- to deny refugees coming via the back door any access to family reunion.

Just as the Hawke government had made policy on the run, flying asylum seekers all over the country, one step ahead of the lawyers, so too the Howard government made policy on the run. This time there was the added spice of an election campaign, an international stand-off on the high seas and a cheque-book approach to mendicant Pacific states willing to detain boat people while their claims were being processed. Everyone knew that such a repressive response could not be maintained for long without doing great harm to the Australian way of doing things and to Australia's reputation in the region. The hope was that the firebreak could be quickly established, that the boats would stop coming, and that the back door would be firmly locked without the need for ongoing confrontations on the high seas, in the middle of the desert and on remote Pacific islands. Everyone would then be able to get back to secure borders and an open front door for those refugees lucky enough to be chosen from the enormous UNHCR caseload.

These were dreadful months for everyone involved, most especially for the terrified people, including children, on boats confronting the Australian Navy, before ending up in Nauru or Papua New Guinea. Meanwhile those who had already arrived on the Australian mainland were in makeshift detention centres stretched to a capacity they had never been intended for. The detention of large numbers of women and children sent shock waves around Australia as many citizens wondered how it had come to this. Prime ministerial expressions of regret, backed by claims that there was no better way, were sufficient to appease, satisfy and even delight many citizens. Others remained troubled that an island nation continent at the end of the earth had to resort to such measures when other first-world countries with far more pressing claims on their borders had never attempted such a firebreak. Surely there had to be a better way. The government remained convinced that if it kept its nerve and stared down those on the boats and the people smugglers then all would be well and there could be a return to a more decent and more humane keeping of the watch.

The Australian stereotype of the boat person in this fourth wave is a young man from a wealthy family who cuts a deal with a people smuggler for transport to one of a range of first-world countries where the young man will be able to settle and provide the option for other family members to join him later. During the course of his journey, the young man will have stopped in various countries where he could have sought and obtained protection. He decided not to do this because he wanted to engage in secondary movement and obtain a favourable migration outcome.

This stereotype was thought to be particularly applicable to the Afghans and Iraqis in 2000 and 2001 because many of them had spent long periods of time in refugee camps in adjoining countries such as Iran and Pakistan. Why didn't they just wait there patiently like their fellow refugees rather than jumping the queue? At this time, Afghans constituted the largest refugee group in the world — 3.6 million or 30 per cent of the global refugee population. People had been fleeing Afghanistan for over 20 years. The second largest group were the refugees from Burundi, concentrated mainly in Tanzania. The third largest group were the Iraqis. People smugglers do not feature much in the journeys of those fleeing Burundi. The people do not have the money and the smugglers do not have the networks there. With the huge out-flow of refugees from Afghanistan and Iraq, people smugglers were able to ply their trade, offering protection in faraway places.

Most of these people who reached Australia by boat were found to be refugees and three years ago they were issued with temporary protection visas. In most cases, the visas were not issued until about a year after the refugee first left home. After a four-year absence, the temporary protection visa (TPV) holders are now expected to prove again that they are refugees entitled to ongoing protection in Australia. If they stayed more than seven days in another country where they could have obtained protection, they are entitled to only another three-year TPV. They are denied a permanent protection visa that would carry with it a right to sponsor family members and a right to travel outside Australia and return.

When they were in detention, the TPV holders would have received legal assistance with the preparation of their claims. Now they are no longer entitled to that assistance. They will have to pay for it them-selves or obtain it with assistance from some community group. If, for example, they are Hazaras from Afghanistan, it was quite simple to ob-tain recognition as a refugee the first time around because, like all Hazaras, they were fleeing from the Taliban regime. There was no need back then to adduce further, more specific evidence about the perse-cution that they, their families and their villages faced by groups other than the Taliban. Now there is a need for such evidence. Much of this evidence will be based on fears about those groups now sharing in gov-ernment who were oppressors of the Hazaras in the pre-Taliban period. It is very traumatic for the young man to provide such evidence when he has had no contact with his family or his village for four years. There is no doubt about his fear. Is his fear caused by his having a real chance of persecution? Does he have a real chance of a fair hearing when he has the Australian government assuring him that it is safe for him to go home because some of his fellow Hazaras have accepted the government's $2,000 offer and returned voluntarily?

When Abdullah Abdullah, the Foreign Minister in Hamid Karzai's Afghan government, visited Australia in November 2002, the Australian government made much of his assertion that there would be TPV holders with false identities, including terrorists and others who were Pakistani nationals. Many Hazaras were terrified by the minister's new-found respectability given their memories of his involvement with the Rabbani government's Defence Minister Ahmad Shah Massoud who authorised Hazara massacres in 1993. It was Massoud who had commissioned the state intelligence service to intensify the conflict between the different ethnic parties. He had espoused ethnic cleansing between Hazaras and Pashtuns, inciting tensions between inhabitants of central and northern parts of Afghanistan, and playing on the differences between Shiite and Sunni Muslims.

The Hazaras are the third major ethnic group in Afghanistan after the Pashtun and the Tajiks. Whereas most of the Pashtuns and Tajiks are Sunni Muslims, the Hazaras are usually minority Shia Muslims. Over the centuries the Hazaras have lost most of their traditional lands. As one TPV holder, Latif Jawadi, described the situation: 'The Pashtun would say to the Tajiks, you have a home land Tajikistan, go home; to the Uzbeks, you have a home land, Uzbekistan, go home; to the Hazaras, you have no home but the cemetery, the graveyard, the land of the dead.'[24] After the fall of the city of Mazar-I-Sharif in 1998, Mullah Manon Niazi, Taliban Governor of Mazar-I-Sharif, had left no doubt in the minds of Hazaras that there was no homeland for them when he spoke to a crowd in a mosque:

> Hazaras, where are you escaping? If you jumped in to the air, we will grasp your legs; if you enter the earth we will grasp your ears. Oh Hazaras! We will not let you to go away. Every border is in our control.[25]

The situation for young Hazara men who joined the fourth wave of boat people to Australia is summarised by Dr William Maley from the Australian Defence Force Academy, an expert on Afghanistan wars:

> Most of the Hazaras are young men, driven from their homes and families by concerted pressure applied by the Taliban, acting in concert with people-smuggling networks and elements of the Pakistani State. Faced with the threat of the forced seizure of their lands and sequestration of their assets, they are casuistically offered a 'safe way out' in exchange for cash payments, with the Taliban, the smugglers, and the Pakistani groups all taking a cut. The cash in question typically comprises the pooled life sav-

ings of elders with a lineage, who recognise that it is the young men of military age in the lineage, bearers of its future identity, who are in greatest danger. These young men are trucked to Karachi, transported by air to Indonesia, and then conveyed by boat to Australian islands and reefs close to the Indonesian archipelago.[26]

It is no answer to say that these young men could have joined the queue at the Australian High Commission in Islamabad where the waiting time for a visa application was two years, Pakistan being no place of safety for an Hazara. In 2000–2001 the Australian High Commission issued only 109 humanitarian visas. Neither could they find protection from the UNHCR even if they knew of the UNHCR's existence. Being swamped with requests for assistance and protection, the UNHCR had to urge Afghans not to approach its office in Islamabad. In Pakistan it was able to process only 2,463 claims in 1999. By September 2001 the High Commission had to close its office in Islamabad for four months, informing asylum seekers that they could present themselves at the Bangkok office on the understanding that there would be some delay with the provision of services due to the increased demand!

One young Hazara, Sha Hussain Hassani, had been on the run in the mountains for months when his father came one night with food and a message. He was to leave with smugglers that very night. His father had sold enough goods to employ a smuggler so that Sha, the eldest son, might leave immediately, he being the one most at risk. Sha's father hoped to be able to afford to have all his family leave Afghanistan eventually. 'There was no place to go and no one to trust any more. It was too dangerous to wait. I had to go immediately.'[27] Sha has heard nothing from his family since that night. He does not know whether they are still in Afghanistan. He does not even know if they are still alive.

Another young Hazara man, Atiq Hashemi, who fled and ended up in Australia, described the beginning of his journey:

The continuation of the family line is very important in our culture, so most of the older sons and their fathers fled to the mountains. We lived in the mountain for a couple of months. We visited our families once a week at night time. My grandfather brought food for my father and I once a week. Finally things got so bad that it was decided that we should get out of Afghanistan. My father could not leave his family so he sent me away by my-

self. This is why I had to say goodbye to my family and my greatest wish
is to be reunited with them where it is safe to be Hazara and we have a
future.[28]

There was no question of planning for the rest of the family to come
to Australia. It was a situation of such desperation that the family made
the decision to save one of their number. Being Hazara, they were not
eligible for Afghan travel documents. They had to leave unlawfully. If
they entered Pakistan they were still terrified of the Pashtun, who pre-
dominated in the west of Pakistan close to the Afghan border. For one
young Hazara, Mohammed Reza Jaffari, the journey to Australia began
with a car journey to the Pakistan border with an Hazara smuggler. His
father came part of the way. Reza had then to cross the Pakistani border
in darkness. He remained in hiding while documents were prepared
for his plane trip to Malaysia.

Sayad Ali Sharaffi came in the back of a jeep hidden under bags of
produce. Others crossed the border by donkey. They crossed where
there were no border guards or where the smugglers could bribe the
guards. Arriving in Pakistan, they had no thought that their journey to
safety could end in the middle of Pashtun country, the birthplace of the

Reproduced with Bill Leak's permission.

Taliban, and most had never heard of the UNHCR. Even those few who knew of the UNHCR in Islamabad entertained no notion of running the gauntlet of Pakistani Pashtun guards outside the office so they could enter their names on a database.

When asked if he could have stayed in Pakistan, Mortaza Ali Askary answered:

> No, because that is not our land and they need documents to say you belong there and we were afraid that if they catch us they would just send us back to the Taliban because they are many of them Pashtun too like the Taliban. We sold our cattle and some of our land and so we wanted to go right away where we thought we would not be sent back to where they would kill us.[29]

When provided with false documents, the Hazaras then made the next step of the journey. Most were flown to Malaysia because there were no visa restrictions on Muslims arriving in Malaysia. Reza described his confusion, fear and ignorance:

> I was alone and I was not allowed to go outside the building because I was illegal in that city in Pakistan. When I had to get on the plane I was so frightened. There was another guy too and the smuggler just said when you get off the plane just wait there and someone will come and pick you up. I landed at Malaysia I think or Thailand, I don't know ... and there was someone waiting at the airport. They took me to another house away from there in the car and we were not allowed to go anywhere in that place.[30]

Those like Reza who had paid the lowest fare to a smuggler had then to make a boat journey to Indonesia:

> From there we went to a boat and they took us to Indonesia, about forty people, families, everyone but I don't know what nationality. I was so frightened, so seasick and I had never seen the ocean and I just didn't want to see the water. I could not swim then. That trip took about two days I think and we landed on a beach near a village, a small village and they took us to another place, a hotel sort of thing. Then one night they took us to the beach and there was another boat and there were many people on that boat. I met Asghar on that boat. It took two and a half days and we landed on Christmas Island. I was so sick and so weak. Asghar saved me I think. He looked after me. When we came to Christmas Island, a boat came and made us stop there.

Most boys realised that their final destination was to be Australia only after they arrived in Indonesia. Families had been promised that their sons would be taken somewhere safe but most were not told exactly where this safety would be. It depended upon the amount of money the family could raise. Europe was a far more expensive trip than the one to Australia and the smugglers simply matched the destination to the funds that the families supplied. Having travelled on false documents, the young men then had their documents confiscated by the smugglers on the last stage of the journey, often with no explanation. They assumed that the smugglers did not want the Australian authorities to discover their *modus operandi*. No one saw any need to retain the documents because they were sham documents anyway. As was the case with every leg of the journey, out of fear and ignorance they did what the smugglers demanded. Mortaza explained:

> The smugglers or their friends, their agents, they had our documents with them until we get on the plane and they had contacts with the Indonesian officers in the airport so that's why we got out of the airport. In Malaysia it was just a transit so there was one smuggler there and he just took us to our plane, to the right plane that we had to catch. We had only the documents when we were in the airport from Pakistan to Indonesia. After that they got the documents. When we got on the plane in Pakistan we had the documents because I was with my older brother and his wife but the other boys didn't get the documents. There was someone with them, a smuggler I think, who had the documents for them because they are too young to know where to go or anything and maybe the smuggler is afraid he will get caught if the boys don't say the things right. When we got to Indonesia, the smugglers they take all the documents from us. We didn't have anything to be tearing or throwing away when we get on the boats. It was like the smugglers they own the documents, not us and maybe they use them again. I don't know. I just wanted to get away and so I had to get the smugglers to help and they do all the document things.[31]

Sayad travelled for two days by road under orders not to speak to his smuggler. He then spent a week locked up in a house somewhere in Pakistan before being taken to the plane in a group of 16. He flew to Malaysia on false documents and 'at no stage did I have control over this journey'. At the airport in Malaysia, they were held in a room until other smugglers came for them 'and escorted us on board a flight bound for Indonesia'. There a group of them were taken by van to a hotel or large house. 'No one dared to leave the building — the smugglers had warned us of the severe trouble we would be in if we went out.' After about a week, they were collected and transported to a boat, being assured that they would be taken to a 'safe place'. This was the first time Sayad had ever heard of Australia. There is no way that he had set out from Afghanistan wanting to come to Australia for a better life, hoping that he would be able to sponsor his family to join him. Like so many others, he left not knowing where he would end up, the one member of his family chosen to survive in the wake of the ongoing murderous Taliban regime. His family was prepared to pool their life savings so that one of their number might survive somewhere in the world.

Even those who are most surely refugees do dream of a better, more dignified life once they reach a place that offers real protection. Reza said:

> No one wants to be frightened of death all the time. No one wants to get, what do you say, stolen or raped. No one wants to be afraid to pray, to be not able to go to someone for protection when you are threatened, to have ... the police beat you if you ask for help, or even kill you. To have no schools and no roads, no hospitals in your area because you are Hazara and no one wants to give anything to Hazaras. Always my grandfather told to me, it has been like this and my mother and father had no education but my father wanted that for his children. He believed that education would change Afghanistan and it could be better for his children than it was for him and for everyone for many years, since my grandfather and before him too.[32]

Mr Ruddock has long been critical of those who arrive in Australia without documents having transited other countries. Here is a typical exchange on Sydney radio station 2GB:

> Mr Ruddock: Everybody's got rid of their documentation before they get here.
> Ray Hadley: That's the point I've been making for the past three years. They get to Christmas Island and it goes floating in some sort of Gucci bag, you know?
> Mr Ruddock: We saw them throwing them over.
> Ray Hadley: Yeah, well, I spoke to one of your people on Christmas Island during that Christmas period two or three years ago who told me that he

saw the briefcases minus the US dollars going west.

Mr Ruddock: That's right.[33]

According to Mr Ruddock, 'For the most part, unauthorised arrivals are not fleeing directly to Australia. Most have lived for extensive periods of time in third countries where documentation supporting their claimed identity and background is often available and have travel patterns into and through the region that would reasonably indicate they possessed formal travel documentation of some sort before arriving in Australia.'[34] Many of the Hazaras who arrived in Australia during the fourth wave had never previously left their local villages. Being Hazara, they could never obtain any form of valid travel documentation whether from the Taliban or their warlord predecessors.

When in Opposition a decade earlier, Ruddock had quizzed immigration departmental officials as to why Australia could not emulate some European countries and deem people to have had the option of protection in safe third countries through which they transited. In 1992 Dr Evan Arthur, director of the department's Determination and Refugee Status Policy Division, explained to him:

> We have done analysis of our caseload and, at the moment — I am not swearing to the total accuracy of this — the number of applicants who would fall into that category is 2 per cent or less. It is something of that magnitude for people who have arrived in Australia via a convention signatory. I think it is a reflection of our part of the world: the nature of the region in, which we live. There are very few signatories of the convention within the Asian region generally and even fewer in the South East Asian region.[35]

The Australian government has continued to claim that it is not in breach of the Refugees Convention. Article 31 provides that a contracting state is not to impose penalties on an asylum seeker for their illegal entry if they are 'coming directly from a territory where their life or freedom was threatened'. The Australian government has been imposing three penalties. First, they have been detaining all such persons until they are granted refugee status. No such penalty is imposed on asylum seekers who enter with a visa. Second, they have been restricting the unlawful entrant to a three-year protection visa without the right of family reunion and without the right to travel outside Australia and return. The refugee who entered Australia with a visa is entitled to permanent residence in Australia, including the right of family reunion and the right to travel from and back to Australia. Third, the government has insisted that any asylum seeker who entered Australia without a visa and who resided in a transit country continuously for more than seven days will never be entitled to permanent residence. The government's reading of Article 31 cannot be reconciled with the UNHCR's Guidelines, which state:

> The expression 'coming directly' in Article 31(1) covers the situation of a person who enters the country in which asylum is sought directly from the country of origin, or from another country where his protection, safety and security could not be assured. It is understood that this term also covers a person who transits an intermediate country for a short period of time without having applied for, or received, asylum there. No strict time limit can be applied to the concept 'coming directly' and each case must be judged on its merits. Similarly, given the special situation of asylum-seekers, in particular the effects of trauma, language problems, lack of information, previous experiences which often result in a suspicion of those in authority, feelings of insecurity, and the fact that these and other circumstances may vary enormously from one asylum seeker to another, there is no time limit which can be mechanically applied or associated with the expression 'without delay'.[36]

When it comes to analysing the government's response to the fourth wave of boat people, it is important to remember that Pakistan, Thailand, Malaysia and Indonesia are not signatories to the Refugees Convention. Those asylum seekers from Afghanistan who have transited through Pakistan, Malaysia and Indonesia have never entered a country bound by the provisions of the convention until they arrive in Australia. Ten years ago, the Australian immigration department thought they had good reasons for not trying to claim that these persons had protection available to them en route. Though none of these transit countries has since signed the convention, the Australian government now tries to argue for de facto protection being deemed to be available unless the applicant disproves it. The applicants are in no position to adduce any evidence about the situation in those countries because they spent their time in isolation under the tight supervision of people smugglers. If they have spent seven days in any of these countries, they are deemed to have passed up the option of protection. They are then labelled as queue jumpers seeking a favourable migration outcome. Contrary to the Refugees Convention, they are penalised for entering Australia without a visa.

CHAPTER 3

Border control

By the time of the fourth wave of boat people, Australia had gone a long way towards perfecting the virtual offshore border, leading the world in setting up a comprehensive visa regime. Australian immigration officials have a better idea than their colleagues do in other governments about who has entered their country and who has left in the past year. Everyone who comes must have either an Australian passport or the equivalent of a visa. Travellers from low-risk countries can now use the Electronic Travel Authority if they are tourists or short-term business visitors. A low-risk country is one that is unlikely to produce refugees or people fleeing disaster. There is a fully computerised Advance Passenger Processing (APP) for most of the major airlines — Qantas, Cathay Pacific, Singapore Airlines, Air New Zealand, British Airways, China Airlines, Air Canada and Thai International. This system provides full synchronisation of passenger listings with the Australian immigration data banks. There are airport liaison officers at the major transit ports in Asia. The result of all these measures is that only 1,193 persons were refused entry at airports in 2001–2002 and only 85 persons arriving at Australian airports in that year engaged our protection obligations.

Undocumented asylum seekers just cannot get through our ports any more. They are stopped offshore at airports like Singapore and Bangkok. In 2001–2002, the airlines carried a record low 3,211 improperly documented people to or through Australia. The airlines are automatically fined for each infringement. Being an island with a computerised visa system and compliant airline operators, Australia is now a secure fortress with the exception of the occasional stowaway on a sea freighter or the occasional wave of boat people. Most who seek asylum come through the front door with a valid visa that was probably obtained under false pretences or without making full disclosure. All these procedures were largely in place before the heightened security concerns that followed 11 September 2001. The only entrants not to appear on the computer lists of visa applicants or of airline manifests are the boat people who have been assisted in recent times by the people smugglers. The boat people are the one group that can bypass the virtual offshore border. In the first year of the fourth wave, 97 per cent of the boats departed from Indonesia and most of them headed for the Ashmore Islands and Christmas Island.

Back in 1999 Prime Minister John Howard established a Coastal Surveillance Task Force which provided greater coordination of surveillance by Coastwatch (a division of the Australian Customs Service) and the defence forces. Boats carrying persons without Australian visas, departing Indonesian ports, were named SIEVs (suspected illegal entry vessels). Each boat was given an identification number. By September 2000 the Australian Federal Police had established a protocol with the Indonesian police to break up people smuggling rackets at work in Indonesia. The Australians paid the Indonesians at least $100,000 to assist with the 'upstream disruption' work. Secrecy was obviously of the essence, in part sparing the Australian police the need to disclose too much murky information to the prying eyes of Australian parliamentary committees. (Strangely, the protocol was suspended in September 2001.) The Australian authorities had no problems with this sweetheart arrangement, but the Indonesian foreign ministry thought that disruption activities should come under a more formal government-to-government agreement. At least, that is the way the Australian police commissioner explained things away when being questioned by senators who were obviously dissatisfied with the responses. A boat (later named SIEV X) carrying twice the usual payload of asylum seekers sank on 19 October 2001 and 353 people died; there were only 44 survivors. Prime Minister Howard said that it was nothing to do with Australia because, he said, the boat had gone down in Indonesian waters. This was not true. As Australian government officials knew on the day the prime minister made this statement, the boat was in international waters under the regular flight path of Australian aircraft carrying out surveillance activities.

In the wake of the *Tampa* incident, the Australian government decided that the Australian Defence Force (ADF) should no longer be just a supporting agency for Coastwatch. The ADF was to become the lead agency for a much more aggressive border-control policy, intercepting boats on the high seas. The operation named Operation Relex lasted four months, including the federal election campaign of 2001. It was a critical part of building the firebreak. As late as 17 August 2001, John Howard had told the voters that 'using our armed forces to stop the people coming and turning them back' was 'not really an option for a humanitarian nation':

> We are a humanitarian country. We don't turn people back into the sea, we don't turn unseaworthy boats which are likely to capsize and the people on them be drowned. We can't behave in that manner. People say, 'Well, send them back from where they came', [but] the country from which they came won't have them back. Many of them are frightened to go back to those countries and we are faced with this awful dilemma of on the one hand trying to behave like a humanitarian, decent country, on the other hand making certain that we don't become just an easy touch for illegal immigrants. Now I believe the government has got the balance about as correct as it can in current circumstances.[1]

Eleven days later, the chief of the Defence Force issued an order that led to the formulation of Operation Relex. Defence Minister Peter Reith approved the rules of engagement for the operation on 1 September. The prime minister's concurrence was sought the next day and the operation commenced at midnight on 3 September 2001. The Air Force would provide aerial surveillance to within 24 nautical miles of the Indonesian coastline. The Australian Federal Police (AFP) already had an agreement with the Indonesian authorities relating to upstream disruption and the sharing of intelligence about activities onshore in Indonesia. Boats would then be tracked, and while they were in international waters the Navy would approach them and warn them not to enter Australian territorial waters. Once a boat was within 24 nautical miles of Christmas Island or Ashmore Reef, the Navy would 'reinforce the warning and turn the vessel around and either steam it out of our contiguous zone ourselves under its own power or — as it happened on a number of occasions — if the engine had been sabotaged in our process of boarding, we would then tow the vessel outside our contiguous zone into international waters'.[2] This cat and mouse game would be played two or three times before authorities in Canberra made the decision as to whether to transport the people to Christmas Island, Ashmore Reef or some other destination such as Nauru or Manus Island. People would be kept on board their own vessels for as long as their boat was 'marginally seaworthy'. At no time would the Australian defence personnel make inquiries about any person's claim to asylum. The head of the Navy, Rear Admiral Smith, told the parliament, 'The status of these people was irrelevant to us.'

Prior to Operation Relex, the Navy would intercept asylum boats only once they entered Australian territorial waters. Now the Navy would be guided by aircraft and would intercept the boats on the high seas, preventing them from entering Australian territorial waters so that ultimately people smugglers would be deterred from using Australia as a destination. Orion aircraft regularly patrolled from Christmas Island to Ashmore Reef and north to within 24 nautical miles of the Indonesian coastline. During the four months of Operation Relex, the Navy intercepted 12 boats, numbered SIEV 1 to SIEV 12. Four were turned back to Indonesia, three sank and the other five were impounded. Those persons who did not return to Indonesia were taken on board the Navy ships and transported to Nauru or Papua New Guinea for processing. These were exercises of high brinkmanship not usually engaged in outside of war. The navy officers knew that the asylum seekers would try desperate tactics to reach Australia, presuming that the Australian personnel would not put life at risk. It was common for boats to be sabotaged by asylum seekers hoping that their stranding would then result in navy transport to Christmas Island.

These antics on the high seas were occurring during an election campaign and the navy commanders were under strict orders not to act without Canberra's approval. Back in Canberra, high-level public servants were meeting with senior military personnel each day to plan the tactics. Rear Admiral Smith told a Senate inquiry, 'Once we had inter-

Sydney Morning Herald, 4 September 2001.
Reproduced with Cathy Wilcox's permission.

cepted, everything that occurred after that in terms of major decisions
— such as boarding, removal of people or whatever it happened to be
— actually came from Canberra.'[3] The humanitarian strain on young
navy officers was immense. For example, on one occasion they had to
keep a boatload of 129 people (including 54 children) in custody on
their overcrowded vessel for ten days. While the asylum seekers were
being transferred to a navy vessel for transport to Nauru, one woman
gave birth.

On 7 October 2001 at 11.15 am, Minister Ruddock, in election
mode, told the Australian public that asylum seekers that very morning
were throwing their children into the sea. Having received information
from his departmental secretary, Mr Bill Farmer, who was attending a
meeting of the government's People Smuggling Task Force, Ruddock
told the media, 'We are not going to be intimidated out of our policy by
this kind of behaviour. I regard this as one of the most disturbing practices I've come across. It was clearly planned and premeditated.'
Prime Minister John Howard came in behind his minister and affirmed, 'Our policy remains quite resolute. We are a humane nation,

but we're not a nation that's going to be intimidated by this kind of behaviour.'[4] As all Australians now know, nothing of the sort was happening. The government saw no need to correct that mistake until after the election. What was happening in the wee hours of that morning under cover of darkness was more frightening, as the log of HMAS *Adelaide* reveals. 'SIEV 4' was a suspected illegal entry vessel carrying 223 persons. The log reads:

6 October:
1813 (AEST 2113) First warning given to master of vessel.
7 October:
0153 (AEST 0453) Second warning issued.
0216 Boarding party ordered by Commanding Officer to prepare to board SIEV 4 when vessel enters Christmas Island Contiguous Zone.
0258 Adelaide made close pass down SIEV 4 starboard side.
0335 Adelaide directed by CJTF to conduct a positive and assertive boarding.
0402 Warning 5.56 mm shots fired 50 feet in front of vessel.
0405 Warning 5.56 mm shots fired 75 feet in front of SIEV 4.
0409 Warning 5.56 mm shots fired 50–100 feet in front of SIEV 4.
0414 Boarding party advised by CO that if 50 cal machine gun warning shots do not stop vessel, boarding party is to aggressively board SIEV 4.
0418–0420 Twenty-three rounds of 50 cal (20 rounds of automatic fire) fired in front of SIEV 4.
0430 Close quarters maneuvering by Adelaide, SIEV passed close astern to Adelaide port quarter and reduced speed/took way off momentarily.
0432 Boarding party issued final warning (to SIEV) indicating that if they did not allow boarding party to board, Adelaide would not let them enter Australian waters.
0442 Boarding party effected a conducted non-compliant boarding of SIEV 4.
0445 Boarding party in control of SIEV 4.

Once on board, the navy officers prepared the sabotaged boat for travel back to Indonesia. People started to jump overboard. Fourteen people were picked up from the sea by the Navy and returned to their boat. The boat headed off towards Indonesia at a slow speed. Within two hours it was dead in the water. Then distress signals were sent up. The Navy appeared again and ascertained that once again the boat had been sabotaged. The boat was now unrepairable. The people wanted to be taken to Australia. The commanding officer, Commander Banks, decided to tow the boat to Christmas Island but, as ever, awaited instructions from Canberra. They then towed the boat for a day. At 2.51 pm on 8 October, the boarding officer asked Commander Banks if the women and children could be removed from the 'marginally seaworthy' vessel. Banks refused because that would have meant the mission had failed. By 5 pm the boat was sinking. Everyone including the children had to go into the water, which would not have been necessary two hours earlier. Commander Banks reported, 'To my personal relief, the unauthorised arrivals' leader confirmed there was no loss of life and, importantly, that no-one was missing.' All this occurred because Canberra was insistent on going to the brink with the asylum seekers, adopting practices that were planned, premeditated and disturbing.

Many citizens agreed with the actions of the government, taking them on trust. Others, learning the facts, regarded this part of the firebreak in peacetime as disproportionate and very un-Australian. There had to be a better way. Most Australians want to believe Rear Admiral Smith's rebuttal of the claim that the Navy could be guilty 'of deliberately turning their backs on people in peril'. In a letter to the *Sydney Morning Herald*, he wrote, 'The Royal Australian Navy is a highly professional service which places the highest importance on the safety of life at sea and, whenever we are able, we will always respond to those in distress.'[5] The secrecy surrounding the arrangements with the Indonesians for upstream disruption and the brinkmanship on the high seas with Operation Relex are activities, which if pursued in the long term, are likely to change the character of Australia's police and military services. They will give some members of the public reason to think about the decency of what is done in the name of the Australian national interest. It ought to be unthinkable that Australian officials could have been party to any action resulting in the tragic loss of life on the boat which sank in international waters under the watch of Operation Relex. It is now imaginable that Australian officials were prepared to turn a blind eye to SIEV X,[6] having underwritten without question whatever the Indonesians thought was appropriate action. The damage to public trust caused by the 'Children Overboard' affair lay in the proof that officials know there are some things the government in

Reproduced with Bill Leak's permission.

Canberra does not want to know and they will go to great lengths to spare their political masters any embarrassment.

The Australian government has now wound down Operation Relex on account of the lack of boats seeking unauthorised access to Australian waters. The government stands ready to engage the defence forces again for such an operation should the boats start reappearing. Our government is prepared to go to great lengths to consolidate Fortress Australia and to ensure that the virtual offshore border is not penetrated by people in boats reaching Australia's outer islands and reefs. Europe and the United States have also designed ruthless strategies for making their borders more secure.

European Union border controls

The European Union is set to increase its member states from 15 to 25 in 2003 and to 27 by 2007. With this next expansion, there will be member states such as Poland and the Czech Republic, which in the past have produced a steady stream of asylum seekers turning up within the existing European Union borders. The European Union has long been seen as Fortress Europe with the desire to create a borderless world within the union. Seeking a Europe-wide area of freedom, security and justice, the member states saw the need to consolidate their external borders. The dual objective of a borderless interior and a strongly bordered exterior could be achieved only if there were agreement among the member states about free trade, commerce and relations between the member states and shared responsibility for the external boundaries. Free human movement among the member states could occur only if there were agreements about shared visas for the entry of third-country nationals and about the processing of asylum claims of third-country nationals and stateless persons within the European Union. With the collapse of the Berlin wall and the breakdown of the USSR, there have been acute new problems for the European Union to confront with asylum.

In 1985 France, Germany, Belgium, Luxembourg and the Netherlands drew up the Schengen Agreement whereby they would honour each other's visas. Third-country nationals with a visa from one of these countries would have free access for up to three months to any other country that was a party to the agreement. The United Kingdom was very wary about this free movement of persons. By 1988 the member states saw the need for some cooperative arrangements regarding refugees and asylum seekers. They did not want asylum seekers to be left in orbit travelling across the free borders once they had arrived in the European inner circle. By 1990, 11 member states had signed up to the Dublin Convention which set down the formula that allowed everyone to work out which member state would be responsible for processing an asylum application.

In 1995 the Council of Ministers made the first attempt to draw up a list of countries that would require visas for admission to any European Union country. The list included those countries affected by civil war or unrest — countries likely to produce a refugee flow. By 1996 all member states except Ireland and the United Kingdom had come aboard with the Schengen and Dublin arrangements. The state most responsible for the presence of an asylum seeker inside the European Union would be the one to process the claim, and a person once in the European Union would be free to travel to other member states without the need for further approval. The member states hoped that these arrangements would put an end to asylum seekers being in orbit within the European Union. To some extent they succeeded, but at the cost of the asylum seekers finding themselves in orbit on the perimeter of the European Union. Member states were negotiating bilateral agreements with neighbouring states outside the European Union on the basis that the neighbouring states were safe third countries where asylum seekers could have obtained protection if they had stayed there and on the understanding that these states would not themselves be producing refugees. Between 1995 and 1997 Germany had paid the Czech Republic 60 million deutschmarks under such an agreement. By identifying neighbouring states outside the union as safe third countries, they were running a refugee auction. Around the European Union was a circle of safe third countries with negotiated readmission agreements.

The member states had originally thought that asylum issues could be dealt with at the national level. All that would be required at the European Union level would be some basic coordination of national responses. When the Maastricht treaty effecting European Union was signed in 1992, asylum and immigration issues were to come under the 'third pillar', which provided only for loose cooperation between member states on issues to do with 'justice and home affairs'. The 'first pillar', including issues such as the internal market, agricultural policy, and economic and monetary union, were to be governed by the European Union institutions. Between the centralised institutions and legislative procedures of the first pillar and the loose coordination of the third pillar was the common foreign and security policy of the second pillar.

When the Treaty of Amsterdam was signed in 1997, asylum and migration issues were brought from the third pillar to the first pillar. The Schengen and Dublin arrangements for visas and asylum became central to the organisation of the European Union. With the desired expansion to 25 states in 2003 and a possible further expansion in 2007, including Bulgaria and Romania, the member states have seen a need for a harmonisation of policy on refugee questions. The Treaty on European Union now provides that by 2004 the European Council should adopt measures on asylum fully in accordance with the Convention on Refugees within the following areas:

- a Dublin Convention mechanism for determining which member state is responsible for processing an asylum claim
- minimum standards on the reception of asylum seekers
- minimum standards about the qualification of third-country nationals as refugees
- minimum standards for procedures designed to grant or withdraw refugee status.

The Council has now completed the first two of these tasks. The Council has also enacted directives about:

- carrier sanctions, setting down a range of penalties for carriers bringing undocumented passengers into the European Union
- the mutual recognition of decisions by member states to expel persons from their territory
- the granting of temporary protection in the event of a mass influx of persons seeking asylum or security in Europe.

In 2000, as an interim measure awaiting the harmonisation of European Union asylum policy, the Council set up a European Refugee Fund to run until 2004, which supports and encourages the efforts made by the member states in receiving and bearing the consequences of receiving refugees and displaced persons. The Council has also established EURODAC, a comprehensive data bank of the fingerprints of all asylum seekers arriving in the European Union after January 2003. Many refugee advocates have been worried that this harmonisation exercise would result in the European Union simply subscribing to the lowest common denominator of present member state practice. To some extent, these fears have been justified. There are many word games played in Brussels. At the same time, major players such as Germany and the United Kingdom have gone ahead and legislated their own reforms, sending a clear message that the harmonisation exercise will not be a one-way street dictating change to the member states.

United Kingdom border control

The United Kingdom does not have as comprehensive a visa system as

Australia. In the last decade the United Kingdom has greatly increased the number of countries on its visa list, which now includes 110 countries. All those countries most likely to produce refugees are on the list. Nationals from countries such as Afghanistan, Iraq and Iran need a visa not only to visit but even to transit Heathrow Airport. Like Australia, the United Kingdom now posts airline liaison officers in sensitive ports, assisting the airlines to make a determination that the intending passenger has the relevant clearance to enter the United Kingdom. There are also steep fines for airline companies that carry people whose documentation is incomplete. The aim is to ensure that people seeking asylum do not turn up on the doorstep. In 1996 the United Kingdom drew up a 'white list' of safe countries that were deemed to be incapable of producing refugees. In a 1999 asylum case, Lord Justice Simon Brown said, 'The combined effect of visa requirements and carriers' liability has made it well-nigh impossible for refugees to travel to countries of refuge without false documents.'[7] On 23 January 2002 the Home Office Minister in the House of Lords was asked 'whether there are any legal means by which an individual can enter this country and claim asylum'. Lord Rooker answered, 'My Lords, I think that the short answer to the noble Lord's question is no.'[8]

Unlike Australia, the United Kingdom receives many foreigners by ship and now on the Eurostar through the Chunnel. This ready channel link renders the United Kingdom much less isolated than Australia. The United Kingdom receives up to ten times more asylum claims a year than Australia. No one knows how many people enter the United Kingdom undetected each year. Since the opening of the Chunnel, there has been a major problem with asylum seekers boarding trains and hiding themselves in lorries. The Red Cross had no option but to provide basic humanitarian assistance to the thousands of people gathering at Sangatte near the French entrance of the Chunnel. During the three years that Sangatte was open, more than 67,000 asylum seekers were given the most basic welfare assistance in horrendously overcrowded and violent conditions. The government still described Sangatte as a magnet for asylum seekers. These people would be seeking entrée to the United Kingdom undetected. Or, if detected, they would often claim asylum. On 2 December 2002, when announcing the closure of Sangatte and closer cooperation with the French authorities,

David Blunkett, the Home Secretary, told parliament, 'The change that has made a difference today is the shifting of the border controls from England to the French coast. We have shifted the immigration and security checks and ensured that people will not get here. Stopping people entering clandestinely has to make more sense than trying to process them and send them back whence they came.'[9] Rarely has a modern first-world government minister made the purpose so clear. The preferred outcome is to move the border offshore so prospective asylum seekers can be turned away before they enter the territory. The British have provided the French with laser heartbeat detectors to check vehicles coming through the Chunnel. There are United Kingdom immigration officers placed at Calais.

In a major overhaul of the United Kingdom migration and asylum program, Blunkett has taken a couple of leaves from Australia's book. He has announced an annual quota of offshore refugees (though only 500 in the first year) and an annual intake of short-term migrants who will work in the needy hotel and restaurant sector. Introducing the Nationality, Immigration and Asylum Bill to the House of Commons on 24 April 2002, he said:

> In enabling people to come to this country for a short or a long stay, and to contribute their diversity and strengths to the well being of our country, we must also strengthen the welcome for those who seek asylum from death and persecution. The new gateways for economic migration and the gateway that we are establishing with the United Nations High Commissioner for Refugees will enable those who face persecution to apply for, and to be granted, such status from outside the country. Those gateways will be crucial in ensuring that we avoid scenes—such as those witnessed last summer and since—of clandestine attempts, often at great personal risk, to enter the country through the channel tunnel and via ferries.
>
> I am proposing that those who currently enter the country clandestinely, with inappropriate papers or by applying for refugee status 'in country', will be able to enter on a managed basis through the UNHCR without needing to put their lives at risk or to present fraudulent papers. In that way, as we gradually build up the process, we can ensure that people can approach this country honestly if they are at risk.[10]

The Australian experience teaches us that the provision of a quota of places for offshore refugees does not put paid to attempts being made by asylum seekers to reach the shores of first-world countries. If they reach a first-world country, they will have a greater chance of resettlement than if they simply waited in the camps in the transit countries.

Since then Blunkett has gone one step further in setting up an orderly offshore migration channel as a moral justification for coming down hard on those who present themselves onshore. There will be a one-off offer of employment places for 1,000 offshore Iraqis, announced at the same time as the closure of Sangatte and increased security measures on the French side of the Chunnel (minimising the prospect of Iraqis and others coming undetected into the United Kingdom and then seeking asylum). There are two possibilities with the political and moral calculus. All these people are only economic migrants, in which case we are entitled to set a quota. Or, providing for 1,000 economic migrants from one country excuses us from giving further assistance to bona fide asylum seekers from that country and many others. Refugee advocates are understandably wary about these new trade-offs. Aware of the Australian rhetoric, they do not want the small new quota of offshore refugees to become a foil for setting up two classes of refugee — the good offshore refugees who respect our borders and sovereignty and the bad onshore refugees who are selfish queue jumpers seeking a migration outcome.

Through its membership of the European Union, the United Kingdom is hopeful that it can shift its border controls for asylum seekers from the United Kingdom to France. Government and Opposition members of parliament are also hoping that one of the positive spin-offs of expanded European Union membership (including Poland and the Czech Republic) will be border controls that can be moved to the outer boundary of the expanded European Union. It will then be virtually impossible for persons from within the expanded European Union states to claim asylum.

In 2002 the United Kingdom was receiving up to 850 asylum claims a month from Czech nationals, especially the ethnic Roma group. These are now presumed to be nationals of a safe country. Though this presumption could be rebutted with evidence presented in an asylum claim, the applicant if refused asylum in the first instance will have to bring any appeal to the decision from overseas. They will not be permitted to remain in the United Kingdom to fight the appeal. The further advantage for government of expanded European Union membership is that asylum seekers turning up in the United Kingdom from other European Union countries can be sent back to a member state where any member of the asylum seeker's family already has refugee status, or where the asylum seeker was previously given a visa or leave to enter.

This combination of measures will help to further isolate the United Kingdom from the mass movements of asylum seekers in the world. British citizens, like their Australian counterparts, will be able to assure themselves that they are doing their part for refugees by taking an offshore quota and by contributing financial and other assistance to the poorer countries which inevitably are the next-door neighbours to the major refugee-producing countries. The ongoing problem for the United Kingdom will be the perception that the United Kingdom is still the most attractive option in the European Union for asylum seekers, especially during the time that their claims are being processed. Even if the accommodation and appeals process is made more stringent, there will always be asylum seekers attracted to a European Union country where English is the spoken language. Even if there are work restrictions for the first six months, asylum seekers continue to see an advantage in being in a country that does not have a universal system of identity cards. Many asylum seekers are also attracted to the country that already has a sizeable group of their own community. It is no surprise that Zimbabwean asylum seekers would flock to London even after the British took the belated decision to require Zimbabweans to have a visa for entry.

While Australia has been dealing with 13,000 asylum claims a year, the British have had to process 92,000 a year. There have been some suggestions that the Royal Navy would be dispatched to the high seas to deter asylum seekers. To date that has not happened. The cooperation with the French authorities has not had any of the hallmarks of the Australian–Indonesian upstream disruption program. Both police forces know that their actions would be subject to parliamentary and media scrutiny.

Germany's border controls

With the collapse of the Berlin Wall and German reunification, the

German nation state found itself sharing land borders with nine countries including Poland and Czechoslovakia. It was inevitable with the collapse of the USSR that there would be major population flows from east to west. Germany's geography and constitutional arrangements conspired to make the country a preferred destination for asylum seekers throughout Europe. After World War II, Germans who had returned from exile during the Nazi regime and citizens traumatised by the State's treatment of the Jews were adamant that the constitution would provide a right of asylum. Article 16 of the 1949 Basic Law provided, 'Persons persecuted on political grounds enjoy the right of asylum.'

Though not viewing itself as a net migration country, Germany has received three main streams of migration since World War II: the Aussiedler (ethnic Germans from elsewhere who had a legal right to return and take up citizenship prior to the building of the wall in 1961), guest workers who came in great numbers from 1955 to 1973, and asylum seekers. More than a million Southern Europeans came to Germany as guest workers. There are now more than seven million non-Germans living in Germany — 9 per cent of the population of 82 million. Once the guest-worker program had been closed down, the asylum route and family reunification (especially after marriage with a German citizen or with a foreigner entitled to a residence permit) were the only ways that foreigners could lay claim to long-term residence in Germany.

With the coming down of the wall, there was a return to the re-entry program for the Aussiedler. There is an annual quota of 220,000 who are permitted to return and take up their citizenship. Under Article 116 of the Basic Law, anyone 'who has been admitted to the territory of the German Reich within the frontiers of 31 December 1937 as a refugee or expellee of German ethnic origin or as the spouse or descendant of such a person' is a German. In the old West Germany, guest-worker agreements had been signed with the governments of Italy, Spain, Greece, Turkey, Portugal, Tunisia, Morocco and Yugoslavia. The old East Germany even had a guest-worker program with the Vietnamese.

In 1990 there were 193,000 people in Germany claiming asylum. By 1993 there were 438,000. More than 60 per cent of all Europe's asylum seekers for the years 1984–1993 were in Germany. During the Bosnian War, half the Bosnians who fled seeking protection ended up in Germany. In 1992 the European Union ministers responsible for Interior Affairs met in London and agreed on a number of 'soft law' options for stemming the flow of asylum seekers in Europe. These options were not binding on the member states but they provided them with room to move, experimenting with national legislation and policy that would not fall foul of the European Union membership. At this meeting, governments decided to close the asylum route for three groups: those deemed to be from safe countries of origin, those deemed to have travelled through a safe third country, and those deemed on arrival to have a manifestly unfounded claim. On 6 December 1992 the Christian, Social and Liberal Democrats announced their decision to use these concepts to restrict the German right of asylum. Despite its post-war commitment to ensure protection for political refugees, Germany extensively amended its Basic Law in 1993, taking unilateral action to reduce access for persons seeking asylum. The German approach has since been replicated by many first-world countries feeling besieged by significant population flows from trouble spots that are not the neighbouring countries but countries that are more accessible with modern communications and transport.

Though the Basic Law still recognises the right of asylum for those fleeing political persecution, someone who enters Germany from a safe third country cannot claim that right. All member states of the European Union are deemed to be safe countries. The Bundesrat (Senate) has the power to declare other countries as safe third countries. The Czech Republic, Norway, Poland and Switzerland are declared to be safe third countries. Now, all countries sharing a land border with Germany are declared to be safe. There is therefore no point in any asylum seeker coming overland and claiming asylum at the German border. They will simply be turned back. If they end up in Germany claiming asylum once they are well away from the border, the German authorities acting on the Dublin Convention will then have the opportunity to return the asylum seeker to another European Union country for processing. Often the asylum seeker will have destroyed travel documents once away from the border. There may then be real difficulty in returning the person to another European Union country.

The 1993 amendment also permitted the Bundesrat to draw up a list of safe countries of origin where because of their legal and political situation there would be a fair guarantee that there would be neither political persecution nor inhuman punishment or treatment. A citizen of such a state could be presumed not to have been persecuted and it would be necessary for the asylum seeker to provide compelling evidence of political persecution. The German list of safe countries of origin presently includes Bulgaria, the Czech Republic, Ghana, Hungary, Poland, Romania, Senegal, and the Slovak Republic.

The Germans also led the way at this time in proposing that persons with manifestly unfounded asylum claims could be removed from the country even if they still had an appeal to the courts pending. The 1993 constitutional amendment permitted procedures for courts to hear non-suspensive appeals, meaning that the removal order would not be suspended while the court considered its decision. The applicant would have to leave the country within a week and await the appeal decision in another country. Only 10 per cent of those who received an initial decision that their claim was manifestly unfounded could convince the courts that they should be allowed to remain in Germany until they had exhausted their appeals.

The 1993 constitutional amendment also envisaged bilateral agreements with other governments permitting the return of asylum seekers to other jurisdictions provided the other government agreed to process the claims and to comply with the Convention on Refugees and international human rights law. Germany has now signed 23 agreements, including agreements with a range of non-European Union countries such as the Czech Republic, Hong Kong, Hungary, Morocco, Norway, Poland, Romania, Switzerland, Vietnam and Yugoslavia. These comprehensive constitutional changes in a member state that had strong historical reasons for honouring the claims of asylum seekers heralded the degree to which the problem had confronted European governments and the lengths to which European governments were prepared to go in reducing the asylum traffic across their borders.

Ever since 1995 the European Union has had an agreed negative list of countries affected by civil war and unrest. Citizens from those countries have required a visa to enter the European Union. Member states can also add to the list for their own purposes. As a result of these changes to the asylum regime in Germany, the government has all but succeeded in closing the legal routes for asylum seekers. Some commentators estimate that 98 per cent of all asylum seekers in Germany gain access to the asylum process illegally and by concealing their route of entry.

The success of first-world governments in closing the legal routes gave rise to the phenomenon of people smugglers who for a fee will engage in criminal behaviour in order to deliver the asylum seeker to a safe country with a transparent asylum process. Countries that do not have a migration program or an offshore refugee processing program would then receive asylum seekers only by the illegal routes. One inevitable consequence was that the citizens of these first-world democracies that had effectively closed the legal route for onshore determination of asylum claims readily suspected that all asylum seekers in their midst were dishonest law-breakers. It would be very easy for politicians and sectional interest groups to exploit community disquiet about these law-breakers in their midst.

Having legally sealed its land borders with a buffer zone augmented by bilateral agreements with nation states surrounding the European Union, Germany then looked to plugging the gap at the airports. The new visa regime helped. Germany adopted a new technique being trialled in France, the Netherlands and Denmark. By law, a part of the airport would be declared an international zone. Asylum seekers landing at the airport would be deemed not to have entered Germany until immigration officers had cleared them. The courts had reservations about this process in the beginning. The government fine-tuned the process to the satisfaction of the courts. At major airports like Frankfurt, asylum seekers without a visa are now regularly held in detention. They are then put through an accelerated procedure, with a decision usually being given within 48 hours. If their claim is rejected as 'manifestly unfounded', they have a week to appeal and the court gives a decision within two weeks. In 2001 the German authorities approved only 25 applications for asylum through the airport procedure. They denied another 234 as manifestly unfounded and turned the applicants around. They admitted 930 claimants to the country so they could put their asylum claims through the usual channels.

US border controls

In August 2001 the Australian government's response to the *Tampa* event seemed ad hoc. Operation Relex and the Pacific Solution had many of the hallmarks of earlier US attempts to deal with the phenomenon of unauthorised arrivals by boat. In fact, the Australian defence personnel looked to an American precedent. Ever since 1981, the United States had a sporadic policy for the interdiction of boats carrying people from Haiti, a voyage of 600 nautical miles to Miami. On 23 September 1981 the United States and the Republic of Haiti had entered into an agreement authorising the US Coastguard to intercept vessels on the high seas and to return any undocumented aliens back to Haiti. The Haitian government of Baby Doc Duvalier guaranteed that its repatriated citizens would not be punished for their illegal departure. For his part, Ronald Reagan and his Executive agreed that the United States would not return any passengers 'whom the US authorities determined to qualify for refugee status'. Reagan issued an Executive Order stating that 'no person who is a refugee will be returned without his consent'. Over the next ten years the Coastguard regularly intercepted boats in international waters and turned them around. In all that time, the immigration officers assisting the Coastguard identified only 11 refugees. More than 23,000 Haitians were sent back home. Then came the coup in Haiti in September 1991. The military ousted Jean Bertrand Aristide. Hundreds of people were killed and thousands went into hiding. Thousands took to boats. Four hundred thousand people were displaced. Six weeks after the coup the Coastguard announced a return to the interdiction policy. Initially the refugee screening was still to occur on the high seas. The acute political situation in Haiti was producing thousands of bona fide refugees who could not be readily assessed on a boat. The precursor to Operation Relex needed to be augmented by a precursor to the Pacific Solution. For eight months following the coup, Haitian boat people were intercepted and taken to the US territory of Guantanamo Bay for processing. More than 34,000 people were intercepted and more than 10,000 of them were screened in as refugees. Then Guantanamo Bay with a capacity of 12,500 was full and the boats kept coming.

In the first three weeks of May 1992, 127 boats were intercepted carrying over 10,000 undocumented aliens. Guantanamo Bay and the Coastguard cutters could not carry any more. President George Bush issued an Executive Order on 24 May 1992 providing interdiction with no interviewing or screening process. The Order stated, 'The international legal obligations of the United States under the United Nations Protocol Relating to the Status of Refugees to apply Article 33 of the United Nations Convention Relating to the Status of Refugees do not extend to persons located outside the territory of the United States.' Article 33 prohibits states from expelling or returning refugees to the territory where their lives or freedom are threatened. Two token steps were taken to offset this drastic measure. The US Administration made announcements in Haiti that asylum seekers could present at the US embassy in the capital, Port au Prince, and lodge a refugee claim. Though all boats were to be returned to Haiti, the Attorney-General, in his unreviewable discretion, could decide that a person who was a refugee would not be returned without his consent. One commentator noted, 'Grace did not abound; all Haitians have been returned under the new order.'[11] This second step was a precursor to the later Australian technique of permitting the immigration minister to grant a humanitarian visa by exercise of a personal, non-compellable, non-reviewable discretion.

President Bush's tough border-protection policy then featured in the 1992 presidential election. Three months out from the election, successful contender Bill Clinton said, 'I am appalled by the decision of the Bush administration to pick up fleeing Haitians on the high seas and forcibly return them to Haiti before considering their claim to political asylum. This process must not stand.'[12] After his election, he told the *Washington Post*, 'I'm going to change the policy.'[13] He did not.

In 1993 the US Supreme Court upheld the validity of the Bush and Clinton policy, with the majority noting, 'The wisdom of the policy choices made by Presidents Reagan, Bush and Clinton is not a matter for our consideration.'[14] Justice Blackmun wrote a stinging dissent:

> The Convention that the Refugee Act embodies was enacted largely in response to the experience of Jewish refugees in Europe during the period of World War II. The tragic consequences of the world's indifference at that time are well known. The resulting ban on *refoulement*, as broad as the humanitarian purpose that inspired it, is easily applicable here, the Court's protestations of impotence and regret notwithstanding.
>
> The refugees attempting to escape from Haiti do not claim a right of admission to this country. They do not even argue that the Government has

no right to intercept their boats. They demand only that the United States, land of refugees and guardian of freedom, cease forcibly driving them back to detention, abuse, and death. That is a modest plea, vindicated by the Treaty and the statute. We should not close our ears to it.[15]

The US government claimed that the policy was working in that fewer people were now making the perilous journey by boat. Whereas over 31,000 Haitians had taken to the high seas in 1992, only 2,400 attempted the voyage in 1993. Then President in Exile Aristide had a brainwave. In April 1994 he unilaterally rescinded the 1981 agreement. The Clinton administration had no option but to recommence more appropriate screening of Haitian boat people. Once again they were taken to Guantanamo Bay and the US administration enlisted the assistance of the UNHCR, seeking regional agreement for the setting-up of safety zones in other countries where people might be denied entry to the United States but guaranteed protection and non-refoulement while their refugee claims were being processed. The UNHCR was worried, observing that 'safety zones should not be allowed to provide a distorted mechanism for offshore processing and detention, or one that consigns refugees to permanent lack of access to international protection with the blessing of the international community.'[16]

The lawyers for and against the US administration had done their homework when preparing for the constitutional showdown on the interdiction policy. They scoured the records of the international meetings that had preceded the drafting of the 1951 Convention and found that the drafting committee had considered, but rejected, a chapter requiring the admission of refugees into a contracting state. The parties were agreed that signature of the convention would not have any adverse impact on their immigration policies. The obligation of non-refoulement could not be applied to a refugee who had not yet entered the territory of a country. The obligations in Article 33 were not to expel a refugee who had already been admitted to a country and not to return a refugee who was already in the territory of a country but not yet resident there. As if foreseeing the possibility of a Guantanamo Bay or a Pacific Solution, prominent international lawyer Louis Henkin, who served on the US delegation to the formulation of the Refugees Convention, had told the delegates in 1950 that a refugee 'must not be turned back to a country where his life or freedom could be threatened. No consideration of public order should be allowed to overrule that guarantee, for if the State concerned wished to get rid of the refugee at all costs, it could send him to another country or place him in an internment camp.'[17] In an affidavit for the Supreme Court proceedings in 1993, Henkin attested that George Warren, who was the official US delegate in 1951, maintained this as the official US position on the meaning of Article 33. Henkin told the court that there was some concern 'that the right of nonrefoulement should not become a vehicle for requiring the admission of massive numbers of migrants'. Many refugee advocates had argued prior to the 1993 Supreme Court decision that there was a need to distinguish a contracting state's power to refuse a refugee admission to its territory (permitted by the Convention) from a state's power to return refugees to countries of persecution. Forced return was not permitted by the Convention regardless of whether the refugees were inside the territory of the contracting state or outside it. The Supreme Court went to great lengths to excuse itself from this politically vexed question, observing:

> The drafters of the Convention … may not have contemplated that any nation would gather fleeing refugees and return them to the one country they had desperately sought to escape; such actions may even violate the spirit of Article 33; but a treaty cannot impose uncontemplated extraterritorial obligations on those who ratify it through no more than its general humanitarian intent. Because the text of Article 33 cannot reasonably be read to say anything at all about a nation's actions toward aliens outside its own territory, it does not prohibit such actions.[18]

Though the compulsory returns policy had withstood Supreme Court scrutiny, it was not politically sustainable, especially for a president who was on record as having said it was unacceptable. When international cooperation for the accommodation and processing of Haitian asylum seekers was not forthcoming, the United States then invaded Haiti in September 1994. As one commentator said, 'The 1994 invasion of Haiti by United States forces was motivated primarily by the objective of migration control.'[19] The stream of boats from Haiti then abated for some years before increasing again in 2000 and 2001. Then on 3 December 2001 a boatload of 187 Haitians was grounded off

Miami, leading the Bush administration to revise the policy on detention and processing of unauthorised asylum seekers.

Conclusions

It is now virtually impossible for a refugee lawfully and honestly to flee directly into a first-world country seeking asylum. Even if the country were a signatory to the Refugee Convention, the migration law and border-control policy will be so tight that the refugee will be required to break the domestic law to seek entry. Often the refugee will be deemed to have fled from a safe country or to have transited a safe third country. Even before the refugees reach the actual border of the asylum country, they will have to get through the virtual offshore border of visa control if they are flying to their asylum destination. If coming to Australia by boat, avoiding the electronic offshore border, the asylum seekers were previously guaranteed humanitarian treatment by Coastwatch and the Navy on the high seas. The Australian government abandoned that guarantee with the introduction of Operation Relex when the prime minister came down off the horns of his dilemma between 'trying to behave like a humanitarian decent country' and 'making certain that we don't become just an easy touch for illegal immigrants'. Having opted for the latter, the government abandoned the former, at least in the short term, revising the strategy once the 2001 election had passed and once the boats in the fourth wave had stopped coming.

When the fifth wave of boat people commences, there is no guarantee that Australia's non-humanitarian antics on the high seas will not recur. Such antics are not illegal and they are electorally popular. Prior to August 2001 these antics were viewed as morally awkward, but no longer. Given the activity of people smugglers, government now takes its moral cue from the smugglers, winning the endorsement of the radio shock jocks. Given the increased security concerns since September 2001, the voters of first-world countries are more likely to endorse the decisions of government, withdrawing humanitarian assistance to asylum seekers on the high seas, engaging in life-threatening brinkmanship, and funding upstream disruption which may result in loss of life.

With the benefits of geographic isolation and a comprehensive visa system, Australia is more secure than most other countries when it comes to asylum seekers wanting access. Our embassies are able

Australian, 23 November 1999.
Reproduced with Peter Nicholson's permission.

accurately to pinpoint those countries that are likely to produce asylum seekers. People from those countries cannot access any automatic visa arrangements. They are closely scrutinised by immigration officers when they apply for visas. Like other first-world countries, we have gone a long way towards setting up a virtual border offshore which is impenetrable for most asylum seekers. Those who bypass the computer net are likely to encounter our Navy on the high seas if they manage to get past the hired sting merchants and disruption agents in Indonesia. Prior to the finalisation of the Comprehensive Plan of Action in 1989, the Malaysians were prominent in threatening boat people who entered their territorial waters. The Americans have done the same from time to time with Cubans and Haitians. The mystery surrounding the sinking of SIEV X, the secrecy even to parliament about upstream disruption activities in Indonesia, and the revelations to the Senate Committee about Operation Relex exposed border control as an Australian obsession in 2001. It is time that border control was once again made a governmental task conducted with decent firmness, providing the necessary humanitarian assistance to those persons in our territorial waters legitimately seeking asylum when they have not found it elsewhere on their journey.

If and when the fifth wave of boat people arrive in our territorial waters from Indonesia, we should have the decency to escort them to a place such as Christmas Island where there might be an initial determination as to whether any persons on board have a credible fear of persecution. If they do, they should be transported safely to the Australian mainland and processed for a protection claim. If they do not, they could properly be made to reboard their vessel and return to Indonesia. Should they refuse to do so, only then should they be taken forcibly by safe means back to Indonesia or to their own country. If a return to moral decency means that we will be viewed as 'just an easy touch for illegal immigrants', so be it. Our geographic isolation has long ensured that we are not a very accessible touch no matter how easy a touch we might be perceived to be.

CHAPTER 4

Reception and detention of unauthorised asylum seekers in Australia

There are three ways in which refugees or asylum seekers come to settle in countries such as Australia. Some are chosen by the Australian government to come after they have been assessed as refugees in need of resettlement, usually while they are waiting in a refugee camp in another country. Some visit Australia having obtained a visa such as a student's visa or a visitor's visa. While in Australia they apply for asylum. They will not be forced to leave Australia until their asylum claim has been processed and until their visa has expired. Unless they are a flight risk or a security risk, they will be permitted to remain in the community until their asylum claim is determined. The others come to Australia, by plane or boat, without a visa, claiming asylum once they have landed. If they have a credible claim, they will be allowed to stay in Australia until their asylum claim has been processed. Countries receiving uninvited asylum seekers have to accommodate the asylum seekers and process their claims. Countries adhering to the Refugee Convention are not supposed to penalise asylum seekers who arrive without a visa or permission provided they have come directly from the territory where they were threatened.

Those asylum seekers who arrive in Australia without a visa are held in detention until their claim is determined and their health and character checked. If they are under 18 and not accompanied by an adult, over 75 or in need of medical help that cannot be provided in a detention centre, they may be granted a bridging visa which entitles them to live in the community until their claim is determined. Or they may be held in an alternative place of detention. Some persons have even been held in hotels or motels under guard supervision. Unaccompanied minors have been fostered out to families and permitted to attend school in the community. The government was lenient towards the one boatload of unvisaed East Timorese who arrived in Darwin on 29 May 1995. All 18 persons were issued with bridging visas within two months. Under the law, they could only be released if they had 'a special need (based on health or previous experience of torture or trauma) in respect of which a medical specialist appointed by Immigration has certified that the non-citizen cannot properly be cared for in a detention environment'.[1] In this instance, the government was responding to public sympathy for the East Timorese. They have not been so gracious in offering bridging visas to boatloads of Afghans and Iraqis who have also experienced excruciating torture or trauma. The ready use of the medical visa for the Timorese may also have been a means for the government to avoid suggestions that they were breaching the Refugees Convention, penalising asylum seekers who had come directly from their country of persecution. As they were fleeing persecution by the Indonesians, there was no country closer to East Timor to which they could have fled.

Rationale for detention of unauthorised arrivals

For a decade both sides in the Australian parliament have supported law and policy that authorises detention of unauthorised asylum seekers at three stages:

- the initial determination of health, security and identity issues at the commencement of the asylum process
- the entire time taken for processing a refugee application and any appeals that may follow
- at the end of an unsuccessful claim, awaiting removal from the country.

The issue of ongoing controversy is the unique Australian solution of mandatory detention during the second stage. Australia is alone in the first world in implementing a legal policy of universal detention for unauthorised asylum seekers from arrival to departure or from arrival until the issue of a visa. A visa is issued to a proven refugee claimant or to one of the handful of persons who convince the minister to exercise his personal discretion for humanitarian reasons.

It has been very difficult to discern a rationale for universal detention during the second stage. The UNHCR's 1999 Revised Guidelines on the Detention of Asylum seekers state that 'As a general principle asylum seekers should not be detained.' The guidelines permit only four exceptions: to verify identity, to conduct the preliminary interview to identify the basis of the asylum claim, to protect national security and public order, and in cases where the asylum seeker does not have proper documentation. But none of these exceptions covers the case of universal mandatory detention during the second stage. Though most boat people have arrived in Australia in recent times without adequate documents, the UNHCR guidelines would not justify mandatory detention throughout the entire second stage except in very rare cases. The guidelines state:

> What must be established is the absence of good faith on the part of the applicant to comply with the verification of identity process. As regards asylum-seekers using fraudulent documents or travelling with no documents at all, detention is only permissible when there is an intention to mislead, or a refusal to cooperate with the authorities. Asylum-seekers who arrive without documentation because they are unable to obtain any in their country of origin should not be detained solely for that reason.[2]

Though no boats had arrived on Australian shores between 1981 and 1989, the government was adamant that once the second wave of boat people started arriving in late 1989 they would be kept in detention, sending a message to other people that there was no point in coming to Australia. In other words, detention was designed in part to act as a deterrent. On 5 May 1992 Minister Gerry Hand told parliament:

> I believe it is crucial that all persons who come to Australia without prior authorisation not be released into the community. Their release would undermine the government's strategy for determining their refugee status or entry claims. The government is determined that a clear signal be sent that

migration to Australia may not be achieved by simply arriving in this country and expecting to be allowed into the community.[3]

The mandatory detention regime was set down by parliament in the Migration Amendment Bill 1992. Sixteen months later, the Department of Immigration and Ethnic Affairs conceded to parliament, 'It is difficult to judge the effectiveness of detention as a deterrence measure per se.'[4] The Secretary of the department told a parliamentary inquiry, 'While there is undoubtedly a deterrence aspect to the policy, it is not by any means the determining or principal factor.'[5]

Detention in remote places has never been an aid to accurate determination of refugee claims. In the initial stages of the detention regime, only three boats arrived between May 1992 and August 1993 when parliament was first reviewing the arrangements. At that time no boat had come since October 1992. Only 23 of the boat people were granted refugee status by the department on the initial interviews and yet 117 of them succeeded at the review stage. The department was clearly troubled by these appalling statistics, but told parliament, 'It is difficult to generalise the reasons for the significant overturn rate at review for the boat people.'[6] The department has always conceded that any detention regime was unsustainable unless there was a prompt and fair decision-making process for the determination of refugee claims. Even by August 1993 the department was reporting to parliament, 'Depression and anxiety amongst some detainees has reached acute levels, necessitating specialised psychiatric treatment and counselling.'[7] There was never any coherent explanation of the need mandatorily to detain boat people and other unauthorised arrivals. The department pointed out to the parliamentary inquiry that there were alternatives pursued by other governments who received far more unauthorised arrivals than Australia ever did. They said, 'A bond requirement in association with a release scheme for unauthorised arrivals would be consistent with practice in the United Kingdom and the United States, and also with practice in Australia in respect of illegal entrants ... The imposition of conditions, particularly reporting conditions, on unauthorised arrivals released into the community would also be consistent with international and Australian practice.'[8]

Under questioning by the Opposition, the department acknowledged, 'There is evidence that people are available for ... assessment.

Our experience in a limited number of cases that are still running is that, while people are in the process of assessment, they are in contact. When the assessment is finished and the decision is negatived, we have to be certain that the great majority of those persons shall remain in contact for a process where that process may be removal from Australia.'[9] Given the lack of a clear rationale for mandatory detention of only one group of persons who were seeking onshore protection, and in the light of the enormous financial and human cost, the department was signalling to its political masters that there were alternatives. However, Chris Conybeare, Secretary of the Department, did tell the inquiry, 'Overseas experience cannot, we believe, be transposed unaltered to Australia, bearing in mind the distinctive features of Australia, such as our geography and our universal visa system.'[10] Conybeare said that the policy of mandatory detention was of course a matter for government but that the department was interested in considering alternatives as long as those alternatives provided 'a similar level of access to persons for processing, both for the refugee determination aspects and for removal where refugee claims are not sustained'.[11] Even though the Deputy Secretary tried to argue that 'the rationale behind detention is not cemented on deterrence', he nonetheless thought it was 'a reasonably significant deterrent' because residents in the detention centres could talk freely to friends and family back home, sending the message that life in an Australian detention centre was not a bed of roses.[12] Under questioning, the departmental officials had to concede that the 81,000 overstayers per year were a greater threat to the integrity of the comprehensive visa system than the 600 people detained as unauthorised arrivals. The distinction in treatment offered by the department was extraordinarily flimsy:

> Certainly, a person who has been issued a visa has satisfied a relevant officer that his or her intent is to comply with the conditions of that visa. His or her intent was not to breach and become illegal. I am not suggesting that means that that was not his or her intent, but that is the test that we apply. Unauthorised arrivals do not submit themselves to such tests.[13]

The department was anxious to downplay the significance of more than 80,000 overstayers, content that by international comparison the figure 'would be regarded as low'. Though they had no objective evidence, they were satisfied from their experience that 'most overstayers did not come with the intent of overstaying'.[14] Be that as it may, surely the relevant comparison in assessing the treatment of the unauthorised arrivals is between them and those who entered on a visa with the intent of overstaying and with the intent of coming for reasons not consistent with the terms of the visa. Presumably there are still thousands of these people. If detention is warranted for the boat people, then why not for the others? For example, why not put all asylum seekers who came on student or visitor visas into mandatory detention (with no provision for release on a bond) once they make their claim?

Back in 1993 it was none other than Philip Ruddock himself (while in Opposition) who highlighted the flimsiness of the distinction:

> In relation to the difference between visa-ed entrants who breach our law by crossing our border and those who breach our law by ignoring the conditions of a visa — those minor distinctions — once you have identified a person and carried out a health check and a character check, how can we characterise them as being different?[15]

Mr Ruddock did not receive a credible answer, except to be told the very obvious: 'If people offshore walked into an Australian embassy and said, "I want a visa to go to Australia to seek asylum" — they would not get it.' Ten years later as minister, he has still not provided a credible answer himself.

In August 1993 the Australian Government Solicitor informed the Immigration Department:

> Article 9 (of the International Covenant on Civil and Political Rights) requires that detention must at all times be reasonable in the circumstances. For example, it may not be reasonable to continue to detain a person who has not been successful in applying for a visa to remain in Australia but who cannot be sent back to his or her country of origin or a third country for reasons beyond his or her control.[16]

The government's lawyers advised, 'It does not appear from the information available that mandatory detention of unauthorised entrants is a widely accepted practice amongst comparable states.'[17] They surveyed the situation in the United States and the United Kingdom and noted the availability of parole in the United States and of bail in the United Kingdom. When discussing the government's legal advice in the Joint Standing Committee on Migration on 12 October 1993, Philip

Sydney Morning Herald, 22 August 2001.
Reproduced with Cathy Wilcox's permission.

Ruddock said, 'I find it surprising that we have such a fixation about these covenants and conventions given the lack of seriousness with which the rest of the world seems to treat international documents … I think it is very useful that we do try to set a positive international example.'[18]

Having just returned from the Vienna Conference on Human Rights, Ruddock made the point that the section on refugees was dropped from the Vienna Declaration in the drafting committee. The officer from the Attorney-General's Department tried to argue that there was still a strong international commitment to refugees. Ruddock retorted, 'I am angry about the extent to which there is an expectation here that we have obligations to honour, not only the letter, the spirit, but provisions that people imagine go well beyond the letter and spirit, when the rest of the world has absolutely minimal commitment to doing anything about refugees at all.'[19]

Gerry Hand's successor as minister, Senator Nick Bolkus, told a news conference on 30 December 1994:

The fact is that we want to send a very clear message to anyone who is intending to come to Australia illegally by boat with no valid claim that the doors are closed. Obviously detention is an important part of our response. Detention has been criticised in the past, but I think the value of detention cannot be underestimated.[20]

The UNHCR continues to say that 'detention should normally be avoided' while noting 'with deep concern that large numbers of refugees and asylum-seekers in different areas of the world are currently the subject of detention or similar restrictive measures by reason of their illegal entry or presence in search of asylum, pending resolution of their situation'.[21] The UNHCR first made this official plea to the governments of the world in 1986, repeating it in 1989 and again in 1998, urging states 'to explore more actively all feasible alternatives to detention'. The UNHCR has never ruled out detention. When people arrive having destroyed all documentation, there are good grounds for holding them in detention until their identities have been established and until health and security matters have been resolved. In 1986 the Executive Committee of the UNHCR published its now famous Conclusion No. 44 conceding that there might be instances when it is necessary to authorise detention 'to determine the elements on which the claim to refugee status or asylum is based'. The UN Commission on Human Rights' Working Group on Arbitrary Detention published ten principles in 1999 as 'criteria for determining whether or not the deprivation of liberty of asylum seekers and immigrants may be arbitrary'. The principles included:

- Any asylum seeker or immigrant placed in custody must be brought promptly before a judicial or other authority, the other authority being one duly empowered by law and having a status and length of mandate affording sufficient guarantees of competence, impartiality and independence.
- A maximum period should be set by law and the custody may in no case be unlimited or of excessive length.[22]

The ad hoc way in which detention was first instituted in Australia made it very punitive. The government's indecent haste in trying to get the Cambodian asylum seekers away from the lawyers resulted in people being flown all over the country, accommodated in ill-equipped facilities and processed very slowly. The public servants and lawyers had to trek many times across the country to prepare cases and hear applications in remote Port Hedland. The Australian parliamentary committee that published its report *Asylum, Border Control and Detention* in 1994 was unanimous in the view that 'the delays in primary processing of boat arrivals prior to 1992 were entirely unacceptable and never ought be repeated'.[23] With a new legislative regime governing detention and processing, including the establishment of the Refugee Review Tribunal, the politicians (except for Christabel Chamarette from the Democrats) were all agreed that 'those who arrive unauthorised at Australia's borders and seek asylum should be detained while their claims to asylum are determined'.[24]

Mr A, who had arrived at Pender Bay and been in detention for more than four years, recounted to the UN Human Rights Committee the saga of his own detention and the protracted and fumbled processing of his case. The UN Committee ruled that the Australian government had failed to advance any grounds particular to Mr A's case which would justify his continued detention for a period of four years, during which he was shifted around between different detention centres. The Committee concluded that his detention was arbitrary within the meaning of the International Covenant on Civil and Political Rights which provides that 'No one shall be subjected to arbitrary arrest or detention.'

By the end of his detention, Mr A had criss-crossed Australia. He had been detained at the Villawood Detention Centre in Sydney. He and his fellow detainees were then flown from Sydney to Darwin thinking they were being returned to Cambodia and not allowed to speak to anyone by phone. They were then detained at what the Human Rights and Equal Opportunity Commission described as the 'totally unacceptable' Curragundi Camp 85 kilometres south of Darwin, and then Berimah camp outside Darwin and ultimately Port Hedland in Western Australia. In its official response to the United Nations, the Australian government said that it did not accept that Mr A's detention was arbitrary or that they had provided insufficient justification for his detention. The exposure of the government's Monty Python tactics in flying asylum seekers all around the country keeping one step ahead of the lawyers was an embarrassment. Australian politicians on both sides of the parliament were delighted to receive the ruling from the UN Committee that 'there is no basis for the claim that it is *per se* arbitrary to detain individuals requesting asylum. Nor can it find any support for the contention that there is a rule of customary international law which would render all such detention arbitrary'.

Unfortunately the Australian politicians decided to overlook the rider added by the UN Committee:

> Every decision to keep a person in detention should be open to review periodically so that the grounds justifying the detention can be assessed. In any event, detention should not continue beyond the period for which the State can provide appropriate justification. For example, the fact of illegal entry may indicate a need for investigation and there may be other factors particular to the individual, such as the likelihood of absconding and lack of cooperation, which may justify detention for a period. Without such factors detention may be considered arbitrary, even if entry was illegal.[25]

The politicians were adamant that the judges were to be kept out of the business of periodic review of migration detention. Without a bill of rights and no equivalent of the European Convention on Human Rights, there was no constitutional requirement that the judges be involved. The politicians wanted detention to last until someone was released on a visa or until they decided to return home. They knew that 27 per cent of lawful non-citizens who had applied for asylum once they had arrived on a visa were never seen again even though they had been refused asylum. They did not want unlawful non-citizens who failed in their asylum claims being added to those who melted into the community.

Back in 1994 our politicians were honest enough to acknowledge the disadvantages of a location such as Port Hedland — its remoteness, inconvenience and problems with accessing appropriate services, the additional travel costs for lawyers and the difficulties for detainees in accessing community support. They thought that these disadvantages were sufficiently offset by 'placing detainees in a centre that is in reasonable proximity to where most of the boat arrivals first land, and where the remoteness of the location provides a disincentive to abscond from the Centre'.[26] No doubt they had new reasons to justify the establishment of Baxter near Port Augusta and the maintenance of Woomera. Baxter is a tailor-made facility from which it will be almost impossible to abscond. Neither place is anywhere near where the boats first land. They are ideal locations for a punitive deterrent. They are bad locations for the provision of legal and community services and contact. They were the key mainland facilities for setting in place the post-*Tampa* firebreak.

A further challenge to the government in building the firebreak was that, though mandatory detention had been in place for almost a decade, the boats were still coming. Back in October 1999 the Howard government had implemented its first raft of changes to build the firebreak. Those arriving without visas, even if they then proved to be refugees, would not be offered permanent residence in the first place. They would be offered a temporary protection visa (TPV) that would last for three years only. After three years their cases would be assessed again and if they were still in need of protection, only then would they be given permanent residence and the right to sponsor their families. One unintended consequence of this change was that the boats arriving after October 1999 carried an increased number of women and children. Presumably these women and children would not have risked the hazardous journey in the past because their husbands and fathers once recognised as refugees would have been entitled to fly them safely to Australia in the foreseeable future. Whereas only 127 children came on boats in the two years before the October 1999 changes, there were 1,844 children on boats after those changes and prior to the *Tampa* affair. After the *Tampa* incident the firebreak was further consolidated by denying the holders of temporary protection visas any prospect of permanent visas with the right to sponsor family if the applicants could have availed themselves of protection in a transit port where they had stayed more than seven days. Of the 1,609 persons held offshore since the *Tampa* incident, 368 of them have been children. Sadly, these aspects of the firebreak set up an attraction rather than a deterrent for women and children to join their men on leaky boats headed for Australia.

Countries that have signed the Refugee Convention are entitled to maintain the integrity of their borders, but Article 31 stipulates that they 'shall not impose penalties, on account of their illegal entry or presence, on refugees who, coming directly from a territory where their life or freedom was threatened … enter or are present in their territory without authorisation, provided they present themselves without delay to the authorities and show good cause for their illegal entry or presence'.

Even though most of the asylum seekers who arrived by boat in Australian territory in these last few years have proved to be refugees, the government argues that they have not come directly from a territory where their life or freedom was threatened. In the government's opinion, most (if not all) the refugees have had protection available to them in some other place en route; they continued their journey not for protection but for a migration outcome, seeking a better life in Australia. The government therefore claims that it is entitled to impose penalties such as detention and the provision of a visa with restrictive and discriminatory provisions given that everyone is presumed to have spent at least seven days in a country where protection was available. According to the government:

> A person to whom Australia owes protection will fall outside the scope of Article 31(1) if he or she spent more than a short period of time in a third country whilst travelling between the country of persecution and Australia, and settled there in safety or was otherwise accorded protection, or there was no good reason why they could not have sought and obtained effective protection there. What amounts to a short period of time will depend ultimately on the facts of a particular case.[27]

This has not deterred the government from arbitrarily setting seven days residence in a country as the cut-off for access to a permanent protection visa, even if protection could have been sought only through the offices of the UNHCR in that country. Does this mean that any refugee who has spent a week en route in Indonesia waiting for a boat to Australia can be penalised and denied a permanent protection visa because they could have gone to Jakarta and joined the queue at the UNHCR office rather than awaiting a boat in precarious circumstances? Given that Indonesia is not a signatory to the Convention and given that the country is not governed by the rule of law, how can it credibly be argued that boat people should stop their journey in Indonesia and enjoy sufficient protection? Mr Robert Illingworth, Assistant Secretary of DIMIA for Onshore Protection, has told the Senate Legal and Constitutional Committee:

> With the agreement of the Indonesian authorities, the UNHCR operates

in Indonesia to identify people in need of protection. As a general principle, the UNHCR is not involved in directly providing physical protection to refugees … The UNHCR can mandate an individual, but in most cases the UNHCR … given that there are 12 million refugees in the world, is not in a position to provide physical protection in the face of somebody intent on persecuting them or refouling them. It relies heavily on the cooperation of states.[28]

Under Indonesian law, all unlawful foreigners who are detected are subject to quarantine detention awaiting deportation. In April 2002 Human Rights Watch conducted extensive interviews with Iraqi and Afghan asylum seekers who had been in transit in Indonesia. During the fourth wave of boat people to Australia, the UNHCR in Jakarta recognised only 476 refugees and only 18 of them were resettled because resettlement countries, including Australia, were just not interested in helping. No wonder those few asylum seekers who knew about the UNHCR's office in the business centre of Jakarta thought it was 'inactive'. Meanwhile the conditions endured by detained asylum seekers in prisons outside Jakarta were often horrendous. Human Rights Watch describes the plight of an Hazara family of four, including children aged 2 and 4:

> They spent three months in a two-metre by two-metre cell in a detention centre based near Jakarta, where each day they received only a cup of water and a dirty fistful of rice, containing ants and rat feces. They were locked in the cell for twelve hours a day and allowed outdoors for just two hours a week. IOM [International Organisation for Migration] did not visit them and their only way to contact the outside world was to bribe the guards. The father repeatedly paid bribes to send faxes to UNHCR officials, who came to see them after two weeks. UNHCR asked him to fill out the form to claim asylum and then a full two months later returned to interview him. By this time his health had deteriorated and he spent most of his asylum interview just begging for release.[29]

What about the Afghan Hazaras in Pakistan who were kept away from the UNHCR queue by the Pashtun Pakistanis? How does one prove or disprove access to appropriate protection through the offices of the UNHCR? Australia's unilateral attempts to design punitive deterrents to secondary movement have not been welcomed by the

UNHCR. The UNHCR's chief, Ruud Lubbers, has told the European Union Justice and Home Affairs Council:

> A major concern today is the issue of secondary movements of refugees and asylum seekers. I am convinced that the international community needs new agreements to deal with cross-cutting issues such as this. These new agreements would supplement the Convention and form part of multilateral frameworks for protecting refugees and achieving durable solutions, primarily in regions of origin.[30]

All governments including Australia should heed Mr Lubbers' caution: 'The current trend towards more unilateralism is adding to the confusion, and needs to be reversed. It can be.' Those who have suffered most as a result of Australia's unilateral action have overwhelmingly been found to be refugees and no security threat at all. Between 2000 and 2002, ASIO, the government's security organisation, had checked 5,986 unauthorised arrivals to assess whether or not they constituted a direct or indirect threat to Australia and found that not one of those persons constituted such a threat. It is in the interests of the

Australian, 2 December 1999.
Reproduced with Peter Nicholson's permission.

refugees of the world that we address the problems of secondary movement. We must heed the warning of Mr Lubbers that we 'build an effective system of international burden sharing, where governments are
discouraged from taking unilateral and punitive action, and where refugees are able to rely on adequate protection and assistance within
their regions of origin. For to take punitive action is to shoot oneself in
the foot. It is not effective, and it only worsens the climate between
North and South.'[31]

The matter is more complex than government apologists like Mr
Paddy McGuinness would have it. He says, 'There is in fact no argument about the right of refugees, as defined in the 1951 Convention, to
arrive without authorisation and claim asylum in the first country at
which they arrive. Few such people actually arrive in Australia and
claim asylum.'[32] He then proposes that all other refugees are false refugees for the purposes of the Convention, and therefore not deserving of
compassionate entrance. What about those refugees who set out on
their journey, not especially seeking an Australian lifestyle, but seeking real protection for themselves and their family, being of the view
that Australia is the first port of call on the only journey available to
them where they think there is the prospect of real protection? Many
Afghan and Iraqi asylum seekers would have gone to Europe if they
could have afforded it. Australia happened to be the cheapest available destination offering the prospect of real protection. Many of them
knew little or nothing about Australia other than the smuggler's assurance that protection was guaranteed. Mr McGuinness thinks that all
refugees are obligated to seek protection 'in the first possible country'.
In recent times, Afghans and Iraqis have gone to any safe country they
can find. It is not as if they have set their sights especially on Australia.
Like the Jews after World War II, they should be accorded some latitude in finding asylum even if there is a country closer to their home
country where some other refugees from their country have found protection. It is wrong for a government to design a punitive deterrent policy based on the simplistic McGuinness presumption that few if any
refugees reaching Australia could be seeking real protection at the
first available port of call. In times of crisis, Australia like all countries
that can offer real protection should be expected to pull its weight in
offering proper assessment and protection to those who come seeking

asylum. We should not go it alone in designing more punitive means for deterring asylum seekers and thereby punishing true refugees as much as the handful of undoubted secondary moving economic migrants.

The failure to provide basic protection and services for persons in immigration detention

The increased number of children who came into Australian waters because their fathers were classed as secondary movers without a right of family reunion then had to be held in detention. They were held in ad hoc facilities which had never been designed for such a number of children. On the mainland, their welfare needs had to be attended to by a Commonwealth government which had never finalised memoranda of understanding (MOUs) or protocols with the state governments for the care and education of children in these facilities. In a federation like Australia, there cannot be regular cooperation between the levels of government for service delivery unless there is a memorandum drawn up in which the governments agree to funding and their respective roles. In areas like child protection, there is then a need for protocols which set out the procedure that public servants and health professionals are to follow if there is state intervention for the well-being of the child. Though children have been detained in immigration detention centres in Western Australia for more than a decade, the Commonwealth has yet to finalise a protocol with the Western Australian government. With the increase in boat arrivals, the Commonwealth decided to open Woomera in South Australia as a detention centre in 1999 and to commission the first purpose-built detention centre at Baxter in South Australia in 2002. In 2001 the Commonwealth government did finalise a protocol for the care of children with the South Australian Liberal government. With a change of government in South Australia in 2002, the new Labor premier blew the lid on the protocol, making a ministerial statement to parliament on 14 August 2002 after he had commissioned a report on children in detention at Woomera. Premier Mike Rann told parliament:

> It is important to note that state child protection workers are only allowed into the Centre with the permission of the Commonwealth and cannot legally enforce their recommendations under South Australia's Child

Protection Act as would be possible in other cases concerning children who are not on Commonwealth land.

There is a need for a protocol to protect and remove children from dangerous situations within the compound to protect children seeing traumatic incidents or being harmed in such incidents.

The following recommendations are made: That the centres develop a protocol by which children are protected and removed from situations of danger and upset within the compound. All of the children in such centres need to be protected from viewing traumatic incidents and the risk of being physically harmed during such incidents. The duty of care to children needs to be effectively managed.

On 15 August 2002 the Commonwealth attorney-general, speaking for Mr Ruddock in his absence, said: 'The Department has a strong and cooperative relationship with the South Australian Department of Human Services and works closely with officials to ensure that the best interests of the children are met.' There is no possible coordinated government response to child protection while one government remains committed to a punitive desert regime without a workable memorandum of understanding (MOU) and protocol being in place. Detention of children in the desert, far removed from regular state children's services and in a political hothouse where there is no agreement between state and federal governments for the delivery of children's services is a recipe for institutionalised child abuse. Another six months later, there was still no agreement between the Commonwealth and the state government about how best to care for children in immigration detention in South Australia. On 17 February 2003 Premier Rann made another ministerial statement to the South Australian parliament reporting on the Child Protection Review by Robyn Layton QC commissioned by the government. He told parliament:

The Layton Review recommends the immediate release of children and their families from the Baxter and Woomera detention centres into the community.

The Review finds that abuse of these children is a direct result of their detention with adults in an inappropriate institutional environment.

To quote from the chapter on children in detention the Layton Review says the effect of detention on children is, I quote, 'so devastating to the well being and development of children and will have such lasting consequences during their lifetimes, which may in fact be spent in Australia, the State Government has a responsibility to take a strong position on this issue'.

These children are subjected to poor health care, poor nutrition, anxiety and significant behavioural problems. The long-term damage to children held in detention cannot be underestimated. The detention of children is a time bomb for the future.

Just as the firebreak required brinkmanship on the high seas, so too it was needed in the detention centres in the desert. The Commonwealth government could not afford to weaken its stance simply because there were many children now in detention. While community groups pleaded that children be released from detention, the government insisted that it was always in the best interests of children that they remain in detention with their parents. The government would not consider release into the community of family groups with children because that would encourage future boat people to bring their children so as to avoid mandatory detention. The government encountered a major problem with unaccompanied minors, whose guardian was the Minister for Immigration. In time most unaccompanied minors, who had been rejected as refugees were released into the community under foster-care arrangements. They were still deemed to be in detention. Within two years some of them were even permitted to attend private schools in Adelaide.

It took the Commonwealth three years to finalise MOUs on education and child protection with the relevant state government authorities in South Australia.[33] The protocol for child protection is completely unworkable from the perspective of the government that must provide the professional staff to care for children at risk. In Western Australia, the Commonwealth government's reckless approach to child detention is even more grave, as there is still no MOU after ten years of the detention regime. The line of authority for care of detainees is even more hazy, given the broad discretion accorded to the detention service provider, Australasian Correctional Management Pty Ltd (ACM).

Let me give one example of the incapacity of the Canberra bureaucracy to deal credibly with reports of child abuse and neglect in detention because of their need to pursue a hot political agenda. I communicated information about injuries to children at Woomera to the Minister and to the Department of Immigration and Multicultural and Indigenous Affairs (DIMIA) on 4 April 2002. Some of this information, including the claim that a seven-year-old boy was hit with a baton and exposed to tear gas, was then published in the *Canberra Times* on 18 April 2002. Within six hours DIMIA had publicly refuted the claim on its website, saying, 'This department has no record of injuries to a 7-year-old sustained during the disturbance at Woomera detention facility on Good Friday ... If Father Brennan has information or evidence of mistreatment of detainees he should report it to the appropriate authorities for investigation.' I had seen the bruises with my own eyes. I had heard reports of tear gas hitting children even from the ACM manager at Woomera. I lodged a complaint about the department's spin doctoring. It took the secretary of the department more than three months to conduct the inquiry. The department could strenuously deny allegations within six hours, then take more than three months to acknowledge their error. The acting secretary of the department explained that their public misinformation occurred because 'a number of communication problems in the Department allowed the matter to escalate to the stage where Mr Foster [Director, Public Affairs, DIMIA] posted inaccurate information'. According to the departmental inquiry, this escalation took place over four days. The public rebuttal was issued within six hours of the publication of my remarks — hardly any time at all for communication problems or escalation to impede the single-minded objective of denying that there had been injury to children.

Mr Ruddock's own chief of staff had referred the matter to the South Australian Family and Youth Services on 29 April 2002 once a new search of medical records revealed there was a problem. On 10 July 2002 the mother reported to the Human Rights and Equal Opportunity Commission:

> My son was with me in Oscar compound during the disturbance in the early hours of Saturday 30 March 2002. He and I were both hit by tear gas even though we were not trying to escape. I was blinded for about a minute and I took my son to my chest and embraced him to protect him. I started to move away from the scene with my son. Then an ACM guard came and bowed over me and struck my son with a baton.

On Tuesday 2 April 2002, I told my story to Fr Frank Brennan and the lawyers at Woomera. I then went to the doctor on Wednesday 3 April 2002. The doctor made a report which I attach to this letter. I asked the lawyers to make a complaint.

One and a half months later, two policemen came to see me. I told them what happened to my son. They said they would return with an interpreter from Adelaide and with Federal Police and someone from Children's Services and with a camera for interview with my son. Then about one week later, and before the United Nations came to visit Woomera, I was interviewed by Geoff Cardwell of the South Australia Police about the incident. He said he was the boss of the other police who had come. He said it was not the responsibility of Federal Police because they would come only for damage to property. He said Child Service would not come because their responsibility is child abuse and relationships between children and parents. He gave me a card with the reference PIR/02/966813. He recorded our conversation. He was interested only in the events which occurred on the evening of Friday 29 March 2002. He told me that the doctor and ACM had not made any report of my son's injury to Children's Services. I asked him about my rights. He told me, 'You can't do anything because you are captive in here and when you get out and get your visa, you can continue your protest and maybe you can get your rights.' He asked whether I saw who hit my son. I said I did not see because the guard was wearing a mask. He said, 'We can't catch him because you didn't see him.' I said, 'It is not important who hit my son, just it is important that ACM action that they hit children, because it is their habit in our compound.'

I trusted the government to protect my son. I hope my complaint can help other mothers and children. I am only a single mother in detention who wants the government to care for us.[34]

On 22 August 2002 Mr Ruddock advised, 'I understand that South Australian police investigations are continuing. Meanwhile, the Department is examining an ACM report into the matter, received on 5 August 2002, to determine what action, if any, is required.'[35] The mother of the boy never received a report on her complaint. On 3 February 2003 the Minister wrote again, advising that 'the matter was referred to the AFP' who 'determined there was insufficient evidence relating to the identity of the alleged offender'. Who does investigate assaults in detention centres? The Australian Federal Police (AFP) or the state police? Or nobody?

The cursory and dilatory nature of DIMIA's inquiry invokes no public confidence that there will not be a recurrence of cover-ups or neglect of credible claims of injury to children in detention, where they are being used as a means to an end. In this instance, the Commonwealth department was guilty of a negligent or willful cover-up regarding the investigation of child abuse in detention centres. If children are to be held in detention with their parents, they should be held in facilities where there is ready access to state Children's Services departments. The policy parameters of their detention should be sufficiently humane to win the support of both the federal government and the state governments, regardless of which party is in power. It is obscene that defenceless children are used as political footballs by political spin-doctors.

The stand-off between federal and state police forces became clearer later in 2002 when Amnesty International urged an investigation of complaints about sexual assaults in the Curtin Detention Centre in Western Australia. There was no demarcation of responsibilities between the police forces, even though there had been Commonwealth detention facilities conducted in Western Australia since 1989.

A female detainee who was a Sabian Mandean from Iran claimed that she had been sexually assaulted at the Curtin detention centre by two Muslim males on the night of 28 July 2002. She claimed that she was the only woman and the only Mandean in a compound with fifty Muslim men. Back in Iran, Sabian Mandeans are a religious minority who follow John the Baptist and who are subject to sustained persecution by the Muslim majority. This Mandean woman claimed that she had been spat upon and had her finger broken during the brutal Muslim attack. The attack was reported to the authorities within hours. DIMIA referred it to the Australian Federal Police (AFP) on 1 August 2002. After the closure of the Curtin Detention Centre, Minister Ruddock wrote to Amnesty International on 18 November 2002 regarding the inquiries into alleged assaults at Curtin, informing them, 'The allegations you refer to have been the subject of an investigation by my Department and the Australian Federal Police.'

The general manager of the AFP wrote to Amnesty International on 20 November 2002, saying, 'The AFP rejected the investigation of this matter as allegations of sexual assault fall within the jurisdiction of State Police Services. The AFP advised both DIMIA and the ACM of its decision not to accept the matter for investigation and also recommended that ACM refer the matter to the Western Australian Police Service.' On the same day, the Western Australian Minister for Police and Emergency Services wrote to Amnesty International, saying, 'The Curtin detention centre was maintained on Commonwealth land. Accordingly, the responsibility for the investigation of criminal activity on such land was vested in the Australian Federal Police (AFP).'

The lack of coordination for basic service delivery between the Commonwealth and the states has caused great harm to detainees in these Commonwealth facilities. It is irresponsible of the Commonwealth to pursue a detention policy without the full cooperation of the states unless the Commonwealth is in a position to make right the shortfall in the basic government services that must be provided for the protection of the basic human rights of those in the government's care. It is imperative that the Commonwealth reaches agreement with the states about the delivery of basic services, including police services.

In the wake of the Christmas 2002 fires in the detention centres, DIMIA moved to commence discussions with the South Australian police, finalising a protocol for routine involvement by South Australian police in the investigation of complaints at the new Baxter detention centre. It is extraordinary that the Commonwealth has been able to conduct detention centres for more than ten years without clarifying the responsibilities of state and federal authorities in relation to criminal offences and child welfare. On 17 February 2003 Minister Ruddock wrote:

> My department is of the view that policing of immigration detention centres for the most part falls within the normal policing responsibilities of the State police services and we therefore rely on these agencies to provide these services within the centres, just as they do within the wider community.
>
> My department continues to work actively with both Federal and State policing agencies to develop formal arrangements. I understand that considerable progress has been made in recent times, particularly in South Australia. Additional resources have also been brought on board to expedite negotiations in Western Australia and I am optimistic that agreements in that jurisdiction will also be finalised before too long. Negotiations in New South Wales are also well advanced.[36]

The legal vacuum surrounding detainees in Australian immigration facilities was further exposed after the 2002 Christmas fires. Detainees were moved from the centres to prisons and police watch-houses without any charges being laid. Strip searches for all men were enforced. People, including local clergy, were denied access to the local watch-house on the basis that the detention was not a matter for the state police but for the ACM guards. These guards unilaterally decided that people would be held in custody, in handcuffs, with no access to any outside persons and prior to any charges being laid. Detainees were held for up to two weeks in solitary confinement in 'behaviour management units'.

The Pacific Solution

Despite mandatory detention and despite the TPV changes in 1999, boat people were still coming to Australia in unprecedented numbers in 2001 because of the adverse situation in Afghanistan and Iraq and because people smugglers were offering cheaper deals to Australia than to Europe. The government needed to remove the two most attractive things about catching a boat to Australia: access to a benign determination process and guaranteed protection and settlement in Australia once refugee status was established, even if you were a secondary mover. Given the remoteness of Christmas Island and Ashmore Reef from the Australian mainland and their proximity to Indonesia, the government saw these places as ideal staging posts in the construction of the firebreak. People could be held there and deemed not to have entered into Australia and they could then be shipped to Pacific countries where their claims could be processed without access to the Australian claims process and court appeals and without the possibility of resettlement in Australia. Also, these people would then be out of sight and out of mind of the Australian public, some of whom were experiencing disquiet at the idea of children behind razor wire. In time, the government would even be able to drop these people out from their detention statistics and from the statistics of those seeking asylum in Australia. Prime Minister John Howard was adamant that none of these people would ever reach Australia. An extra $159 million was allocated to DIMIA for 'offshore asylum seeker management' during the financial year 2001–2002.

This was bold thinking and it required some very fancy footwork given that an election was to be held on 10 November 2001. The government and public service had to go into caretaker mode at 12 noon on 8 October 2001. There was not a minute to lose. Even the fledgling nation state of East Timor was sounded out as the Timorese were going to the polls for their first elections. Jose Ramos Horta was publicly gracious in offering assistance to a needy neighbour who had done so much to assist East Timor in the previous two years on its road to freedom and independence. All around Dili, people were incredulous that such a suggestion could be made, given the lack of infrastructure and the chronic water shortages and electricity restrictions in East Timor.

The Australian government was fortunate to finalise cheque-book solutions with the governments of Nauru and Papua New Guinea. People from the *Tampa* were transported to Nauru for detention and processing under an agreement that provided some additional financial assistance to Nauru and some of its prominent citizens. Australia undertook to provide Nauru with an extra $26.5 million in development assistance. Several Nauruans were flown to Sydney for surgery at St Vincent's Hospital as part of the package. President Rene Harris himself needed some heart surgery. Australia also offered to double the number of educational scholarships for Nauruan students. The formal agreement with Nauru provided that the asylum seekers would be processed within six months 'or as short a time as is reasonably necessary for the implementation of this memorandum'. The initial agreement with Papua New Guinea was finalised by Mr Max Moore-Wilton, the Secretary of the Australian Department of Prime Minister and Cabinet, thirty minutes before the government went into caretaker mode, thereby avoiding the need to consult with the Opposition. The initial agreements with both countries were then renewed for an additional twelve months, given the difficulty in finding resettlement places for the proven refugees in countries other than Australia, and also given the delay with those who have had their claims rejected making a decision to return home voluntarily.

In 2003 Australia was paying the International Organisation for Migration (IOM) US$54 million for what the IOM Budget describes innocuously as the 'management and processing of Australia-bound migrants in an irregular situation'. Far from abandoning the Pacific Solution as quickly as possible, the Australian government has increased

its budgetary allocation for 'offshore asylum seeker management' from
$159 million to $240 million in 2002–2003.[37] The DIMIA portfolio
budget statement for 2002–2003 contains forward budget figures up to
2005–2006, with more than $100 million per year being provisionally
allocated for offshore reception and processing. The department confidently claims that in future years it could save up to $86 million per
year in the cost of onshore processing. This saving does not offset the
ongoing cost of the Pacific Solution, because there are also the added
costs of more than $120 million per year budgeted for the reception
and processing of boat people on Australia's external territories such
as Christmas Island. The department is also proposing to build a $200
million processing facility on Christmas Island. If onshore asylum
seekers were not being kept in detention on the mainland during the
second stage of processing, the onshore costs would be much less and
the cost of the Pacific Solution even more difficult to justify.

The detention of asylum seekers is contrary to the constitutions of
Papua New Guinea and Nauru. Imagine if every first-world country decided to engage in this sort of unlawful people trading. Mr Ruddock's
first defence to this suggestion is to claim that the facilities in those
places are not detention centres, despite the *Migration Legislation
Amendment (Transitional Movement) Act 2002* speaking of 'the detention of the person in a country in respect of which a declaration is in
force' (s. 198D(3)(c)). The bill's digest for the Migration Legislation
Amendment (Transitional Movement) Bill 2002 speaks of the removal
of persons 'to a place such as a "Pacific Solution" detention facility on
Nauru or Papua New Guinea'. The minister's chief of staff explained
the situation:

> Asylum seekers on Nauru and Manus are NOT detained. IOM do not run
> and manage detention centres. There is a fence around the compound but
> it is single strand in most cases and ringlock in others.
>
> You may wish to consider this detention — however it most clearly is
> not, either technically or practically. Hence neither we nor the Nauruan
> and PNG governments are in breach of constitutional law. However I
> do understand that our particular frame of reference will determine
> our perception of these issues.[38]

It is interesting to note the chief of staff's assurance that the IOM
does not manage detention centres. The IOM describes its role as hav-

ing been 'tasked with the management of the centres' but 'in coordination with the relevant agencies of the Australian government and host governments who are responsible for the overall security of the facilities'. The local police forces are complemented by the Australian Protective Services (APS) who are tasked with keeping the asylum seekers inside the facilities as well as keeping others from gaining access without approval. A short time after the chief of staff's statement, the Australian government's website was changed so that there were no longer references to persons being 'detained' in facilities under the Pacific Solution. Now they are 'accommodated'. Not everyone in the Australian government has been sensitive to the semantic changes. Senator George Brandis, who led the charge for the government in the Senate Select Committee on a Certain Maritime Incident, and Mr John Hodges, the head of the government's Immigration Detention Advisory Group (IDAG), referred during the inquiry to the 'detention centres' in those places and the 'detainees' kept therein. In his evidence on 1 May 2002, Mr Hodges said, 'Curtin is a lot better than Manus Island and Nauru in terms of accommodation. Nauru is by far the worst of the detention centres.'[39] The Senate committee's terms of reference, which did not evoke any protest or correction from the government at the time, included a consideration of 'the agreements between the Australian Government and the Governments of Nauru and Papua New Guinea regarding the detention within those countries of persons intercepted while travelling to Australia, publicly known as the "Pacific Solution".' The minister has continued to claim that asylum seekers are not detained in Nauru or on Manus Island.

The semantics of detention were exposed after the minister insisted on the SBS Dateline program on 29 January 2003 that no persons were detained in the processing centres on Nauru. Two days later he published a detailed ministerial response to the program, saying, 'People have from time to time been taken to the Nauru police cells for breaching their Nauru visa conditions, which restrict their movement to the processing centres.' If a person is liable for arrest and imprisonment for leaving a processing centre, they are properly classified as being detained in the processing centre. The UNHCR Guidelines on Detention define detention as:

confinement within a narrowly bounded or restricted location, including prisons, closed camps, detention facilities or airport transit zones, where freedom of movement is substantially curtailed, and where the only opportunity to leave this limited area is to leave the territory.[40]

Even Mr Ruddock's finely honed legal vocabulary is strained to refute the assertion that asylum seekers on Nauru and Manus Island are held in detention.

Mr Ruddock's next defence is to claim that it is not for the Australian government to tell other governments how to interpret their constitutions. He says, 'The constitutionality of the arrangements for accommodation of asylum seekers in Nauru and Papua New Guinea is a matter for the Governments of the countries concerned.'[41] The Constitution of Nauru is very specific in the way it details the conditions in which a person may be held in detention. The constitutional founders of Nauru and Papua New Guinea did not contemplate the Pacific Solution. For example, Article 5 of the Nauruan Constitution provides:

(1) No person shall be deprived of his personal liberty, except as authorised by law in any of the following cases:
(a) in execution of the sentence or order of a court in respect of an offence of which he has been convicted;
(b) for the purpose of bringing him before a court in execution of the order of a court;
(c) upon reasonable suspicion of his having committed, or being about to commit, an offence;
(d) under the order of a court, for his education during any period ending not later than the thirty-first day of December after he attains the age of eighteen years;
(e) under the order of a court, for his welfare during any period ending not later than the date on which he attains the age of twenty years;
(f) for the purpose of preventing the spread of disease;
(g) in the case of a person who is, or is reasonably suspected to be, of unsound mind or addicted to drugs or alcohol, for the purpose of his care or treatment or the protection of the community; and
(h) for the purpose of preventing his unlawful entry into Nauru, or for the purpose of effecting his expulsion, extradition or other lawful removal from Nauru.

(2) A person who is arrested or detained shall be informed promptly of the reasons for the arrest or detention and shall be permitted to consult in the place in which he is detained a legal representative of his own choice.

(3) A person who has been arrested or detained in the circumstances referred to in paragraph (c) of clause (1) of this Article and has not been released shall be brought before a Judge or some other person holding judicial office within a period of twenty-four hours after the arrest or detention and shall not be further held in custody in connection with that offence except by order of a Judge or some other person holding judicial office.

(4) Where a complaint is made to the Supreme Court that a person is unlawfully detained, the Supreme Court shall enquire into the complaint and, unless satisfied that the detention is lawful, shall order that person to be brought before it and shall release him.

Detention of asylum seekers in Nauru is contrary to the Nauruan Constitution. By offering financial and personal incentives to Nauruan politicians, the Australian government has engaged in unlawful people trading. The UNHCR has informed the government and now the Senate about its concerns with the detention regime under the Pacific Solution. In its submission to the Senate's Legal and Constitutional References Committee on the excision of more islands from Australia's migration zone, the UNHCR has said:

Detention or similar restrictive measures applied to asylum seekers are inherently undesirable and should normally be avoided. If necessary, detention may be resorted to only on grounds prescribed by law to verify identity; to determine the elements on which the claim to refugee status or asylum is based; or for reasons of national security or public order. Detention, where this lacks appropriate safeguards such as humane conditions and access to periodic judicial review, may be considered arbitrary.

Of concern to UNHCR in the cases of Nauru and Manus Island is that refugees who have been recognised and therefore have had their status regularised remain detained until a durable solution is found. This detention is without time limits or periodic review. The ongoing detention of persons recognised as refugees is a restriction of freedom of movement in breach of Article 26 of the 1951 Convention. Furthermore, such detention is not consistent with Article 31(2) of the Refugee Convention, which provides that restrictions of freedom of movement shall not be applied until the status of refugees in the country is regularised. Even though these recognised refugees are no longer on Australia's territory, Australia's obligations under the Refugee Convention continue to be engaged until a durable solution is found.[42]

If other countries were to emulate the Pacific Solution, asylum seekers would be routinely traded across the world by first-world countries anxious to maintain the integrity of their borders. Asylum seekers would be exported to third-world countries desirous of improving their terms of trade. In the Pacific region, a country like New Zealand would never contemplate such a solution. Neither should Australia.

Conclusions

During the firebreak period, the government made an example of the Afghans, the Iraqis and the Iranians in detention. If they had been released into the community while their cases were being determined, they could have commenced their orientation to life in the community, given that most of them would be staying at least three years on a temporary protection visa. The modest number whose claims were rejected could have been treated in the same way as all other onshore asylum seekers. Their numbers would not contribute significantly to the 60,000 overstayers in the community.

There can be no objection to detention while a person is awaiting removal from the country once a decision on refugee status is made. There is no case for detaining one particular group before a decision is made when that group is known historically to contain a much higher percentage of refugees than all other groups. There is no case for detaining them further while their appeals are processed, especially when it is known that they are at least six times more likely than other asylum seekers to succeed on appeal. The injustice of this discriminatory detention would be heightened if, as is likely, the detention in remote places were contributing to more regular bad decision making at the primary stage.

If the government's chief concern was to limit the number of unlawful overstayers in the community, the savings from not holding unlawful arrivals in protracted detention during the processing stage could be devoted to increased surveillance of all overstayers in the community. This would facilitate the orderly departure from Australia of the overstayers, regardless of their racial, national or religious identity. Though there are 60,000 overstayers a year, our government locates only about 15,000 of them a year. The Australian public's fixation with boat people is highlighted when you consider that only 308 unauthor-

Australian, 29 December 2001.
Reproduced with Peter Nicholson's permission.

ised boat arrivals were removed from Australia in 2001–2002, while
another 10,894 persons who had no authority to be in Australia were
removed. Where are the other 49,000? Would it really have mattered if
those 308 boat people had been in the community rather than in detention at taxpayer expense? There is no coherent rationale for keeping all
unauthorised asylum seekers in detention during the second stage of
their processing. After ten years of such detention, there is no proof
that it operates as a deterrent. With the fourth wave of boat people,
mandatory detention was imposed on a group of whom 90 per cent were
proved to be refugees.

Even after ten years of mandatory detention, the Australian government has been unable to finalise appropriate arrangements with state
governments for the delivery of child welfare, police and education
services. In 1978 Malcolm Fraser had threatened to take over the running of Aboriginal reserves in Queensland. He had to drop the proposal when the Queensland premier made it clear that Queensland

would not deliver basic state services, and the Commonwealth was not equipped to fill the gap. Commonwealth governments should have made a similar assessment when they decided to set up immigration detention centres in the more remote, less-populated states. As the Commonwealth had no capacity to deliver the basic services, and no intention of doing so, it should have proceeded only with the agreement of the states for the delivery of those services. After ten years we still do not know which police force is responsible for investigating assaults in immigration detention centres. State child protection services say that they cannot discharge their responsibilities to the children being held in detention.

The Pacific Solution has been so harshly administered that women and children in Nauru are unable to join their husbands and fathers who are lawfully residing in Australia on temporary protection visas. They ended up in Nauru only because they wanted to be reunited with their husbands and fathers who were lawfully on the Australian mainland enjoying protection but not the right to family reunion. The government rhetoric about commitment to family values and honouring our obligations as a good international humanitarian citizen has been strained to breaking point.

On 29 January 2003 the SBS Dateline Program featured seven Iraqi women with their children in detention on Nauru. They were failed asylum seekers who would have been granted refugee status if they had reached Australia. Having been intercepted by the Navy, they were transported to Nauru for offshore processing to a jurisdiction where their husbands were not residing as refugees. Until the Pacific Solution was set up, Australia's law and policy had honoured the principle of the unity of the family, which Australia had voted for at the Conference of Plenipotentiaries in July 1951. That Conference, which finalised the Refugees Convention unanimously, resolved that governments should ensure 'that the unity of the refugee's family is maintained particularly in cases where the head of the family has fulfilled the necessary conditions for admission to a particular country'.[43] While the Australian government signed up to President Bush's Coalition of the Willing, these women and children were held in detention on a remote Pacific outpost unable to join their refugee husbands and fathers lawfully residing in Australia. Mr Ruddock says, 'There is no obligation

under the Refugees Convention to provide for family reunion. As TPV
holders are not permanent residents of Australia they are not eligible
to sponsor members of their families for migration.'[44]

In June 2002 the UN Working Group on Mandatory Detention completed a visit to Australian immigration detention facilities. In their
report of October 2002 they stated at paragraph 15:

> During talks conducted with government officials it became obvious that
> one of the goals of the system of mandatory detention and the way it is im-
> plemented is to discourage would-be immigrants from entering Australia
> without a valid visa.[45]

This was a reasonable conclusion for the group to draw, given that
they had met with Alexander Downer, the Australian Minister for Foreign Affairs, on 5 June 2002. The next day, Downer, in answer to a Dor-
othy Dixer, told parliament that he had emphasised to the group 'that
detention is essential to enable appropriate health, security and identity checks to be carried out and that we would be continuing with this
policy also in order to stop the flow of illegal migrants coming to our
country'.[46] The UN group had no objection to detention for health security and identity checks. Their objection was to detention aimed at deterring other asylum seekers from coming. Mr Downer had told them
that Australia had no intention of changing its detention policy, 'because to do so would undermine the integrity of our orderly migration
system'.

As soon as the UN Working Group had circulated its report to
government (and even prior to its formal publication), the government
responded on its website to paragraph 15:

> This is an incorrect assumption. Detention is for the purpose of ensuring
> unauthorised arrivals are available for the processing of any claims to stay
> in Australia, for their identity to be established and for appropriate clear-
> ances for health, character and security to be obtained. In addition, deten-
> tion ensures that people are available for removal if they have no grounds
> to remain in Australia.[47]

Are we meant to believe that neither the Minister for Foreign Affairs
nor the UN visiting delegation that met with Downer and Ruddock on 5
June 2002 accurately understood the limited and proper rationale for
Australia's mandatory detention policy? Then again, presuming the

absence of government deceit or incompetence, there may not be a coherent rationale for the government policy once it moves beyond detention for initial checks on health, security and identity and for removal. There just is no coherent rationale for detention during the processing stage. Sometimes government spokesmen have justified detention during the processing phase as a deterrent for others contemplating illegal entry to Australia. At other times, government spokesmen have insisted that such detention is the thing furthest from their minds, that it is only incidental. But incidental to what?

It may be reasonable and necessary to keep people in detention at the reception stage in order to determine identity, health and security issues, especially if they have arrived without documents, which they may even have deliberately destroyed. It may also be reasonable and necessary to keep people in detention during the removal phase. Even then, there may be individual cases for which detention would not be justified, for example if there was absolutely no risk of the person absconding. It is a quantum leap to claim, as no other first-world country does, that mandatory detention is reasonable and necessary at the processing phase. Rather it may be arbitrary and excessive. The House of Lords has set down a useful test of proportionality in these instances. To decide whether some limitation of freedom is arbitrary or excessive, you ask whether:

- the legislative objective is sufficiently important to justify limiting a fundamental right
- the measures designed to meet the legislative objective are rationally connected to it
- the means used to impair the right or freedom are no more than is necessary to accomplish the objective.[48]

The legislative objective is to ensure that people are available for processing. Given that these individuals have applied for refugee status, they generally have a personal motivation for presenting themselves for processing. The detention measures in Australia include detention in remote places, removed from ready access to legal and other services. It is a comprehensive detention regime, not simply a hostel arrangement with strict curfews and reporting conditions. There is no rational connection between these aspects of the measures and the legislative objective, despite DIMIA's misleading assurance that 'every effort is made to ensure detainees are able to go about their daily lives with as few restrictions as possible'.[49] If the legislative objective were very prompt processing (as we will see with the Oakington model in the United Kingdom), there might be a case for a brief period of detention. Detention in places as remote as Woomera and Port Hedland would still not make much sense. We know from the appeal records that the primary decision making in detention cases is more often in error than in those cases where the applicant is free to live in the community, arranging their case with the ready assistance of migration agents, friends and community groups. The means used, including the long-term detention of dependent children, is far more than is necessary to accomplish the objective.

The only other arguable legislative objective for detention at the processing stage is to ensure that the unsuccessful applicant is available for removal at the conclusion of the process. This is akin to arguing that everyone should be taken into custody once they have been charged with an offence. Applicants usually present voluntarily during the processing phase. In the last couple of years the overwhelming majority of detainees have been proved to be refugees. Yet even these refugees have had to endure ongoing detention (with their children) to ensure that the remnant of unsuccessful applicants would be available for removal. Meanwhile, most unsuccessful asylum applicants are not detained during the processing of their claims because they happened to have entered the country on a student or visitor visa, having failed to disclose that the seeking of asylum was their primary motivation in coming to Australia.

On a visit to the memorial at the Changi war prison in Singapore, I realised that the abuses of detention are always more aggravated when the jailers are people of another race. Most of the Afghans and Iraqis held in these desert camps have been genuine refugees with every right to be integrated into the Australian community. Ninety-seven per cent of the Iraqi boat people were ultimately recognised as refugees. One hundred per cent of them started life in Australia in detention. What have we done to each of them? What have we done to ourselves? The Europeans and Americans will not be copying us, because our solution could only be devised by an island nation that does not have much of a problem. Australia has designed a large sledge hammer to crack a small nut. It is a hammer that would wreak havoc in those countries with significant asylum-seeker populations. It has devastated the fresh beginnings of some of our newest Australians. This policy requires geographic isolation, mendicant island neighbours, and a compliant, unaccountable police force in the neighbouring, transit country. It also requires plenty of space and a politicised public who are not too perturbed to learn, to quote the minister's modulated phraseology, 'The longest recorded period for any minor asylum seeker in detention was 1998 days. This minor would now be 12 years old, is the child of the above female and was included in the same application. Immigration detention ceased 29 days after the family member's litigation was completed.'[50] It remains only to add that the litigation resulted in the issue of a visa to the family member and the family now lives in Perth. When asked for further details about this case, the minister's spokesman told the *Age* that the child 'was born in Australia of a Chinese family who pursued every legal avenue and went to the High Court twice in their fight to avoid deportation'.[51] Chen Shi Hai was born in detention. His family won their case in the Federal Court and they could then have been released. The minister appealed to the Full Federal Court. Having failed there, the minister appealed to the High Court where he once again lost and had ultimately to release the family.[52] Chen Shi Hai will carry the scars of our detention policy for the rest of his life. We all carry the shame, knowing that there is no coherent rationale or national interest in a policy that results in Chen Shi Hai being born in detention and not being able to step outside the razor wire for the first five and a half years of his life.

CHAPTER 5

Reception and detention in Europe and the United States

EU reception and detention

Germany, the United Kingdom, France and Italy have the greatest voting power in the European Union. On asylum issues, Germany and the United Kingdom call the shots because they receive such a large number of asylum seekers. Under the Treaty of Amsterdam, the United Kingdom has a choice whether to opt in and be bound by any particular directive on asylum issues. The United Kingdom has always opted in, but has used this capacity as a further lever for getting its way. Germany, on the other hand, has exercised its leverage by insisting on particular procedures for the implementation of the new asylum directives, and has got its way. Under the 2001 Treaty of Nice, there is a special arrangement for the European Council to adopt asylum measures setting down the minimum standards on reception of asylum seekers and their processing, the qualifications for refugee status, and the minimum standards for giving temporary protection to those in need of humanitarian assistance. No community legislation defining the common rules and basic principles governing these issues can be passed unless it has the unanimous support of the Council of Ministers. Everyone, including Germany, has a veto. This explains why the two main players, Germany and the United Kingdom, have been happy to proceed with their own comprehensive redrafts of asylum law and policy. They know that the smaller players will be forced to adopt their standards in the interests of having these thorny issues resolved in the time frame. Even if the common rules and basic principles are not agreed in the five-year time frame, there will still be a need for unanimous resolution by the Council of Ministers. Only once the common rules and principles have won unanimous support is it possible for the European Union then to fine tune the detail, with legislation passed by a qualified majority of the Council after the usual consultations with the European Parliament and the Conciliation Committee have occurred. Karl Kopp from the German refugee agency 'Pro Asyl', who sees Germany acting as a brake on a sensible European asylum policy, explains the politics of this complex legal arrangement:

> The balance of power between the three central actors, parliament, council and commission, is represented as follows. The commission supplies partially refugee-friendlier suggestions. These fail however because of the resistance of individual states. The European Parliament takes comments on the suggestions, but does not have the right to participate in the decision; it possesses only a hearing right. The resolutions of the parliament remain to a large extent unconsidered. Thus the practice of the Union remains further on shaped by national particularistic interests. The all-blocking unanimity principle is almost a right of veto and prevents a brisk transfer to common, international law.[1]

Even before agreeing to a wholesale expansion of member states, the European Union saw the need for a harmonisation of refugee and asylum law and policy consistent with the Convention on Refugees and the European Convention for the Protection of Human Rights and Fundamental Freedoms (ECHR). Under the Treaty on European Union, the European Council of Ministers is supposed to reach unanimous agreement by May 2004 on:

- criteria and mechanisms for determining which member state is responsible for considering an application for asylum submitted by a national of a third country in one of the member states
- minimum standards on the reception of asylum seekers in member states

- minimum standards with respect to the qualification of nationals of third countries as refugees
- minimum standards on procedures in member states for granting or withdrawing refugee status
- minimum standards for giving temporary protection to displaced persons from third countries who cannot return to their country of origin and for persons who otherwise need international protection.

If agreement has not been reached, the treaty sets down a complex procedure for breaking the deadlock after May 2004. Proposals come to the Council of Ministers through a circuitous route. The Director General of Justice and Home Affairs in the European Commission first drafts a proposal and circulates it for comment. The draft is then submitted to the European Parliament. The Commission then considers any amendments proposed by the Parliament before the final draft is then submitted to the Council of Ministers. In a policy area as controversial as refugees and asylum seekers, the real horse-trading commences behind closed doors with the Council of Ministers. Ultimately the directive is published in the Official Journal of the European Union. Member states are then expected to enact their own laws in compliance with the directive within two years of publication of the directive. Within three years they are to report on the workability of the directive and propose amendments. The Commission is then expected to report to the European Parliament and to the Council of Ministers after another six months.

The European Union has conducted a long-time debate trying to find the right balance, setting minimum standards for reception of applicants for asylum, while maintaining adequate border protection. The Council of Ministers issued a directive prescribing minimum standards on the reception of asylum seekers in member states on 27 January 2003. The Commission proposal was first circulated in April 2001 and approved by the European Parliament in April 2002. In November and December 2002 the original proposal was extensively amended by the Council of Ministers and agreed to with minimal public discussion on 28 November 2002. There was extensive horse-trading about the question of detention. Regardless of an asylum seeker's mode of entry to a member state, the Commission had proposed that member states were to agree that they 'shall not hold applicants for asylum in detention for the sole reason that their applications for asylum need to be examined'.[2] It was impossible to win a consensus on this ban on detention. The final directive simply provides:

> Member states may decide on the residence of the asylum seeker for reasons of public interest, public order or, when necessary, for the swift processing and effective monitoring of his or her application.[3]

The directive does permit detention for the purpose of making an accelerated decision, as at Oakington in the United Kingdom. As a concession to the Germans, the directive permits a member state to confine applicants and their accompanying family members to specific areas of their national territory so that government can disperse the asylum population to more remote places. Applicants can request permission to make visits outside the specified area for personal, health and family reasons as well as for the preparation of their applications. If the request is denied, they will have a right of appeal.

As with asylum seekers in Australia who are on bridging visas, European governments want to retain a broad discretion about whether to provide a right to work. In Australia, the asylum seeker who enters with a visa will usually have the right to work if the application for asylum has been made within 45 days of arrival. There has been a wide variety of practice in Europe regarding the right to work. The Greeks and Italians would not contemplate it. Originally, refugee advocates were optimistic that the European minimum standard would permit applicants access to the labour market at the latest six months after the lodgment of their application. The government would still have full control of the internal labour market, being able to specify the types of work, the hours of work and the skills necessary. The European Parliament was even minded to reduce to four months the maximum time that an asylum applicant could be excluded from the labour market. As the proposal came closer for determination by the European Council of Ministers, that maximum exclusion time was blown out to a year.

In the end, the Commissioners who were responsible for taking the proposal to the Council of Ministers could read the signs and dropped altogether the restriction on member states being able to exclude applicants from the labour market. Member states retain the unilateral discretion to deny work rights to an asylum seeker, even if the application for asylum has not been decided for over a year, and through no fault of the applicant. This was a major setback to those wanting to set minimum standards that were more than the lowest common denominator. Two of the main reasons for seeking a harmonisation of minimum standards have been the need to arrest secondary movement within the European Union and the need to be fair to asylum seekers who because of the Dublin Convention will have no choice where their claim is processed. It was only reasonable that there be the same right to work for asylum seekers in all member states — taking away one of the major reasons for secondary movement and ensuring equality of treatment for all applicants in the European Union while they await a decision about their claim.

Though there is an agreed minimum standard for the reception of asylum seekers, the ongoing wide variety of state practices regarding work rights (especially with the expansion of the European Union to 27 members) will still cause significant secondary movements within the Union. Article 11 of the final directive provides:

1. Member states shall determine a period of time, starting from the date on which an application for asylum was lodged, during which an applicant shall not have access to the labour market.
2. If a decision at first instance has not been taken within one year of the presentation of an application for asylum and this delay cannot be attributed to the applicant, member states shall decide the conditions for granting access to the labour market for the applicant.
3. Access to the labour market shall not be withdrawn during appeals procedures, where an appeal against a negative decision in a regular procedure has suspensive effect, until such time as a negative decision on the appeal is notified.
4. For reasons of labour market policies, member states may give priority to European Union citizens and nationals of States parties to the Agreement on the European Economic Area and also to legally resident third-country nationals.

When it came to minimum standards for 'material reception conditions', the European Union also dropped the bar very low. Originally the Commission had proposed a wording that was consistent with the Universal Declaration of Human Rights. It would have required member states to provide material conditions 'to ensure a standard of living adequate for the health and the well being of applicants and their accompanying family members as well as the protection of their fundamental rights'. In the end they were required only to provide conditions for 'a standard of living adequate for the health of applicants and capable of ensuring their subsistence'.[4] Though there are detailed provisions about the standards of housing and health to be provided, these standards are applicable only if the asylum applicant has promptly made a claim for protection on arrival in the member state. A government is entitled to refuse even the minimum conditions of support and assistance if the applicant fails to demonstrate that the asylum claim was made as soon as reasonably practicable after arrival.[5] Governments are insistent on these limitations because they are concerned that people who make belated asylum claims are often economic migrants who are simply seeking another means of remaining in a country once they have come to the attention of the authorities or once they have exhausted all other lawful means of remaining in the country. Originally member states were to permit vocational training for asylum seekers after six months. Now there is no minimum standard for access to vocational training.

Everyone agrees that this first minimum-standards exercise reached a conclusion only because the Council of Ministers was prepared to water down key standards proposed during the consultations. The Belgian, Spanish and Danish presidencies of the Council of Ministers were happy to claim the credit for a prompt, watered-down outcome. They trumpeted that all member states accepted the principle 'that destitute asylum seekers who are allowed to stay in the country to wait for the outcome of the procedure are entitled to a reception (which includes housing, food, clothing and an allowance of the daily expenses)'.[6]

While the European Union is concluding its harmonisation of policy and practices relating to asylum seekers, governments are proceeding with bilateral negotiations trying to bed down lowest-common-denominator procedures in the hope that such agreements will consolidate their bargaining position at the European Union table. The United Kingdom Home Secretary has told the Home Affairs Select Committee of his parliament:

There is a new spirit in terms of recognising that we must work together on this ... I am not waiting for European-wide agreement on anything. Waiting for Dublin II is a bit like 'waiting for Godot', so we have to make what progress we can as quickly as we can bilaterally and trilaterally based on what we are anticipating on a Europe-wide basis.[7]

Meanwhile the major organisations in the United Kingdom advocating the refugee cause and providing refugee assistance have expressed cautious optimism about the harmonisation process. Keith Best of the Immigration Advisory Service told the Committee:

What we are ending up with, though, is that very often the EC Draft Directives that are coming out in this field are ones that do have adequate safeguards and are ones that many of us could live with quite happily, but by the time individual ministers have got their hands on it, they are being cut down to such minimum standards that they are not harbouring the safeguards that we would want to see in a common European policy.[8]

Nick Hardwick from the Refugee Council told the committee:

Clearly it is a good thing to move in that direction. I think some of the proposals coming out of the Commission are quite positive. If we simply go down to the lowest common denominator, it will be a missed opportunity. I would say about a harmonisation process that it is not a panacea. We do not think that is going to solve everything and make the whole system work better right across Europe and make it perfect, but I think it would help.[9]

The whole harmonisation exercise will not be complete until 2004 at the earliest. The changes to the first agreed directive are a sure sign that the exercise will not result in higher standards for the processing of asylum claims. The European Council on Refugees and Exiles (ECRE) is the peak body of refugee advocacy groups in Europe. ECRE is rightly concerned that the process for this first directive resulted in further negotiations by the governments of member states reopening provisions on which there was already agreement. In each instance the result was a watering down of the standards originally proposed. ECRE observed, 'The events of September 11th have cast a shadow on the European Union's discussion on asylum.'[10]

It is one thing to ensure that asylum applicants are not unnecessarily taken into detention. It is another to provide adequate facilities for asylum seekers who continue to reside in the community when they are denied permission to work, to study or to engage in vocational training.

Such permission will be increasingly withheld in Europe in an attempt to reduce the pull factors for persons from the third world jumping the queue of economic migration and seeking a place in a first-world society regardless of their asylum needs.

Australia falls short in compliance with these European Union standards. Contrary to the ECHR, it keeps unlawful non-citizens in detention. Also, destitute asylum seekers who are resident in the community on a bridging visa (often having come to Australia on a visitor's visa or a student's visa) are usually not eligible for any assistance from the government's Asylum Seekers Assistance Scheme until six months after the lodging of an asylum claim. This scheme, administered by the Red Cross, has provided assistance to 2,100–2,800 applicants per year over the last three years. The financial assistance provided is 89 per cent of the standard welfare payments that would be payable to a citizen in equivalent circumstances. Once an applicant has had a rejection of the asylum claim from the primary decision maker, the applicant will no longer be eligible for the assistance even if he or she is awaiting an appeal to the Refugee Review Tribunal (RRT). The best the Red Cross can do is to request that the RRT give priority to the applicant's hearing. If the applicant made the asylum claim more than 45 days after arrival, usually the applicant then will have no right to work and no access to Medicare. The Immigration Department can exempt an applicant from the six-month waiting time for benefits on account of financial hardship, age, inability to work, parenting or caring responsibility, or pregnancy. The Red Cross cannot give the exemption. As the European Union works on its other directives setting minimum standards, we Australians would do well to ensure that our laws and practices at least comply with the European lowest common denominator. If our laws and practices fall short, we will have no claim to be acting as a good international citizen sharing the burden.

UK reception and detention

The British would never contemplate mandatory detention for the processing of asylum claims by all those arriving in lorries, on the Eurostar, in containers, on ships or by plane without documents or with forged documents. Such action would be contrary to the European Convention on Human Rights. In any event, responsible politicians in the United Kingdom would regard such a course as financially irresponsible, administratively impossible and morally repugnant. The United Kingdom government has become a greater practitioner of detention, and they have now decided to withdraw all welfare and accommodation assistance from applicants when the government officials are not satisfied that the claim was made as soon as reasonably practicable after the person's arrival in the United Kingdom. No one yet knows how liberally this restriction will be applied. The National Asylum Support Service (NASS), which provides the assistance, estimates that the restriction will affect about 100 asylum cases a day. Given that applicants are prohibited from working for the first six months, there will be many impoverished and needy asylum seekers on the streets seeking charity assistance. Even though the Secretary of State can deny welfare benefits to an asylum seeker who does not lodge a claim as soon as practicable, he retains the legal power to avoid any breach of the asylum seeker's rights under the ECHR.[11] On 19 February 2003 a judge ruled that the welfare restrictions breached the human rights entitlements of six destitute asylum seekers. Home Secretary David Blunkett reacted angrily: 'If public policy can always be overridden by challenge through the courts, then democracy itself is under threat.' He said:

> This measure is an important part of our asylum reform programme, which is dealing with widespread abuse of the system and reducing unfounded claims. It is simple common sense that asylum seekers should lodge their claim as soon as they arrive if they expect support from the government.[12]

Barry Stoyle, Chief Executive of the Refugee Legal Centre, was delighted with the court's ruling. He said:

> Denial of support will leave many asylum seekers without a roof over their head and without any money to feed themselves. Since they are prevented from working to support themselves, many without family or friends in this country will be left destitute. Many of the clients we see are traumatised, and face great difficulties in recounting their experiences at the best of times. This task is made more difficult when they are hungry, cold and destitute, and having to think more of their day-to-day survival on the streets.[13]

The Court of Appeal unanimously rejected Mr Blunkett's appeal on

18 March 2003 noting that the legislation was crafted to ensure that there was no infringement of the rights of asylum seekers under the European Convention. The three law lords said that it was for the asylum seekers to prove that they had made a prompt asylum claim. The judges posed the question: 'On the premise that the purpose of coming to this country was to claim asylum and having regard both to the practical opportunity of claiming asylum and to the asylum seeker's personal circumstances, could the asylum seeker reasonably have been expected to claim asylum earlier than he or she did?'[14] If the asylum seeker could have been expected to claim asylum earlier, there would be no claim for state assistance unless its withdrawal, in light of the absence of the right to work, would subject the asylum seeker to inhuman or degrading treatment. If the state officials rejected an applicant's claim for assistance, they would need to show that they acted fairly. They would need to explain clearly to the applicant the purpose of the interview for assessing the claim for asylum assistance. The judges noted that 'fairness required the interviewer to try to ascertain the precise reason that the applicant did not claim asylum on arrival, which called for interviewing skills and a more flexible approach than simply completing a standard form questionnaire'. In light of the way the case went during argument in the Court of Appeal, the government undertook to overhaul its determination processes.

Most people who seek asylum on entry or shortly after arrival in the United Kingdom are not taken into detention. There are usually about 1,000 asylum applicants each night being held in detention in prisons around the country. The government has also constructed a handful of detention centres that are now being renamed 'removal centres'. In theory, people are not taken into detention except in preparation for their removal from the country. Immigration officials sometimes interpret the law such that preparation for removal commences when the applicant arrives in the country, given that the applicant is presumed to have a hopeless case.

There have been four major overhauls of the United Kingdom law and policy for asylum seekers in ten years. Though there is no system of automatic detention for unlawful entrants even if they are asylum seekers, back in 1993 there would have been only about 250 asylum seekers in detention at any one time, whereas in 1996 there were 850, and now there are over 2,000. Detention with limited access to bail is becoming more commonplace in the United Kingdom even though the government manuals state that there is still a presumption in favour of temporary admission. Refugee advocates say that detention decisions at ports by immigration officers are inconsistent and ad hoc. They compare a detention rate of 2 per cent at Waterloo Station with a rate of 18 per cent at Stansted Airport. At different times there have been policy decisions 'to detain all Chinese asylum seekers until further notice'. 'If we're told to do that we do it.'[15] Zimbabweans were regularly taken into detention on arrival during 2001. Though bail is often available in theory once someone is in immigration detention, there will be a demand for sureties of thousands of pounds, an amount obviously beyond the reach of an asylum seeker who has no family in the country and no right to work.

Under the latest model, an asylum seeker will usually be taken to an induction centre near one of the ports for a stay of about seven days. In that time there will be basic health checks and briefings on the asylum process. The NASS will then decide if the applicant is in need of accommodation or welfare assistance. Applicants will be issued with an Application Registration Card that carries relevant information including fingerprints. Those who will then be living independently will be required to report regularly to the authorities. They may be eligible for welfare assistance. Those dependent on the state for accommodation will be dispersed to centres mainly in the north of England and in Scotland. The four new centres will each accommodate up to 750 persons, being modelled on the centres in Finland and Sweden. It is expected that applicants will be processed through the centres within six months. Refugee advocates, the Conservative Opposition and the House of Lords have been critical of the size of these centres, arguing that smaller clusters would have been better for assisting people to integrate into the local community. The government is proposing that children be educated in the centres rather than at local schools. The Home Secretary, David Blunkett, got himself into deep water when he said that local schools and medical practices were afraid that they could be swamped by clusters of asylum seekers coming into their midst, and that that was why he wanted centres large enough to provide their own cost-effective medical and educational services. No matter what the size of the centres, the government knows that there are always problems with the NIMBY ('not in my backyard') voters, who argue that their own neighbourhood should be spared the strain of a large number of foreign, welfare-dependent people who will remain for six months with no intention of settling permanently in the area. Most asylum seekers will still be dispersed into the community to find their own accommodation with the assistance of local charities and local councils. On present figures, there could be up to 80,000 asylum seekers dispersed in the community at any one time awaiting determination of their cases. There will be 6,000 a year going through the accommodation centres, 7,000 a year through the Oakington centre (see later) and a few thousand a year spending most of their time in detention during the processing of their claims. Applicants who are uncooperative with the authorities or who do not give accurate information about their journey to the United Kingdom or about their residence and activity since arrival in the country can have their NASS assistance withdrawn.

The asylum seeker can be asked to fill out a 19-page form outlining the basis of the asylum claim. The form must be submitted within ten days. Often there will be a detailed interview with a Home Office officer. In 2001 there were about 120,000 decisions made, half of them within two months. Only 11,000 (7%) were found to be refugees. A further 20,000 (17%) were granted 'exceptional leave to remain'(ELR). Seventy-four per cent were refused any status and were expected to depart the United Kingdom within 28 days unless they appealed.[16] Refugees are granted permission to remain in the United Kingdom. Those with ELR have initial approval to remain only for four years. Though not refugees, they are judged to be deserving of humanitarian assistance, being allowed to remain in the country presumably until it is safe for them to return to the place from which they came. Sixty-one per cent of Afghans who applied for refugee status in 2001 were granted ELR. In future, those who have come from a 'safe third country' will not be permitted to remain in the United Kingdom only to lodge an appeal against the refusal of refugee status. The government can also certify that other cases are so unfounded that the applicant cannot delay the removal back home by lodging an appeal.

In March 2000 the government decided to establish a 'fast track' procedure for some asylum cases that could be resolved within seven days. The government hoped to process 13,000 applications a year through the fast track centre. Detention of the applicants was a critical element in the process because applicants had to be on hand for interviews and meetings. They were sent to the specially designed Oakington Detention Centre near Cambridge. Most cases there were presumed to be manifestly unfounded. All services were provided, including comprehensive legal assistance. This created the ironic situation that legal assistance was to be provided for the cases that were said to be self-evidently unfounded. Ninety-one per cent of cases do get resolved in the seven-day period. The other 9 per cent prove more problematic than first thought. Initially the government intended that Oakington should be only for people from countries that were unlikely to produce refugees. With more places available, the government decided it should also be for straightforward cases for processing. The Bail for Immigration Detention (BID) group has been very suspicious that Oakington has routinely been filled with asylum seekers simply for administrative convenience, often with no regard to the actual merits or straightforwardness of a case. They quote one case when the United Kingdom Immigration Service officer was naive and honest enough to admit that an asylum seeker had been placed in Oakington because he was 'Young single male. No ties in the United Kingdom'.[17] If cases could not be resolved in the seven days, applicants were to be moved to another place of detention or granted 'temporary admission', which is a convenient legal fiction permitting the person to live in the community while being deemed not yet to have entered the country. Eighty-two per cent of those who have their claim refused at Oakington are then certified so that they can be removed from the United Kingdom even if they have an appeal pending. Should they later win their case, they would be entitled to return to the United Kingdom.

There are compelling administrative reasons for this limited form of detention — a seven-day limit (which sometimes blows out to ten days) for a targeted group of asylum seekers who have little chance of success and who can readily be shown to have little chance of success. In the United Kingdom, even this degree of detention caused concern. When Oakington was opened, there were 280 Iraqi applications a month for asylum. Four Iraqis appealed the legality of their seven-day detention all the way to the House of Lords. Such a case would have caused uproar in Australia, with allegations that legal aid funds should not be wasted on such an unmeritorious claim and that judges have no business to be ruling on these matters. The court hierarchy of the United Kingdom, all the way to the top, had to give serious consideration to the case because of the European Convention on Human Rights. The four Iraqis included a doctor who had arrived lawfully, flying into Heathrow, and three others who had arrived unlawfully hidden in the backs of lorries. Imagine the outcry from Minister Ruddock if an Australian court dared to offer the observation of the House of Lords that 'they arrived in this country concealed in the back of a lorry, a course understandable in view of the conditions and the risk of persecution under which some would-be asylum seekers lived'.[18] The House of Lords pointed out that, though they had entered unlawfully, they had immediately sought asylum from the appropriate authorities and therefore they were seeking authorised, lawful entry. There was no suggestion that they were likely to abscond while their applications were being processed. The court upheld the legal validity of the scheme, holding that the ECHR permitted detention for the purpose of inquiring whether an applicant should be granted asylum. The only contentious issue was whether the detention in this sort of case was proportionate to the end to be achieved. Lord Slynn of Hadley concluded:

> I do not see that either the methods of selection of these cases (are they suitable for speedy decision?) or the objective (speedy decision) or the way in which people are held for a short period (i.e. short in relation to the procedures to be gone through) and in reasonable physical conditions even if involving compulsory detention can be said to be arbitrary or disproportionate.
>
> It is regrettable that anyone should be deprived of his liberty other than pursuant to the order of a court but there are situations where such a course is justified. In a situation like the present with huge numbers and difficult decisions involved, with the risk of long delays to applicants seeking to come, a balancing exercise has to be performed. Getting a speedy decision is in the interests not only of the applicants but of those increasingly in the queue. Accepting as I do that the arrangements made at Oakington provide reasonable conditions, both for individuals and families, and that the period taken is not in any sense excessive, I consider

that the balance is in favour of recognising that detention under the Oakington procedure is proportionate and reasonable. Far from being arbitrary, it seems to me that the Secretary of State has done all that he could be expected to do to palliate the deprivation of liberty of the many applicants for asylum here.[19]

The system of universal detention for all unlawful non-citizens in Australia (regardless of the likelihood of success of their claims or of the straightforwardness of their case), being confined for months not days, in remote places deliberately far removed from lawyers and do-gooders, would not pass muster with this test of proportionality.

The Australian government has continued to defend the detention of whole families in the name of maintaining the stability of the family unit, even justifying the ongoing detention of children with the detained parent while the other parent was living lawfully in the community. In the United Kingdom, the Operation Enforcement Manual for the Immigration Service states: 'It would generally be disproportionate to detain an entire family when any risk that the family would not meet the conditions for temporary admission or release would be successfully countered by the detention of one person only (i.e. the head of the household).'[20] Now that the capacity for family accommodation in detention has been increased, the UK government considers 'that the interests of the children of such a family are best served by detaining the family together rather than separating parents from children'.[21] Given governments' capacity to argue the case either way, you would have thought that the best way to resolve this Solomon's choice in good faith would be to leave the choice to the parents.

One of the effects of institutionalising people when those who do it are also institutionalised is that everyone assumes that people are not able to make a decision in their own best interests and that of their children. The Australian political debate has been marked by the major political parties insisting on the need for mandatory detention subject to exceptions, the exceptions being the point of party political controversy. The United Kingdom debate has been marked by unanimity that asylum seekers should be at liberty, subject to some contested exceptions, until detention is warranted for their removal. When debating the 2002 legislation in the House of Commons, the Minister, David Blunkett, and the Shadow Minister, Oliver Letwin, had this exchange, which would have caused government and opposition members in Australia to think they were simply naive:

> Simon Hughes (government member): May I press the hon. Gentleman on his and his colleagues' view on this issue? Is it his view, as it is ours, that, until the end of the process, or just before it, the presumption should be that asylum seekers are not detained and are at liberty—that the loss of liberty should come only at the end, or just before the end, of the process of applications?
> Mr Letwin (Shadow Minister): Subject to the requirement for judicial oversight and to there being particular cases in which it is judged that there is a serious risk, my answer is yes.
> Mr Blunkett (Home Secretary): To be even more helpful, may I clarify a point so that there is no misunderstanding? Habeas corpus still applies. People are entitled to that, and the real problem is those who are held inappropriately before they reach the point at which removal is required.
> Mr Letwin: That is exactly my view. Having said that all those things are welcome and having congratulated the Home Secretary on the manner in which he is pursuing this whole endeavour, I must add that good intentions and an appropriate means of debate are not enough. To produce the results that he and I desire—namely, to create harmony where there is discord and to deny the extremists the purchase that they have or might have on the minds of some voters—we must not merely try hard and in the right spirit, but succeed.
>
> We must take a system that the Home Secretary has correctly described as chaotic—it was not in perfect working order in 1997, but it has got substantially worse—and turn it into an orderly system that achieves the two results that he and I share the desire to achieve. Those are the rapid, effective admission of refugees fleeing dreadful persecution and the equally rapid and effective removal of those seeking to use this as opposed to other, legitimate means to enter the country, getting round rather than facing the immigration rules.[22]

In the United Kingdom, there is no party political point-scoring about insisting on the need to detain all unvisaed asylum seekers for months on end in the name of border security. The mandatory detention of men, women and children is just not an option, despite the enormous problems there are in accommodating destitute asylum seekers and in finding and removing failed applicants.

Once asylum seekers had arrived in the European Union, it was thought that the major attraction for many of them wanting to head for the United Kingdom was that they would be entitled to work after six months even if their asylum claim had not been finalised. The government decided to put paid to that by denying all asylum seekers the right to work. David Blunkett told the Home Affairs Select Committee of Parliament:

[The right to work after six months] was an incentive for people not to want an early decision. Secondly, it sent all the wrong signals *apropos* what happens in other European countries. I do not think we should under-estimate the critical importance of signals that are sent. With countries now evaluating their own policies, we can see and we can track the change in direction of particular nationalities dependent on what they think is available to them. We want to say to people, 'If you want to claim asylum, then you should use the legitimate asylum route. If you want to work you should use the economic migration work permit route.' That is why, contrary to those who are against any form of inward migration — and there are people now promoting this quite heavily and we will see more of it in the media through the months ahead — I believe that we need a managed economic migration policy in order to welcome people in the country. It has to be robust and managed. At the moment a very large number of people seek asylum as a route to migration and we should discourage that.[23]

Once the government has set up its new regime, there will be a series of induction centres, detention processing centres such as Oakington, residential processing centres dispersed throughout the country, and removal centres where failed applicants will be held in detention awaiting their removal from the country. Though there is no prospect of universal detention from arrival until removal for any asylum seekers unlawfully entering the United Kingdom, there will be ongoing pressure to round up failed asylum seekers. There will also be increased social tension and law and order problems as a result of the increased number of homeless, destitute asylum seekers on the streets without the right to work. The present Home Secretary had confidently predicted that he will be able to remove at least 20,000 failed asylum seekers a year. He is often taunted by the Conservatives on the Opposition benches that, with up to 29,000 asylum applicants each quarter and only 3,500 removals, there will be 25,500 net additions from asylum in that period. The Opposition claims, 'With roughly 70% of asylum applicants finally refused asylum, we face the prospect of 700,000 additional people, who are failed asylum seekers, coming to this country and remaining in it for the next 10 years.'[24] A particular problem has been the number of unaccompanied minors arriving in the United Kingdom as asylum seekers. The government spends more that 100 million pounds a year caring for these children.

Germany's reception and detention

Germany has the greatest restrictions on the movement of asylum seekers in the European Union. It could never contemplate going down the path of universal mandatory detention of all those asylum seekers inside the country without a visa. The security guards are quite punitive along the Poland and Czech borders. Once asylum seekers have made it into Germany beyond the airport or beyond the border, they will be made to reside in a reception centre. The Germans have received 130,000 applications a year on average for the last four years, despite the fact that those coming overland claiming asylum will be immediately returned to the safe third country from which they have come. If the safe third country refuses to take the person back, claiming there is no evidence that the person really came via this country, the person's application is decided in Germany. All asylum seekers must stay in one of the 32 initial reception centres around the country. There are over 20,000 beds available in the reception centres. Asylum seekers are not detained, but it is compulsory for them to reside in one of these centres during the first three months. Unaccompanied minors are accommodated in children's homes.

Applicants are then dispersed to one of the 16 federal regions (known as 'Landers') unless their case is judged to be manifestly unfounded, in which case they are given a week to leave the country, and have very limited appeal rights. Usually the lodging of the appeal in this situation does not operate to suspend the decision to remove the applicant. Applicants can apply to the court for permission to remain in Germany until the appeal is determined. If they are judged ineligible for asylum in Germany because they came from another European Union state or through some safe third country, they can appeal to the local administrative court but the lodging of the appeal does not work to suspend the decision. The removal from the territory can proceed. If the case is not rejected on the basis that it is manifestly unfounded, or because the applicant came from a safe country of origin or through a safe third country or another European Union member state, the applicant will be moved to an accommodation centre or to private accommodation in one of the 16 Landers. Within each Lander, there are subdistricts to which an applicant will be confined — spreading the load throughout the country. Some applicants are confined to areas no greater than 15 square kilometres. Eighty per cent of asylum seekers are allocated to Landers in the old West. The facilities for asylum seekers in the old East were very poor but they have improved of late.

Usually the applicant will have to stay in an accommodation centre. If there is no room or if there is a special reason, the applicant may be permitted to stay in private accommodation. Bear in mind that Germany had 438,000 asylum claimants in 1992 following the war in the former Yugoslavia. Asylum seekers are not allowed to work for a year and may leave their allocated district only with permission. They have to stay in the accommodation allocated while their application is finalised, and this can take from two to seven years. They receive vouchers and limited welfare assistance equivalent to about 80 per cent of the base social welfare payment for needy citizens. After three years of waiting for the processing of their claims, asylum seekers are entitled to the regular social security payments and medical care. In the first year, the only medical and dental care is for emergencies, serious illness and acute pain. There is provision for psychological help for torture and trauma victims. Children have access to education.

After the initial three months in a reception centre, applicants may be given permission to work provided an assessment is made that they would not be taking the jobs of any local citizens. Those who end up with 'Duldung' status, not being refugees but being unable to leave Germany, are often refused the right to work by a special decision of the Aliens Office if they have concealed their identity or not cooperated in getting the appropriate travel documents. These people will often have to remain in the district to which they were first allocated. Those given temporary asylum to escape war or civil war are also required to reside in the Lander to which they were first allocated. After hosting so many Bosnians and then so many Kosovars, the Germans have retained a special three-month temporary protection status for the victims of civil war. Protection is then extended until the state decides it is safe for these victims to return home.

Even those persons awaiting deportation can be detained only by a court order. Usually detention will be authorised only if there is a history of the person having left the Lander without approval or having sought to escape detection. These people can be detained for up to six months. If they have refused to cooperate with their removal to another country, they can be detained under a court order for a further year. If the authorities have still failed to remove the applicant, the authorities can approach the court for another detention order of no more than 18 months duration.

United States reception and detention

In 1996 the Clinton administration conducted a major overhaul of its onshore asylum policy and procedures, having a backlog of 425,000 cases. One of the major problems was that any person in the United States could obtain the right to work immediately by lodging an asylum claim. The law was changed so that the right to work could no longer be obtained until asylum had been granted or until 180 days had passed since the lodging of the claim. The number of INS (Immigration and Naturalization Service) asylum officers was doubled and the number of immigration judges increased.

Congress passed a special law for undocumented Cubans. Under the 'wet foot/dry foot' policy, Cubans intercepted at sea are assessed. Those with refugee claims are brought to the United States or resettled in third countries. Those without a claim are returned to Cuba. Any undocumented Cuban who manages to land in the United States will inevitably be paroled (unless a security risk or a criminal) and entitled to permanent residence after one year. Except for Cubans, aliens arriving in the United States without travel documents or who were engaging in fraud or misrepresentation would now be detained and placed in an expedited removal procedure. An asylum officer would judge if the person has a credible fear of persecution. If the officer judges the claim to be unfounded, the applicant has the right to an immediate appeal to an immigration judge. If the judge agrees that there is no credible fear, the applicant will be removed from the United States. If there is a credible fear, the asylum seeker will have his or her case determined by an immigration judge in the ordinary way. INS district directors have a discretionary authority to release an applicant on parole prior to the conclusion of these proceedings. Directors in Miami are more likely to exercise the discretion benignly than directors in New York and New Jersey.

The 1996 legislative changes in the United States have permitted the INS an increased reliance on detention. On any day there will be 20,000 people in immigration detention. Sixty per cent of the detainees are held in state and county jails because there is insufficient room in immigration detention facilities. Up to 5,000 children a year now spend some time in immigration detention. The main groups detained are resident aliens facing removal as a result of a criminal conviction, undocumented workers apprehended at work sites, and insufficiently documented asylum seekers. About 70,000 resident aliens are removed each year after they have served time for criminal offences. There are more than 80,000 new asylum claims filed each year. About 20,000 onshore asylum claims are approved each year and there are more than 300,000 claims outstanding. Given the huge costs of detention, the INS commissioned the Vera Institute in New York to conduct a three-year study of alternatives when the legislative changes commenced. The study concluded: 'Asylum seekers do not need to be detained to appear for their hearings. They also do not seem to need intensive supervision. Detention of asylum seekers is particularly unnecessary and unfair since they are so willing to attend their hearings and since so many of them win their cases.'[25]

The Vera study found that 'in most districts around the United States, the INS paroles many asylum seekers who are found to have a credible fear of persecution. In the New York district, however, most asylum seekers are detained throughout their proceedings.' Some undocumented arrivals at New York airports are released from detention on humanitarian grounds even before they are assessed as having a credible fear. They are simply given a court date and they attend their immigration interviews while living in the community.

On the fifth anniversary of the 1996 reforms, the INS claimed to have struck a more appropriate balance, providing safe refuge for asylum seekers while at the same time reducing the number of unmeritorious claims. Between 1993 and 1999 the number of asylum claims fell from 127,000 to 30,000, while the approval rate escalated from 15 per cent to 38 per cent.

From 1996 until late 2001 the INS policy for undocumented Haitians was to grant virtually automatic parole so that they could live in the community while their asylum claims were being processed. But then, on 3 December 2001, a boat carrying 187 Haitians was grounded off Miami. Eighteen people escaped and two drowned. The country was focused on security and border concerns after September 11. About 2,000 Haitians had been intercepted at sea during 2001, 600 more than the previous year. The new Bush administration decided that the time had come to change the parole policy for Haitians. Just as the Howard government had done with *Tampa* three months earlier, the Bush administration thought it was time to send a message, fearing further mass movements from Haiti. Previously the Haitians benefited from a blanket policy that guaranteed their release from detention pending an asylum claim. Now they were to receive more adverse treatment than other undocumented arrivals, with the administration removing even the local discretion of INS district directors to grant parole, except in the most demanding humanitarian circumstances. Even though all but two of the asylum seekers interviewed were found to have a credible fear of persecution, only five pregnant women and ten unaccompanied minors were released on parole. Lawyers for the Haitians claimed that this was discrimination. They claimed that prior to the grounding of this ship, 95 per cent of all asylum seekers who established credible fear were released into the community within five days. Now the Haitians were being singled out for adverse treatment. Unlike the Australian government, which, for constitutional reasons, claims that detention is not a deterrent, the US administration was very upfront in justifying the new detention policy as a reasonable step to discourage other Haitians from risking the perilous voyage. On 21 February 2003 the 11th Circuit Court of Appeals affirmed that the courts had no jurisdiction to overrule the INS policy of mandatory detention for Haitian boat people, even if it were racially discriminatory.

Meanwhile, the Bush administration had decided that Haitians who did not make it to shore would be repatriated. On 29 October 2002 an overcrowded wooden boat carrying over 200 Haitians arrived at Miami. Those who made it ashore were taken into detention for the processing of their claims. Nineteen less fortunate ones who did not make it ashore were immediately repatriated to Port Au Prince. Marleine Bastien, spokeswoman for the 'Haitian Women of Miami', said, 'This is really a travesty of justice because their reasons for leaving Haiti have not changed, whether they arrived on land or not.' President Bush and his brother, Governor Jeb Bush, tried to reassure the Haitian community in Florida that all would be well. The President said, 'Haitians and everybody else ought to be treated the same way, and we're in the process of making sure that happens.' He just forgot to tell them that the same treatment for everyone (except the Cubans) was going to be achieved not by restoring the discretion to release undocumented Haitian asylum seekers on parole but by introducing a policy of mandatory detention for all undocumented asylum seekers (except the Cubans). The White House's spokesman said the new policy 'treats all people seeking to come to America illegally by sea the same'. He added, 'The president believes Haitians ought to be treated fairly and humanely.' In answer to the claim that the administration was now treating Haitians much worse than Cubans, the administration explained, 'We treat everybody not as well as Cubans. That is because Congress has created a statutory difference for Cubans.'[26] Cubans aside, the Australian government now finds company with the Bush administration with a policy that comes close to mandatory detention for unauthorised arrivals.

On 8 November 2002 the INS announced that 'all individuals who arrive illegally by sea will be placed in expedited removal proceedings and during their legal process will remain in detention at the discretion of the INS and Department of Justice'.[27] It remains to be seen whether the departmental discretion is exercised so as to take away the semblance of mandatory detention during the processing of asylum claims. The official INS announcement notes that 'individuals may be released for humanitarian reasons at the discretion of the INS'. With none of the Australian sensitivities about the constitutionality of such detention, and with the added September 11 concerns, the INS says, 'The assessment of the US is that releasing these aliens would encourage additional illegal migration. Such a surge in migration threatens our national security as well as the safety of these smuggled aliens.'

An alien arriving at the US border without a permit to enter will now be held in detention until an INS officer exercises the discretion to parole the person, allowing them to enter the country. This decision is made 'on a case by case basis for urgent humanitarian reasons or significant public benefit'. Immigration judges have no power to release the person from detention at this point in the process. If the unauthorised entrant seeks asylum and passes the credible fear test, the INS is supposed to grant parole unless the person poses a flight risk or is a danger to the community. Once a person is in the process of having their asylum claim adjudicated, they can apply to an immigration judge for release on a bond or on their own recognisance. In Miami, Haitian boat arrivals are now being fast-tracked. Immigration judges are forcing lawyers to proceed with their cases even though the lawyers have only just met their clients. The INS has closed the pro bono legal office at the Krome detention centre. Even if Haitians win their initial asylum claims, they may still be detained while the INS appeals the decision. No other racial group is treated like this in the United States. Haitians arriving by boat are now subject to mandatory detention.

Conclusions

Mandatory detention during the processing phase is not reasonable, necessary or allowable under the European Convention on Human Rights (ECHR). The Australian government continues to tell the Australian public that 'Australia's border management strategies are increasingly being looked at by other countries as a model on which to base the development of their own programs.' They even tell us that Mr Ruddock's 2002 seminar in London 'was acknowledged by the audience as very relevant to their own border management issues'.[28] The English are interested in our annual quota of offshore refugees. They have no interest in our upstream disruption program conducted without parliamentary scrutiny. Though they have considered placing Royal Navy patrols in the Mediterranean, they have no interest in the excesses of our Operation Relex. They have expanded the use of detention. They know they cannot withdraw from the ECHR so that they might keep all unlawful non-citizens in detention for the entirety of their processing regardless of whether there is any risk of their absconding. Admittedly Tony Blair did flirt with suspending the operation of the ECHR after three Algerian asylum seekers were linked to the discovery of the poison Ricin in a London flat and to the murder of a Manchester policeman. This would have meant the repeal of his Human Rights Act, one of his proudest legislative achievements.

The Europeans cannot believe that we would proudly market the Pacific Solution. Australia's evangelism for increased detention has had some effect in the international community, providing an opportunity for those countries that do not have a bill of rights or a robust tradition of individual liberty to practise more widespread detention of asylum seekers. The Americans with their long land border with Mexico and steady stream of Haitian boat people are increasingly using detention at the outset when unauthorised persons arrive at the border. Once an asylum seeker is in the determination process, the INS and the immigration judges have the power to supervise the detention and some discretion to release the applicant regardless of their age or medical condition.

The Executive Committee of the UNHCR decided in 2002 to work on a statement on the reception of asylum seekers in the context of individual asylum systems. On 26 June 2002 the Executive Committee published its Agenda for Protection as a follow-up to the consultations for the 50th anniversary of the Convention. One item on the agenda was: 'States more concertedly to explore appropriate alternatives to the detention of asylum seekers and refugees, and to abstain, in principle, from detaining children.'[29] In part as a response to Australia's evangelism on detention, the UNHCR circulated a draft conclusion on 23 August 2002 listing general considerations that should guide the reception of asylum seekers. One of those considerations was: 'Open reception centres, which provide basic services and an adequate degree of privacy, are the preferred form of accommodation for these asylum seekers who are unable to sustain themselves. When restrictions to freedom of movement prove necessary, for example, for reasons of public order, asylum seekers may be confined to a particular place of residence in accordance with international refugee law and human rights law.'[30] By the time the document saw the light of day on 8 October 2002, this consideration was dropped completely. The Executive Committee was still prepared to recall its famous 1986 Conclusion 44 on the detention of refugees and asylum seekers but then decided to remain silent on the presently controversial issue of the increasing use of detention of asylum seekers. Australia's lowering of the bar has had an effect in the international community. It is opening the door for other countries to experiment with further detention of asylum seekers within their constitutional constraints. Sadly for asylum seekers in Australia, there are next to no constitutional constraints provided the Minister continues to state that detention is not, nor is it intended to be, a deterrent or a punishment. The English and the Americans do think it is a deterrent. Because their detention regimes permit bail and parole in some circumstances, there is no legal or constitutional problem with their politicians adopting a deterrence strategy and rhetoric, whether or not it works.

The German and United Kingdom experience highlights that release from detention is not an answer to all the pressing social problems confronting an asylum seeker awaiting a decision on migration status. The abysmally low minimum standards adopted by the European Union ensures that many asylum seekers throughout Europe will continue to eke out a miserable existence with little access to the employment market while they await the determination of their claims. Such a punitive regime may help to cull out those asylum seekers who are more truly classed as economic migrants. It does nothing to assist the most deserving asylum seekers during the first critical months when they are trying to put their lives back together, often having fled torture and trauma. Accommodation in remote hostels can be very difficult for such people. It is still preferable to detention in Woomera or Baxter or on Nauru.

CHAPTER 6

Courts and the adjudication of asylum claims

All first-world countries that take seriously their commitment to the proper processing of onshore asylum applications have had problems with unsuccessful applicants wanting to access the courts simply to delay their departure. Attempting to stop the abuses, some governments have gone too far in reducing the role of the courts, thereby putting at risk those genuine asylum seekers who then have no appeal against shoddy decisions. In the wash of the *Tampa* incident, the Howard government thought it had a great opportunity to exclude the courts once and for all from the refugee determination process. The High Court struck back in 2003, putting beyond doubt the ongoing function of the courts in a constitutional democracy. Even when a government sets up a system of tribunals to review refugee decisions, there is a need for the courts to ensure that the decision makers and the tribunals correctly interpret and apply the law. As well as trying to limit appeals to the courts, the Australian Parliament has attempted to constrain the courts so that judges are unable to give broader, more compassionate readings on what constitutes persecution, membership of a particular social group, or non-political crime for the purposes of the Refugees Convention.

Usually when a government prescribes detention for asylum seekers or for those awaiting removal from the country, courts will also have some role in supervising the ongoing detention, ensuring that it is lawful and not arbitrary. In some countries, even failed asylum seekers will be able to apply for bail awaiting their removal provided they are not a flight risk or a security risk. Since September 11 it has become more difficult for western governments to move some asylum seekers who need to return to the Middle East. In countries with a bill of rights, it will be necessary for the courts to determine if the open-ended detention of persons in these circumstances is authorised. In Australia, where there is no bill of rights, there was a series of test cases in the Federal Court in 2002. Initially Palestinians and Iraqis were having some success in winning their release from protracted detention. Because the government could not remove them, their ongoing detention was not related to a migration purpose. The government was successful in convincing the courts that the Australian legislation, in the absence of a bill of rights, was sufficiently watertight. Failed asylum seekers could be kept in detention for years on the direction of the government and without a court order until they could be removed. If there was evidence that the public servants seeking removal agreements with foreign governments were dragging their feet, an applicant could apply to the court for a court order requiring the relevant public servant to remove the applicant 'as soon as reasonably practicable'. The courts even declined to order the government to release a failed Iraqi asylum seeker from detention though the government was planning and executing a war against Iraq, rendering a return in the foreseeable future a hazardous undertaking. Eventually, in March 2003, a full bench of the Federal Court reconfirmed the power of judges to grant habeas corpus when government had no realistic prospect of removing a failed asylum seeker from Australia.

In the refugee domain there is plenty of opportunity for tension between government and the courts. Countries like Australia, having signed the Refugees Convention, are expected to comply with the minimum standards set down in the UNHCR's *Handbook on Procedures and Criteria for Determining Refugee Status*. If the competent state official charged with determining refugee status gives a negative decision, the applicant has to be given a reasonable time 'to appeal for a formal reconsideration of the decision, either to the same or to a differ-

ent authority, whether administrative or judicial, according to the pre-
vailing system'.[1] Unless the initial claim was 'clearly abusive', the
applicant should be allowed to remain in the country while the initial
decision and appeal are decided.

Offshore asylum seekers who are processed by the UNHCR would
usually be interviewed by a case officer who would make a decision.
When the decision is negative, there would at least be an appeal to another case officer. Onshore asylum seekers in Australia have had access to a more refined decision-making process and appeal system. It
is not surprising that those who are rejected as refugees will often pursue all possible appeals. Since 1989 governments of both political persuasions in Australia have been trying to streamline the appeal
process and reduce the access to the courts. It was Robert Ray, Labor
Minister for Immigration, who first decided to reduce the political and
administrative discretion in the Australian immigration system. He
wanted to achieve two goals that on their face almost seem contradic-
tory. He wanted to codify the law and procedures while at the same
time reducing the access to the courts. Usually you would expect that a
new codification of laws would result in increased litigation, at least
during the teething period, while everyone determined the meaning
and limits of the detailed provisions in the code. Robert Ray explained
his purpose to parliament:

> Immigration is an unusual jurisdiction in that delay in decision making
> can be to the advantage of the applicant. Delay is compounded where the
> same matter is repeatedly reopened through fresh applications, reviews
> and appeals. The new [merits] review system proposed in the Bill aims to
> ensure that cases are resolved fairly and speedily.[2]

In 1985 the Australian courts had started granting judicial review of
migration decisions under the comprehensive *Administrative Decisions (Judicial Review) Act*. Under this Act, the courts were able to review decisions by public servants and tribunals and set aside those
decisions if there had been a denial of natural justice or if the decisions
were judged to be so unreasonable that no reasonable person could
have made the decision. In 1989 a code for decision makers in the
migration area was enacted in legislation in the hope that when the decision makers followed the code there would be little chance of successful appeals to the courts. Those persons wanting to extend their

stay in Australia by delaying a final decision would have less access to the courts. In 1993 the Refugee Review Tribunal (RRT) was established in the hope that all failed asylum seekers would be able to access the tribunal, which would be able to give quick, fair and transparent decisions, reducing the need for any access to the courts.

Though Australia does not have a bill of rights, section 75(v) of the Constitution does provide: 'In all matters in which a writ of mandamus or prohibition or an injunction is sought against an officer of the Commonwealth, the High Court shall have original jurisdiction.'

The effect of this clause is that, when a decision is made by a Commonwealth public servant (including the RRT), the person affected by the decision has the right to appeal to the highest court in the land, claiming that the decision was not made in accordance with the law. Usually, the judges and politicians are agreed that it is not a good idea to have the time of the High Court taken up in considering such applications in the first instance. The jurisdiction is transferred to a lower court and the High Court retains its traditional role as the ultimate court of appeal.

When the courts have shown a willingness to overturn refugee decisions, the politicians have been less than impressed. For more than a decade Philip Ruddock has been very impatient with the role of the courts. Back in March 1992, while in Opposition, he told the Joint Committee on Migration Regulations, 'I have said to people that if we want the High Court of Australia to concentrate its mind on these matters, we should let 23,000 applicants put their cases to the High Court. It would quickly find a mechanism for dealing with them.'[3] He went on to say:

> I am still one of those who would be quite happy to remove that matter from the purview of the *Administrative Decisions (Judicial Review) Act* and leave the courts to see whether or not they would like to use their original jurisdiction. The High Court could willingly do that, I suppose. I guess that is the matter that the Government was not prepared to bite the bullet on, was it?[4]

For some years the politicians were concerned that the Federal Court was making decisions too favourable to asylum seekers and was reviewing too many decisions of the DIMIA case officers who were rejecting refugee claims. The politicians took a gamble and restricted the jurisdiction of the Federal Court hoping that the High Court itself would not want to fill the gap. The High Court made it clear that it had no option but to exercise its constitutional jurisdiction if the politicians were not going to allow lower courts to perform the role.

Ultimately, the parliament in the wake of the *Tampa* incident decided to try and oust the jurisdiction of all the courts, including the High Court, with the use of a 'privative clause' which purported to exclude decisions under the *Migration Act* from judicial review by the courts. Minister Ruddock was furious when some of the Federal Court judges continued to overturn migration decisions on the basis that his privative clause did not exclude all review by the courts. On 30 May 2002 he told the Channel 9 *Today* program:

> What we are finding is that, notwithstanding that legislation, the courts are finding a variety of ways and means of dealing themselves back into the review game.
>
> And what I have said to the Parliament is, look, we've passed this legislation, this was a decision of the Parliament. The High Court of Parliament is saying decisions of the Tribunal should be final and conclusive and if we need to give the court some further advice we may need your support again.

Earlier he had told the Commonwealth Lawyers Association in London that it should be parliament that decided the laws and not the 'unelected and unresponsible officials' of the courts. This Ruddock approach would be arguable if Australia did not have a Constitution that sets limits even on the powers of a popular government and on an unsympathetic parliament acting against unpopular groups. Ultimately it is justices of the High Court who are charged with the constitutional function of ensuring that all persons and all institutions are subject to the law.

There was a time when the Commonwealth conducted itself as a model litigant before the courts. Because of the politics of refugees, those days have gone and we now pay the price of losing such sensible conventions. When the Federal Court constituted a special five-member bench to consider appeals on the new privative clause provision, Chief Justice Michael Black saw fit to call Minister Ruddock to account for his public statements critical of the courts. He addressed the Solicitor General of the Commonwealth:

Despite these statements I have not previously responded to any of them publicly. The most recent statement however raises a new issue since it would appear that it could only refer to the issues before the Court on these appeals — appeals to which your client is a party. He is the respondent in four appeals, in which he was successful before the trial judge, and he is the appellant in one appeal in which he was unsuccessful before the trial judge. The statement was made only a matter of days before the date fixed weeks ago for the hearing of the appeals.

You would of course know, Mr Solicitor, that the court is not amenable to external pressures from Ministers or from anyone else whomsoever, but we are concerned that members of the public might see the Minister's statements as an attempt to bring pressure on the Court in relation to these appeals to which he is a party.[5]

All this simply earned Mr Ruddock a pat on the back from the prime minister and a round of applause in the party room. Ex–Chief Justice of Australia, Sir Gerard Brennan, explained the matter to an Indonesian legal audience:

There has been much controversy about the laws relating to the mandatory detention of people who arrive in Australia without the requisite immigration permits. The Government and the Parliament of the Commonwealth assert that those laws are essential to preserve both the integrity of the national borders and the policies which govern a generous immigration program. Some of those who arrive without permits are refugees seeking asylum and who are entitled to asylum under Australian law. The laws are controversial because many Australians regard the laws as offensive to the human rights of those who flee from other countries, particularly children and those who are genuine refugees within the definition of that term in the International Convention relating to the Status of Refugees.

The Government has been critical of Federal Court decisions which, it is said, have been too generous in determining refugee status. Laws have been passed restricting the jurisdiction of the Federal Court to judicially review decisions on refugee status, but the Constitution precludes the passing of laws restricting the jurisdiction of the High Court in any case in which judicial review is sought against an officer of the Commonwealth. Although the effect of the restrictive laws has been an increase in the High Court's workload, the importance of the Constitutional provision has been illustrated. This provision is a constitutional guarantee of equality under the law: any person in Australia may invoke the High Court's jurisdiction if that person claims to be adversely affected by an exercise of Commonwealth executive power.[6]

Sir Gerard described this as 'a dramatic example of the tensions that can exist between the Executive Government and the judiciary and of the ultimate constitutional protection of the rule of law as defined by the High Court'.

In February 2003 all seven justices of the High Court threw out Minister Ruddock's attempt to deny asylum seekers access to the courts.[7] The government's intention was that once the Refugee Review Tribunal had reviewed a decision to refuse a protection visa there would be no appeal possible to the courts. In the main test case on the privative clause, a Bangladeshi person who was refused a protection visa appealed to the courts on the ground that he was denied natural justice. He argued that the tribunal took into account adverse material that was relevant to his case without giving him notice of the material and without giving him any opportunity to address it. The High Court has said that persons in this situation can still appeal to the courts. They can appeal not only to the High Court but also to the Federal Court and the new Federal Magistrates' Court. Importantly the High Court, despite attempts by the government to stop this practice, can still remit such matters to lower courts to avoid the High Court being clogged with such cases.

Chief Justice Gleeson insisted on the need for decision makers not only to act in good faith but also to act with fairness and detachment: 'the requirement of a fair hearing is a limitation upon the decision-making authority of the Tribunal of such a nature that it is inviolable'.[8] The Chief Justice said that the broad reading, which the Commonwealth tried to give to its privative clause, was inconsistent with four principles of statutory interpretation:

- If the words are ambiguous, the court should interpret the words consistent with Australia's international obligations.
- The court should not impute to the Parliament an intention to abrogate or curtail fundamental rights or freedoms.
- The Australian Constitution is framed on the assumption that the rule of law applies to actions by the executive government.
- The court presumes that the parliament does not intend to deprive a

person of access to the courts except to the extent expressly stated or necessarily implied.

It is not enough for the immigration officers or the RRT simply to establish that they acted in good faith. Asylum seekers, like the rest of us, are entitled to expect fairness. The Chief Justice concluded: 'Parliament has not evinced an intention that a decision by the Tribunal to confirm a refusal of a protection visa, made unfairly, and in contravention of the requirements of natural justice, shall stand so long as it was a *bona fide* attempt to decide whether or not such a visa should be granted.'[9]

Five of the other justices pointed out that the *Migration Act* is a very complex piece of legislation and any decision made by the minister or the RRT must be 'a decision made under the Act'. They said, 'It is impossible to conclude that the Parliament intended to effect a repeal of all statutory limitations or restraints upon the exercise of power or the making of a decision.'[10] As the *Migration Act* and Regulations contain an exhaustive list of the criteria for the grant of various classes of visa, Justices Gaudron and Kirby pointed out that the privative clause could not be invoked to shield a wrong decision on the basis that the decision maker had acted in good faith when failing to be satisfied that the conditions for the grant of the visa had been fulfilled. If the criteria for the grant of a visa have been misconstrued or overlooked, the decision maker's error is a jurisdictional error reviewable by the courts.[11] Also, the courts retain the power to review RRT decisions that have been reached without according procedural fairness to an applicant. The privative clause comes into play, excluding court review, only if the error made by the decision maker is a 'non-jurisdictional error', that is, an error made within the jurisdiction that the decision maker has. The Australian Constitution guarantees that Courts must always be able to assess whether a Commonwealth decision maker has made a decision within their jurisdiction. Five of the justices were very scathing in stating that 'the fundamental premise' for the privative clause legislation was 'unsound'. They went out of their way to make it plain that the litigation was not a mere word game. They said:

It is important to emphasise that the difference in understanding what has been decided about privative clauses is real and substantive; it is not some verbal or logical quibble. It is real and substantive because it reflects two fundamental constitutional propositions, both of which the Commonwealth accepts. First, the jurisdiction of this Court to grant relief under s 75(v) of the Constitution cannot be removed by or under a law made by the Parliament. Specifically, the jurisdiction to grant s 75(v) relief where there has been jurisdictional error by an officer of the Commonwealth cannot be removed. Secondly, the judicial power of the Commonwealth cannot be exercised otherwise than in accordance with Chapter III. The Parliament cannot confer on a non-judicial body the power to conclusively determine the limits of its own jurisdiction.[12]

There is guaranteed constitutional access to the courts to correct jurisdictional errors by the RRT and the minister. This guarantee covers any application based on the claim that the minister or the tribunal has not acted with fairness and detachment. Back in 1994 the parliamentary committee investigating mandatory immigration detention in remote areas had acknowledged the inconvenience and problems associated with accessing appropriate services, including the additional travel costs for lawyers. Justice Callinan highlighted the constitutional problem:

> There are certain matters which cannot be ignored for the purposes of judicial notice. Those matters include that the persons seeking the remedies may be incapable of speaking English, and will often be living or detained in places remote from lawyers.[13]

Justice Callinan pointed out that parliament could not even set time limits on access to the courts 'as to make any constitutional right of recourse virtually illusory'.

How then did the government get it so wrong? Weren't they warned? Yes, they were. Locking out the courts has been one of Minister Ruddock's abiding passions. He first tried introducing this legislation in June 1997, and again in September 1997. Back then, the Labor Opposition opposed the legislation and accurately predicted that 'the Coalition will probably fail in this objective. The jurisdiction of the High Court cannot be totally excluded.'[14] Mr Ruddock claimed that the legislation had been given the tick by a bevy of silks including Tom Hughes QC, once a Liberal attorney-general.[15] That seemed a dubious claim once Mr Hughes had appeared before the Senate committee in January 1999, saying, 'the entrenched constitutional jurisdiction of the High Court to grant what is called prerogative relief ... cannot be eradicated and abrogated, except by passage of legislation after a referendum'. He warned that the 'passage of this bill would produce the altogether undesirable effects to which two former chief justices, Sir Anthony Mason and Sir Gerard Brennan, had alluded'.[16] A month before Mr Hughes had come out and given evidence in his personal capacity, Minister Ruddock was so cocksure of his position (which has now been discredited 7–nil in the High Court) that he told parliament, 'My good friend Sir Gerard Brennan has misunderstood in part the nature of the provisions that we are proposing.'[17] Hughes, Mason and Brennan understood all too well.

It was only in the aftermath of the *Tampa* incident that the government was bold enough and the Opposition defeated enough for the parliament to retreat from legal principle, enacting the ambiguous and suspect privative clause. There will continue to be added uncertainty with future litigation, because the government wanted to play fast and loose, tampering with constitutional principle despite all the warnings. Now disaffected asylum seekers can appeal to the courts (including the Federal Magistrates Court) alleging that they have been denied a fair hearing before the RRT. A week after the High Court decision on the privative clause, the government published some information for the thousands of TPV holders who were applying for renewal of their visas. They were told:

> A TPV holder whose application for another protection visa is refused will have the right to seek review of the decision from the Refugee Review Tribunal or the Administrative Appeals Tribunal.
>
> If the review fails, or they decide not to seek review, they will need to leave Australia once any review proceedings have been completed.[18]

What will be the situation for those persons seeking judicial review of their RRT rejection? Will they be removed from Australia? Will they be taken back into immigration detention? Will they be eligible for a bridging visa? If so, will they have to provide a bond or security? Will they have the right to work? These are not academic questions, given that the appeals process could take some time. It is conceivable that some TPV holders who have been living in the community for three years might now take many more years to exhaust their appeals in the courts once the RRT has rejected the renewal of their visa.

Rather than complaining about this outcome, Minister Ruddock should heed the call of Tom Hughes when he addressed the Senate Committee four years ago:

It seems to me that the driving force behind this proposed legislation is economy of administration—a very laudable objective in itself, although perhaps it can sometimes be carried as an objective to undue lengths. What the committee might like to ask itself, looking at the matter on a more general level than the strictly legal, is this: we are, as I said, an affluent and a free society. It is in the nature of things, that being such a society, people claiming to be oppressed and to be the victim of injustice in their own countries will be forever knocking on our doors. It is one of the burdens of being a free society that we should, you may think, provide a system of dealing with persons claiming to be refugees which is as legally certain as any branch of the law can be and that has established and clearly understood legal criteria of exemption or liability.[19]

Now that the High Court has established beyond doubt that a privative clause cannot be devised to exclude refugee decisions from the courts, it is time for the executive government to design a process for the orderly determination of these matters in the courts. Back in September 1997 Mr Ruddock told parliament that he would look after matters once the courts were excluded:

I do not intend to leave the system flawed. I intend to ensure that the system is run with integrity. I intend to ensure that the former government's measures to contain abuse of our judicial system are given effect. I want to assure the House that I am intent on ensuring that those people who are genuine are accommodated and at the end of the day there is a safety net; and that safety net is me, as minister.[20]

Unfortunately, the other decision delivered by the High Court on the same day as the test case on the privative clause revealed that the minister is not your ordinary safety net. Mrs Bakhtyari and her five children were denied a protection visa by the safety-net minister. It was revealed in the course of the litigation that Mrs Bakhtyari learnt two days after the RRT decision that her husband was lawfully resident in Australia on a TPV. He had already applied for a permanent protection visa. The minister's department knew this but did not see fit specifically to inform the RRT, presumably because the department harboured doubts about whether Mr Bakhtyari was a refugee from Afghanistan or an economic migrant from Pakistan, having fled Afghanistan many years previously. If the RRT had known that Mr Bakhtyari already had a visa, the RRT would have issued the family with protection visas as a matter of course back in July 2001 on the basis that their spouse and father was already recognised as a refugee. Instead the woman and five children spent an additional 18 months in detention in Woomera and Baxter. The South Australian Family and Youth Services (FAYS) reported to the state premier in August 2002 that the antisocial behaviour of the boys was a coping mechanism 'that can be seen as basically "healthy" within a hostile environment (i.e. detention). However, they are maladaptive behaviours that, outside of detention, would be seen as indicating disturbance.'[21] The RRT, Mrs Bakhtyari and her children were left in the dark about their lawful entitlement to be issued with the same visa as the spouse and father. Presumably, the departmental officials decided not to reveal the lawful presence of Mr Bakhtyari in Australia because they suspected that his

Australian, 24 August 2002.
Reproduced with Peter Nicholson's permission.

protection visa had been obtained under false pretences. Government officials often have information available to them which is not in the public forum and which is adverse to the interests of asylum seekers. In this case, journalist Bob Ellis got hold of a statement by Montezar, one of the Bakhtyari children, and published it in the *Canberra Times* a year after the RRT had given its decision. Montezar had told his lawyer in July 2002, 'I do not know the date of my birth but I know that I am 12 years old. In Afghanistan the way we count our ages is by the winters passing.' He 'was about 7' when he left Afghanistan. He had been in Australia in detention for 18 months at this time. He said:

> When we left Afghanistan we went to Pakistan. My family and I were hiding in a room all the time. We were there a long time and we did not go out very much. I remember that my father was with us for a while in Pakistan. My dad's mother and my dad's brother were also in Pakistan with us. I remember that they left and went back to Afghanistan.[22]

These statements confirmed the departmental suspicion that the family had been living in Pakistan for some years and that the father had gone ahead of them to seek a better life in Australia. These statements, if true, put in doubt the RRT's finding that Mrs Bakhtyari 'is not an Afghan national and there is no evidence the children have any nationality other than hers (the Tribunal does not accept that the husband is an Afghan national as there is no evidence supporting this claim)'.[23] There are many Afghan nationals who have been living in Pakistan for years having fled persecution in Afghanistan.

In 2002 DIMIA chartered a plane and took Mr Mohib Sarwari and his family into detention, flying them from their home in Launceston to the Baxter detention centre. The government claimed that Mr Sarwari was a brother of Mr Bakhtyari and a Pakistani national. The local community in Launceston was so outraged by the government's high-handed, presumptuous detention of community members that it raised the money for refugee advocate Marion Le to fly to Afghanistan so she could obtain first-hand evidence about the nationality and background of the Sarwari family from their local village near Kabul. She returned with irrefutable evidence which was presented to the RRT and the minister. The family was then released and returned to Launceston. In this case, the government's witch-hunt had badly misfired. The strands of the minister's safety net were looking distinctly frayed.

An appropriate safety net for asylum seekers demonised by the nation's radio shock jocks requires four strands: public servants with integrity, a dispassionate minister, an informed tribunal and accessible courts. It is time for the executive to respect the role of the courts. Despite ten years of fine tuning the decision-making system, the government has not been able to get it right. There is an ongoing need for court supervision, especially of decisions relating to boat people who, despite the government claims that their detention makes them more available for prompt processing, are more susceptible than other asylum seekers to wrong decisions being made about them. Given the government and popular hostility to boat people, it is essential that the process for determining their claims be supervised by judges with secure tenure rather than by RRT members whose appointments expire in June 2004. The statistics continue to reveal a systemic problem with the determination of claims of those in detention. If court supervision of the RRT were removed, it would be only a matter of time before tribunal members, hand-selected by the government on short-term contracts, sitting in private, were assessing the claims of those in detention more in conformity with the views of the departmental case officers.

Since the establishment of the RRT in 1993, 60 per cent of all appeals have come from asylum seekers from six countries — China, Indonesia, Philippines, Sri Lanka, India and Fiji. Only 3 per cent of the cases from these countries have been detention cases. The RRT is used mainly by asylum seekers living in the community who have entered Australia on some other form of visa. Since 1993 the RRT has heard 53,711 cases. The Afghan, Iraqi and Iranian caseload has been a modest 2,434 cases, of which 1696 (70%) were detention cases. The detention caseload from all other countries was only 4.5 per cent.

From 1 July 2001 to 30 June 2002 the RRT found fault with the refugee assessment in 44 per cent of the detention cases that were appealed to the tribunal. In cases where the applicant was not in detention, the tribunal found fault with the public servants' initial decision in only 6.6 per cent of the cases. In that year the RRT set aside 62 per cent of all Afghan decisions appealed and 87 per cent of all Iraqi decisions appealed. This means that Afghan asylum seekers got it right 62 per cent of the time when they claimed that the departmental decision makers had got it wrong. The public servants got it wrong 87 per cent of the times that the Iraqi applicants claim to have been mistakenly assessed. Meanwhile the RRT set aside only 7.9 per cent of decisions appealed by members of other ethnic groups. In the last three years of the fourth wave of boat people, 82 per cent of all Afghan and Iraqi applicants were found to be refugees by the primary decision makers (7,330 out of 8,965 applicants). Back in 1999 applicants had to wait 32 weeks on average in detention before getting the primary decision. It is concerning that the primary decision makers got it wrong so often when they rejected an Afghan or Iraqi claim. Those ethnic groups living in the community who most often appeal to the RRT have little chance of success. Most of the boat people held in detention during the firebreak period were proved to be refugees. When they failed on the first round, they had a very good chance of success on appeal. They then had to wait in detention an extra 10 weeks to get the right answer.

The appalling results in relation to those held in detention are nothing new. Back in 1993 when he was the Opposition spokesman, Philip Ruddock asked two questions of departmental officials appearing before the Joint Standing Committee on migration:

> The approval rate for boat arrivals since 1989 was 4.2% at the primary stage; 25.9% at the review stage. The approval rate for non-boat people for the corresponding period was 5.4% at the primary stage; 3.1% at the review stage. I simply ask the question in relation to those who are boat people: how did the department get it so wrong at the primary stage? How could you have a situation where you reject 95% and, when the cases are reviewed, 25% get through, yet the figures for those covered by the other range reflect much the same sort of numbers?[24]

Whether it is 1993 and Mr Ruddock is seeking answers or 2002 and Mr Ruddock is being asked, there is no credible answer.

There is a big resource problem for the courts, with asylum seekers in Australia accessing the courts for judicial review of their decisions when they have very little chance of success. No doubt many asylum seekers do apply to the courts in order to delay their removal from Australia; some no doubt do it simply to exhaust all available remedies given that they do not have to pay for the legal proceedings. In 1993–94 there were only 381 applications to the courts; in

2001–2002 there were 1,423. In 2001–2002 the courts dismissed 1,221 of these applications. Of the 1,904 cases resolved before the courts during 2001–2002, only 111 applicants won their cases. Even if an applicant does succeed in the courts, this does not mean that a visa is necessarily granted. It simply means that the RRT has to reconsider the application in the light of the law as set down by the court.

When the government was trying to exclude all judicial review of refugee decisions back in January 1999, Dr Nygh, the principal member of the RRT, presented the Senate committee with compelling statistics.[25] At that time the RRT had decided 26,401 cases since it commenced in 1993. There were 1,837 Federal Court appeals. In only 276 cases had the RRT decision been set aside. Even in those cases, the court had the power only to send the matter back to the tribunal for a new decision in conformity with the law as stated by the court. In only 48 cases did the RRT finally reverse its decision and grant the asylum seeker a protection visa. According to Dr Nygh, there was a difference in the ultimate decision in only 0.2 per cent of the cases. This set of figures does nothing to discount the fact that a tribunal subject to judicial review is likely to produce results that are fairer to the applicants and more consistent with the law than a tribunal that is free to make decisions in secret, without court oversight, and where the tribunal members have been appointed on short-term contracts by the government of the day which then conducts quality-control assessments of their decisions.

The cost effectiveness of removing the courts from the supervision of the correctness of these decisions is obvious. However, people would feel more comfortable with such a move if they could be convinced of the professionalism and independence of the primary decision makers and of the public accountability and security of the RRT members. When 18.2 per cent of RRT decisions appealed to the Federal Court have been set aside in a year, there are good grounds for concern when the Parliament attempts to limit judicial review of RRT decisions. Justice McHugh, hardly an expansionist High Court judge, told the Australian Bar Association Conference in July 2002:

> Even if 30 per cent of applicants have commenced proceedings 'as a means of prolonging their stay in Australia', it seems a small price for a just and prosperous country to pay for maintaining the rule of law.

The frustration of the Executive as the result of applicants abusing the judicial review system is understandable. But Parliament and the Executive should never forget the statement of Sir William Wade, the doyen of administrative lawyers, that 'to exempt a public authority from the jurisdiction of the courts of law is, to that extent, to grant dictatorial power'. Review of a public servant's decision by an administrative tribunal, whose members do not have the same security of tenure and independence as judges, is no substitute for review by a court. In principle, even a national emergency should not be a sufficient basis for refusing to permit the courts to examine the legality of the conduct of the Executive Government.

Under the separation of powers doctrine, the principal function of the judiciary is to uphold the rule of law. It is a corollary of that doctrine that the judiciary cannot be deterred from exercising that function by criticisms of the Executive branch even if the Executive's criticisms have the support of the general public. The Judiciary has to apply the law, not public opinion.[26]

There is a serious problem. The Federal Court, the country's second most senior court, has been swamped with appeals on migration matters in recent years. Back in 1987–88 the court received a modest 84 applications under the *Migration Act*. Six years later there were 320 applications. Another six years later there were 934 applications. By 2000–2001 there were 1,312 applications. The Howard government had sound policy reasons for wanting to limit the appeals to the Federal Court. It had reached the stage that in most months the majority of Federal Court appeals were migration matters, in a court with a broad federal jurisdiction including the burgeoning area of native title as well as the time-honoured jurisdictions of administrative law, trade practices and taxation. As recently as 1998–99 migration matters were only 23 per cent of the Federal Court's appeal docket. By 2001–2002 they were 56 per cent.

The High Court has upheld the constitutional entitlement of asylum seekers to review RRT decisions in the courts. The courts must ensure that the decision maker acts in good faith, with fairness and detachment, being satisfied that the detailed criteria for a visa are fulfilled, those criteria having been properly construed and fully considered. Parliament still has the capacity to ensure that not every minor point is appealed to the courts. The government needs to respect the constitutional limits set by the High Court and the political constraints that the Senate will rightly apply to any new law limiting appeals.

There is a need for continued alignment of the grounds on which any court in the hierarchy can grant relief such that 'there is no advantage for an applicant making an application under section 75(v) of the Constitution to the High Court' (to quote Mr Ruddock).[27] There is no point in cutting back appeal rights to the lower courts while failed asylum seekers have guaranteed access to the High Court. Within a week of the High Court restricting the scope of the government's privative clause, the court sent 586 cases down the line to the Federal Court, which now has the power to send them further down the line to the newly created Federal Magistrates Court.

The government's privative clause, though valid, has little work to do. Its wording is simply an invitation to further litigation about its meaning. It should be scrapped. The surest path to more efficient and expeditious disposition of these cases is likely to be procedural. Hopeless cases should be rejected at the threshold. Courts could insist that no appeal would be possible unless the court gave leave to appeal. Courts could also insist that some applications be put in writing without the need for an oral hearing. The provision of legal advice about the limited scope of judicial review would also help potential appellants to make better informed decisions.

In going down this path the government would not be riding any of the populist wave of appeal in the wash of the *Tampa*. It might be able to design a system of review that respects the Constitution and the traditional Australian way of considering fundamental rights and interests. It is time for politicians to heed the 1994 cry of Senator Barney Cooney, a lawyer:

> The courts are charged by society with the task of restraining arbitrary action, whether public or private, directed by one person against another. They stand between government and those it seeks to detain. People in Australia, whether legally or illegally, are entitled to have this safeguard retained to protect their civil rights. To remove it would diminish the quality of the liberties available in Australia.[28]

The government is right to claim that many unsuccessful applicants will appeal all the way to the High Court if it buys them more time in Australia and if they can buy time with no financial cost to themselves.

The minister himself has also been pursuing higher court appeals rather than having matters resolved promptly on the merits. His motivation is even more base and questionable than the motivation of those who desire to extend their stay in Australia. The human cost is unbearable. One graphic example will suffice.

An Iranian single mother attempted suicide in June 2002 at Woomera. This happened after the minister lodged an appeal to the Full Federal Court against her successful appeal to a single judge of the Federal Court. The judge had ordered that her matter be sent back to the RRT to be decided in accordance with the law set down by the High Court in a case that had been decided after the RRT had considered her case. In her favour, Justice Tamberlin had observed:

> In this case the RRT member dismissed, without any consideration, the possibility that the applicant could be a member of a particular social group which may be either women in Iran or divorced women in Iran. The reasons for decision focus only on the question whether the added references to possible harm could define a social group. In so doing the decision fails to come to terms with the central issue of group identity. Until this issue has been addressed and determined it is not possible for the decision-maker to determine whether there is a real chance of persecution as a consequence of being a member of that group. Furthermore, the RRT decision does not make a determination as to the availability of protection by the State or State agencies against violence or threatened violence to women in Iran.
>
> In my opinion the failure by the RRT to consider and determine the applicant's claims in relation to membership of a particular social group is a fundamental error of law because it demonstrates that the essential issue for determination by the RRT has not been considered.[29]

The judge had simply remitted the matter to the RRT, ordering that the RRT determine the matter consistent with the principles set down by the High Court. In the *Khawar Case*, decided in April 2002, the High Court had said that abused women could constitute a particular social group for the purposes of the Refugee Convention.[30] Chief Justice Gleeson had said:

> In my view, it would be open to the Tribunal, on the material before it, to conclude that women in Pakistan are a particular social group. The size of the group does not necessarily stand in the way of such a conclusion.

There are instances where the victims of persecution in a country have been a majority. It is power, not number, that creates the conditions in which persecution may occur. In some circumstances, the large size of a group might make implausible a suggestion that such a group is a target of persecution, and might suggest that a narrower definition is necessary. But I see nothing inherently implausible in the suggestion that women in a particular country may constitute a persecuted group, especially having regard to some of the information placed before the Tribunal on behalf of Ms Khawar. And cohesiveness may assist to define a group; but it is not an essential attribute of a group. Some particular social groups are notoriously lacking in cohesiveness.[31]

Regardless of the minister's personal opinion of the High Court decision, surely it was in everybody's interests, especially the mother and her accompanying seven-year-old son at Woomera, that this reconsideration by the RRT proceed as quickly as possible without further proceedings in the courts. If the minister had been concerned about Justice Tamberlin's interpretation of the scope of the privative clause, there were at that time many other cases on appeal that would have been sufficient vehicles for him to obtain clarity on that aspect of the law.

Once a court had had the opportunity to scrutinise the woman's RRT decision and to find it inconsistent with a subsequent High Court decision, nothing was to be gained by any party, including the minister, proceeding with an appeal to the Full Federal Court. The only conceivable gain to the government would be if an alternative outcome were to be obtained by upholding the original RRT decision and reasoning without the benefit of the High Court's guidance in *Khawar*. That would be a travesty of justice highlighting the injustice of the outcome.

The minister has constantly told parliament and the public that he is more concerned with a just outcome in a particular case rather than elaborate and legalistic appeal points. Yet he could not concede that this was an appropriate case for prompt determination by the RRT rather than further Federal Court litigation with the prospect that the matter would be eventually returned to the RRT in any event.

The government had a medical report indicating that, after the minister lodged his appeal, the Iranian applicant 'made a serious attempt to kill herself by cutting a vein in her arm. This was in the context of now wanting her son to be fostered out to an Australian family and she thought that if she died that this is what would happen to him.' The psychiatrist had observed, 'Her determination to find a way of getting her son out of the Detention Centre is strong and in this context, she is quite capable of further significant acting out behaviour and is ultimately at serious risk of suicide.'[32] The government's lodgment of a Full Federal Court appeal, thereby postponing or avoiding the RRT deciding her case consistent with the High Court decision in *Khawar*, could only add to her anxiety and desperation. The human cost of the Australian government's litigation strategy is too high.

European Union

One of the greatest problems confronting all democratic countries that pride themselves on the rule of law is how to process asylum claims effectively. They need to ensure fair decision making for the applicant without at the same time providing opportunities for unsuccessful applicants to exploit the appeals process so as to extend their stay. The EU Commission has found it very difficult to draft a proposed council directive on the minimum procedures to be used by member states in granting and withdrawing refugee status. The Commission's first attempt underwent 106 amendments when it reached the European Parliament. Europe is now contemplating a two-track system for processing asylum claims: a normal procedure and an accelerated procedure. In every case, the applicant would be entitled to remain on the territory of the member state until the primary decision maker had made a decision to grant or refuse protection. If the applicant were being put through the accelerated procedure, there would usually not be any right to remain in the country while the appeal was being heard and determined. For example, if the claim related to alleged persecution in a country that was listed as a safe third country, the applicant would have no right to remain. The accelerated procedure would be available to member states not only in the usual types of cases when it is asserted that the claim is manifestly unfounded but also in those frequent cases when 'there are serious reasons for considering' that the applicant has 'in bad faith, destroyed or disposed of an identity or travel document that would have helped establish his/her identity'. What would constitute bad faith in these circumstances? Often the people smuggler has ordered the destruction of documents. On other occasions people just think they will be maximising their chances of asylum by destroying their documentation, especially if some of the documentation is forged. Is that bad faith?

Consistent with the directive on reception of asylum applicants, this proposed directive on procedures for granting refugee status reaffirms that member states should not hold applicants in detention solely because the application needs to be examined before a decision is taken. There are only two circumstances in which a member state may hold an applicant in detention during the processing of the claim. The first is the Oakington type situation (see Chapter 5), when it is 'objectively necessary for an efficient examination of the application'. The second is when in the particular case there is a strong likelihood of the applicant absconding. The assessment must be made 'on the basis of the personal conduct of the applicant'.[33] The European Union knows that this attempted harmonisation of the procedure for granting refugee status is fraught with difficulty. The Commission proposes that the directive be reviewed every two years.

In the light of the protracted European negotiations on this part of the harmonisation exercise, one can have sympathy for those governments that are concerned by the burgeoning lists of court appeals from failed onshore asylum seekers. Something needs to be done to reduce the consumption of precious court resources and the drain on the treasury coffers, especially when most appeals do not result in a reversal of the finding about refugee status. Even in the small percentage of appeals that succeed, it is usually the case that the primary decision maker or administrative tribunal is asked to review the matter again but this time according to the law set down by the court. This does not usually result in a change to the final decision. The draft European directive provides much latitude for member states to experiment with different appeals mechanisms before the European directive is passed.

United Kingdom

The United Kingdom Home Secretary, David Blunkett, has shared the concern of Australia's Philip Ruddock that too many court resources have been dedicated to fruitless refugee appeals that bring satisfaction to the legal purists but little change to the outcome in the particular cases. Meanwhile these appeals provide the non-paying, failed applicant with more time to remain in the country. *The Nationality, Immigration and Asylum Act 2002* provides a more restrictive range of appeals to the courts. Asylum claims in the United Kingdom are determined by public servants who act in the name of the Secretary of State. The Secretary of State either grants the asylum claim, rejects it or grants the applicant leave to enter the country or to remain in the country for a set period of time (what used be called 'exceptional leave to enter' or 'exceptional leave to remain' [ELE or ELR]). An asylum seeker can appeal on the basis that the original decision was unlawful or that the person taking the decision should have exercised differently a discretion conferred by immigration rules. If the decision was to remove the applicant from the United Kingdom, an appeal may be brought to the adjudicator on the basis that the removal would be a breach of the country's obligations under the Refugees Convention or under the *Human Rights Act 1998*.

If the original decision maker decided to refuse a claim for asylum and instead decided only to grant leave to remain in the United Kingdom for one year or less, there is no appeal to an adjudicator. However, if the applicant later applied for an extension of the leave to remain and that extension was refused, with the result that the applicant was liable for removal from the United Kingdom, it would be possible to appeal to an adjudicator.

If the adjudicator refuses to grant asylum, there is no further right of appeal. The applicant may appeal further to the Immigration Appeal Tribunal if the Tribunal gives its permission for the appeal. The appeal can be only about a question of law. There is no way that the Tribunal will involve itself with the merits of the applicant's claim. If the Tribunal declines to give permission for an appeal, the applicant can go to a court and seek a review of the Tribunal's action. A single judge who will decide the matter on receipt of written submissions constitutes the court. The judge will not hear oral evidence and the judge's decision is final.

If the applicant gets permission for an appeal but then fails before the Tribunal, the applicant may appeal further to the Court of Appeal but only if the Tribunal or the court gives permission. Once again the court will consider only questions of law. The aim of these provisions is to give the failed asylum seeker one appeal to an adjudicator who can consider whether the decision maker exercised the discretions under the rules correctly and whether the decision maker made a decision within the law. It is not for the adjudicator to say that another decision would have been preferable. If the original decision maker could have come to that decision acting lawfully, that is the end of the matter. The failed asylum seeker has further appeals but only if the argument is restricted to the original decision maker's and the adjudicator's interpretation of the law.

A failed asylum seeker may not bring an appeal while remaining in the United Kingdom if the Secretary of State issues a certificate indicating that another member state of the European Union has responsibility for the processing of the claim, or if the applicant can be removed to another country with no risk of refoulement or threats to life and liberty. Even if the failed asylum seeker is bringing a human rights claim, departure from the United Kingdom can still be a condition for the hearing of an appeal if the Secretary of State certifies that in his opinion the human rights claim is clearly unfounded. By certifying that an asylum claim or human rights claim is clearly unfounded, the Secretary of State can require the departure of the applicant before any appeal proceeds. There is no question of the court or tribunal having the discretion to decide whether the applicant's presence would be helpful for the determination of the appeal. The only long-term safeguard is that the Secretary of State has to appoint someone to monitor his exercise of this certifying power. The monitor is then to report to parliament at least once a year. If the asylum seeker is entitled to reside in one of the ten proposed new member states of the European Union, the Secretary of State must require the departure of the applicant unless he is satisfied that the claim is not clearly unfounded. The UK government sees two advantages in an expanded European Union: there will be no prospect of asylum claims coming from the new member states, and there will be every opportunity to return asylum seekers from other countries if they have even a right of residence in one of the new member states. The legislation permits the Secretary of State to add other states to the list of safe residence countries. The Secretary of State can even obtain the removal of the applicant before the hearing of an appeal. He certifies that the applicant will be removed to a country other than the applicant's country and that 'there is no reason to believe that the person's rights under the Human Rights Convention will be breached in that country'.[34] The government assumes that most appeals brought by applicants from outside the United Kingdom will be abandoned by the applicants.

If the Secretary of State or immigration officers think that an appeal is being brought only to delay removal from the country, they may sign a certificate that results in the appeal being discontinued. If they think that the original immigration decision being appealed relates to a matter that could have been raised in an earlier immigration appeal by the applicant, they may also issue a certificate discontinuing the appeal.

Given the post–September 11 concerns, there are also provisions that allow the Secretary of State to discontinue appeals if he certifies that the original reason to deny asylum was that it would be in the national interest that the applicant be removed from the United Kingdom, or even that it would be in the interests of the relationship between the United Kingdom and another country. The Secretary of State can also stop an appeal if he certifies that the original decision to deny asylum was based on information that should not be made public, or if he certifies that the original decision to deny the asylum claim was made personally by him on the ground that the applicant's exclusion from the United Kingdom was 'conducive to the public good'. Even worse, an appeal can be denied if the decision to deny asylum was made by a public servant in accordance with a direction given personally by the Secretary of State identifying this particular applicant. Australia is not alone in going to great lengths to limit the appeal rights of asylum seekers.

United States

As in Australia, there has been a tussle between the judiciary and the executive about the extent to which aliens awaiting deportation or removal from the country can be held in detention, especially when there is no reasonable prospect of the alien being removed to another country. Not having a bill of rights, Australia has a very simplistic law passed by the parliament providing that unlawful non-citizens who cannot obtain a visa must be kept in detention until they are removed from Australia or deported. The US Congress could never pass such a law because the due process clause of the Constitution forbids the government from depriving any person of liberty without due process of law. The US Congress passed a more complex law. During removal proceedings, a person could still be released on parole. Once a court has made a removal order, the person must be held in detention for up to 90 days awaiting removal from the country. If the authorities have been unable to remove the person, the law provided that any alien held in custody would be transferred to a post-order detention unit where the Immigration and Naturalization Service (INS) would conduct an initial custody review within another 90 days. A two-member panel of INS officers would then interview the alien and make a recommendation to the INS headquarters, having regard to the alien's criminal history and flight risk. If detention were ongoing, there would have to be an annual review of the detention, with the alien being given 30 days notice of the reviews and the opportunity to submit any relevant material.

These checks and balances were not sufficient for the law to pass constitutional muster. By the narrowest margin of 5–4, the US Supreme Court in 2001 struck down this legislative arrangement because it would have permitted indefinite detention of some aliens who could not be removed to any other country.[35] The Court read an implicit limitation into the law so that the post-removal period of detention after the initial 90 days was a period reasonably necessary to bring about that alien's removal from the United States. The government was able to invoke only two reasons for indefinite detention: ensuring the appearance of aliens at future immigration proceedings and preventing danger to the community. If there were no reasonable prospect of removing someone, there would be no reasonable prospect of future immigration proceedings. The court reaffirmed a 1972 decision that 'where detention's goal is no longer practically attainable, detention no longer bears a reasonable relation to the purpose for which the individual was committed'.[36] The majority was adamant that 'once an alien enters the country, the legal circumstance changes, for the Due Process Clause applies to all "persons" within the United States, whether their presence here is lawful, unlawful, temporary or permanent'.[37]

The court was careful to make it clear that the choice was not between indefinite detention and freedom within the United States but between indefinite detention and 'supervision under release conditions that may not be violated', thereby substantially reducing any danger to the community. In Australia, the Executive has been spared any judicial insistence that unlawful non-citizens be treated with due process because there is no bill of rights. However, the Federal Court of Australia has followed the US jurisprudence. When the Australian parliament enacted the law for mandatory detention until removal, it 'must be taken to have intended that the power to detain be limited to the period during which the Minister is taking reasonable steps to secure the removal and be exercisable only for so long as removal is reasonably practicable'.[38] There must be a real likelihood or prospect of removal in the reasonably foreseeable future. After the Federal Court had given decisions to this effect in Iraqi and Bidoon[39] cases as well as the initial Palestinian test case, Minister Ruddock still declined to release other members of these national groups who had exhausted all remedies. He declined even to offer an identity card to those released by the courts on the basis that the courts should accept responsibility for those whom they ordered released into the community without ministerial approval. Instead he appealed the original Palestinian decision to the Full Federal Court. Though the Palestinian had long since returned to the Gaza Strip, the minister was anxious to pursue the litigation to retrieve his costs and to get a Full Court decision limiting the capacity of individual judges to grant habeas corpus.

On 15 April 2003, the full bench of the Federal Court unanimously dismissed Minister Ruddock's appeal in the Palestinian test case. All three appeal judges agreed with Justice Merkel that there must be 'a real likelihood or prospect of the removal of the person from Australia in the reasonably foreseeable future' if the detention were to be lawful once a failed asylum seeker has formally requested removal from Australia.[40] The appeal judges considered Australia's international obligations under the International Covenant on Civil and Political Rights when interpreting the statutory power to detain an asylum seeker and concluded, 'conformably with Australia's obligations under Art 9(1) of the ICCPR, it would be necessary to read it as subject, at the very least, to an implied limitation that the period of mandatory detention does not extend to a time when there is no real likelihood or prospect in the reasonably foreseeable future of a detained person being removed and thus released from detention'.[41] Migration detention is reviewable by the courts and subject to *habeas corpus* when the minister is unable to return a failed asylum seeker back home or to a third country after the applicant has requested removal from Australia. The minister and his department are now rendered more accountable to the courts for the protracted detention of failed asylum seekers. Following the High Court's decision on the privative clause, this was Mr Ruddock's second major setback in the courts in 2003. He had to release into the community another eight Iraqis and Palestinians who were lauguishing in detention centres with no hope of returning home in the foreseeable future. The judges have started to set legal limits on the Howard/Ruddock post-*Tampa* firebreak.

Conclusions

In all first-world countries there is a major problem with failed asylum seekers pursuing every available appeal avenue, often only to delay their removal from the country. However, decision makers and administrative tribunals cannot be kept accountable unless the lawfulness of their decisions is reviewable by the courts. In Europe it is now common to permit the removal of failed asylum seekers while their appeals to the higher courts are being processed.

Judicial review of migration decisions is here to stay in Australia unless the major political parties were successfully to propose a constitutional referendum taking away the High Court's inalienable jurisdiction to supervise the lawfulness of the actions of Commonwealth public servants and tribunals. That is not very likely. For over a decade politicians like Philip Ruddock have thought that their problems would be solved if they could convince parliament to pass a privative clause excluding court review of refugee decisions. This has proved a dead end.

Politicians on both sides of the parliament need to accept the constitutional guarantee of access to the courts for failed asylum seekers. With this access, the courts must ensure that the decision maker acts in good faith, with fairness and detachment, being satisfied that the detailed criteria for a visa are fulfilled, those criteria having been properly construed and fully considered. Our politicians are right to insist on parliament's capacity to ensure that not every minor point is appealed to the courts. But the government needs to respect the constitutional limits set by the High Court and the political constraints that the Senate will rightly apply to any new law limiting appeals.

With the establishment of a Federal Magistrates' Court, much of the review of the RRT could now be transferred from the overtaxed Federal Court. There ought to be an automatic right of appeal on points of law to the Magistrates' Court. There should then be an appeal to the Federal Court but only with leave being granted by a single judge of the Federal Court. The Americans have long lived with a detailed system of court appeals. In the United States, a failed asylum seeker will have his or her case referred to an immigration judge. If the judge also refuses to grant asylum, there is an automatic appeal to the Board of Immigration Appeals. If there are complex questions of law, the case can then be heard by one of the thirteen Federal Circuit Courts of Appeal.

The Australian technique of the last decade of attempting to remove all administrative discretions, to codify with increasing complexity the criteria for the grant of a visa, and to remove the courts from the role of supervision has failed. The RRT should be resourced with country information that is known to be reliable because it has been provided by sources that are credible and mandated to provide objective, up-to-date information. There should be an automatic right to appeal questions of law to the Federal Magistrates' Court. There should be no further appeals allowed except with leave of the court. The government could be given the option of applying to the court that any further appeal proceed only once the applicant has been removed from Australia. With proper court supervision, the prospect could then be avoided of complex appeal points being formulated by lawyers only to assist the applicant to remain longer in the country when there is little likelihood of a protection visa being granted at the end of the judicial and administrative process.

If failed asylum seekers unable to return to their country are held in endless detention, there must be a regular review of their detention by the courts. Even without a bill of rights, our judges have still been able to restrict the law on endless detention, as has the US Supreme Court. A federal magistrate should be commissioned to conduct regular hearings about the ongoing detention of asylum seekers who cannot be removed from Australia. If there is no reasonable prospect of their removal within a reasonable period of time and if they are not a flight risk or a security risk, they should be released into the community on bail awaiting notification of their renewed detention prior to their immediate removal from Australia.

CHAPTER 7

Refugee and humanitarian status

Most first-world countries have signed the Convention Against Torture and the International Covenant on Civil and Political Rights as well as the Convention on Refugees. These countries need to extend protection to persons in their territory who would face torture, death or cruel and degrading treatment on their return home. It is not enough simply to determine whether someone is a refugee. For example, the human rights record of a regime may be so bad that no person could be safe on return even if they were not part of some persecuted religious or ethnic minority. Countries of asylum nowadays need a process for determining these humanitarian protection claims as well as the refugee claims. Often these countries will argue correctly that there is no obligation to grant permanent residence to someone in need of humanitarian protection. Though in the past it was customary to grant permanent residence to refugees, there was no obligation in international law to do so. Increasingly governments are looking at the option of short-term protection for refugees who enter a country without a visa, especially if they had the option of seeking protection in some place closer to home. Australia has been active in seeking options to permanent residence for refugees who have entered uninvited and without a visa. Though willing to grant humanitarian assistance to persons fleeing torture or degrading treatment, the Australian government has been anxious to keep the courts out of any consideration of humanitarian cases that do not raise legal questions about refugee status.

Prior to the blow-out of onshore protection claims in Australia caused by the prime ministerial edict of Bob Hawke that Chinese students would not have to go home post—Tiananmen Square, those who were granted protection in Australia used to be given the right of permanent residence. This was the case whether they came to Australia through the offshore humanitarian program or through the onshore determination process. Trying to cope with the large onshore component after the Hawke decree that the Chinese students could stay, the Immigration Department convinced the government that only temporary visas should be issued to some onshore applicants. The department thought that this would help to avoid a permanent skewing of the migration program by permanent protection holders being able to sponsor their families to join them in Australia. The government proposed four-year temporary visas. By the time these visas came up for renewal, Paul Keating was prime minister and he broke the news in the Chinese-speaking newspapers that the Chinese students would be entitled to the automatic issue of a permanent visa. Between March 1994 and October 1999 all applicants for protection to whom Australia owed protection obligations were granted a permanent visa.

The Howard government when elected appropriated to itself some key elements of the policy of Pauline Hanson's One Nation Party. With the commencement of the fourth wave of boat people, the parliament enacted legislation that would grant onshore asylum seekers who had come without a visa only a three-year temporary protection visa. When reviewed after 30 months, the visa could be made permanent if the asylum seeker still engaged Australia's protection obligations.

Terms and conditions of temporary protection visas in Australia

Traditionally, Australia has prided itself as a nation that does not have second-class citizens or residents. There has never been a guest-worker program except for Queensland's nineteenth-century system of indentured labour for South Sea Islanders who came mainly from Vanuatu. There were discriminatory labour laws that permitted

Chinese labourers to work in sweatshop conditions. After World War II, when the major migration program was instituted, all political parties agreed that migrants would have the same labour and social security rights as citizens.

In recent years there have been major changes made to the social security, labour and health-care entitlements of new migrants. For example, some people wanting to sponsor their parents to live in Australia can do so only if they assume responsibility for their health care. Most visitors to Australia no longer have the right to work. In the midst of all these changes, Australia has maintained a generous list of entitlements for those granted permanent residence through the offshore refugee and humanitarian program. Those granted permanent protection visas have access to all government employment assistance programs. They receive free tuition under the Adult Migrant English program. They are able to sponsor their family members in the same way as a citizen could. They are eligible for the full range of social security benefits and Medicare, including torture and trauma counselling. On arrival, they are provided with orientation assistance in finding accommodation through the migrant resource centres funded by government. They are eligible for HECS (Higher Education Contribution Scheme) rather than having to pay full up-front fees for tertiary education. They are free to travel overseas and return. The whole emphasis is on providing maximum opportunity for the newly settled refugees to settle into Australian life, enjoying the benefits and opportunities of life in their new country.

Those who apply for asylum onshore, having arrived without a visa, are treated very differently now. The rationale for the discriminatory approach is that the government has no intention of allowing the uninvited and unvisaed onshore asylum seeker to become a permanent member of the Australian community; the onshore asylum seeker just happens to be someone who chose Australia as the country to honour its protection obligations; the only responsibility of government is to grant protection — not to grant permanent residence or the services normally associated with permanent incorporation in to a new community. The government is adamant that it honours its international protection obligations to the letter, while being at liberty to cut back on other entitlements.

Onshore asylum seekers who arrive in Australia with a visa are eligible for permanent residence. They are able to apply for asylum having lawfully entered Australia on some form of temporary visa. If they apply within 45 days of arrival, they will retain the right to work while their application is being processed. If their visa has expired, they will usually be able to reside in the community on the payment of a bond provided they are not a flight risk and provided there is no perceived danger to the community. Those who come to Australia without a visa are classed as 'unlawful non-citizens' and they are held in detention while their refugee claims are processed. If they are under 18, over 75 or in need of acute medical assistance, they may be eligible for a bridging visa.

If the 'unlawful non-citizens' are successful in claiming asylum, they will be granted a temporary protection visa (TPV) which is valid for three years only. They are not eligible for any Commonwealth-government-sponsored settlement services. They will have the right to work but no access to the government employment assistance programs. They will not be eligible for English language tuition. They will be eligible only for restricted social security payments.[1] They will be eligible for Medicare if they have submitted an application for a permanent protection visa for which they may be eligible after the three-year visa has run its course. They would have to pay full up-front fees at the rates applicable for international students if they were to pursue tertiary education. Some state governments and community groups have come to the rescue and provided assistance to TPV holders in need. Regardless of the help they receive from others, they are not eligible to sponsor members of their family to join them. This is one of the reasons that there was a steep rise in the number of women and children in the fourth wave of boat people. In the past, their husbands and fathers would have had the right to sponsor them to come to Australia so they could fly here in safety. Also, TPV holders have no right to go and visit their family. Or more accurately, they have no right to return to Australia should they choose to depart at any time during the term of their TPV.

Minister Ruddock remains adamant that the Convention on Refugees does not require a government to provide a person with the right to travel in and out of the country while protection is being provided.

There is no doubt that Australia is in flagrant breach of Article 28 of the Convention that provides:

> The Contracting States shall issue to refugees lawfully staying in their territory travel documents for the purpose of travel outside their territory, unless compelling reasons of national security or public order otherwise require, and the provisions of the Schedule to this Convention shall apply with respect to such documents.

The Schedule of the Convention then stipulates that the travel document should state that the holder is authorised to return to the country that has issued the document. The Schedule stipulates:

> Each contracting state undertakes that the holder of a travel document issued by it in accordance with Article 28 of this Convention shall be readmitted to its territory at any time during the period of its validity.[2]

Once a TPV has run for 30 months, holders are eligible to apply for a renewal. Should they convince the decision maker that they still engage Australia's protection obligations, they will be eligible for a permanent visa unless the decision maker decides that they resided for a continuous period of at least seven days in a country where they could have sought and obtained effective protection. If the decision maker thinks that the applicant could have obtained protection en route to Australia, either from the government of a country or from the UNHCR, the applicant will be eligible only for another three-year TPV with its ongoing limitations. If the minister thinks that it is in the public interest, he can permit any TPV holder to be granted a permanent visa even if the holder did have access to protection en route to Australia.

Those TPV holders who came by boat and were then held in detention were eligible for legal assistance with the processing of their original claim for a visa. However, they are not eligible for free legal advice for the renewal of their visa even though there may now be difficult questions to decide, including whether they had the opportunity to avail themselves of protection en route to Australia. Having travelled for months and having then been in detention for many more months, some will have been absent from their countries for four years before they come to argue their case again for protection. On 3 February 2003 Mr Habib Wahedy, a 46-year-old Hazara man whose TPV was about to expire, received a letter from the government offering him $2,000 to return to Afghanistan. He had spent six months in detention in Port Hedland before being granted his three-year TPV, and he had moved to Murray Bridge in South Australia for employment. On receipt of the letter, he climbed on to overhead power lines and committed suicide. He left a tape-recording saying, 'Because I am under a lot of emotional pressure I have done this.' Mr Dale West, the State Director of Centrecare, a church agency providing assistance to TPV holders, explained the death in these terms: 'The final straw was a letter offering voluntary return to Afghanistan. It's mental jail having a TPV hanging over your head.' Minister Ruddock replied, 'There is a range of support services that are there and we are not going to be able to put in place systems whereby we have a counsellor beside every temporary protection visa holder, to hold their hand through the process.'[3] For many TPV holders, the government's three-year reconsideration of their refugee claim is itself a very traumatic experience, often reviving the trauma of their past. The offer of $2,000 to return home has to be set against the thousands of dollars that will have to be repaid to family and friends who paid for the people smuggler in the first place. For

Australian, 10 April 2002.
Reproduced with Peter Nicholson's permission.

many, no financial offer will still their concerns about their safety were they to return to Afghanistan. No wonder so few have accepted the government's financial offer. The government is hopeful that more Afghans will choose to return home once they are again taken into detention in places like Port Hedland where they can make what the government regards as a more realistic choice about their future options.

Subsidiary protection in Australia

Because of the increasing intervention from the courts in the review of migration decisions from 1985 onwards, the Labor government restricted the access to onshore humanitarian assistance for those persons who were found not to be refugees. Anyone pleading to stay on humanitarian or compassionate grounds who was not a refugee and who had not qualified for a standard migration visa would have to apply to the minister to exercise his personal, non-reviewable, non-delegable, non-enforceable discretion. This form of protection is often referred to as 'subsidiary protection'. Any government which prides itself on adherence to the protection of human rights needs some machinery for determining the claims of people wanting to remain in the country because on return they would face torture, cruel or degrading treatment, civil war or some horrendous natural disaster. Australian governments of both political persuasions have been convinced that this sort of protection can be provided efficiently and fairly only if the minister and his department can be spared interference by the courts. In the event of a mass influx of persons in need of humanitarian assistance, the government is able to issue temporary safe-haven visas. These visas have been issued to East Timorese and Kosovars on the understanding that the people are to return home once the Australian government determines that it is safe for them to do so. Individual applications for humanitarian assistance are then dealt with by departmental officers who decide whether to recommend that the minister look at the file and consider exercising his personal discretion. The departmental officers follow a seven-page ministerial guideline in which Philip Ruddock informs them of 'the unique or exceptional circumstances in which I may wish to consider exercising my public interest powers ... to substitute for a decision of the relevant

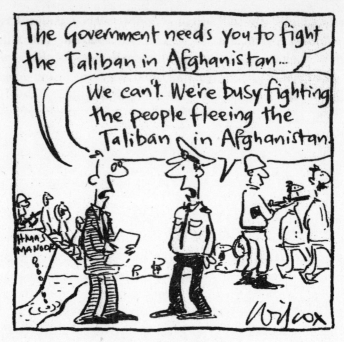

Sydney Morning Herald, 20 September 2001.
Reproduced with Cathy Wilcox's permission.

decision maker, a decision more favourable to the person concerned in the particular case'.[4] No doubt there are public servants and ministers who are very scrupulous in exercising this difficult national responsibility. When something goes wrong in an individual case, the systemic shortcomings in such a system are revealed.

In the 1980s Australian politicians felt they had lost control of the decision-making process regarding onshore humanitarian claims. Visitors to Australia would come on a permit or visa with the right to stay for a fixed period. At any time while their permit was still valid they could apply to the minister for a further permit if there were 'strong compassionate or humanitarian grounds for the grant of an entry permit'. If the minister refused an application, the person could then appeal to the courts. Ultimately this led to a blow-out in entry permits and visas granted on humanitarian grounds. Politicians became convinced that judges were a soft touch.

The problem that the government encountered with the courts is graphically highlighted by a decision in the Federal Court relating to a 24-year-old Czech woman, Gabriela Surinakova, who came to Australia on a six-month visitor's permit to care for her aged grandparents. She arrived in April 1989 and applied for permanent residence on humanitarian and compassionate grounds in June 1989. Under the 1980 legislation her entry permit could be extended or made permanent if there were 'strong compassionate or humanitarian grounds'. Due to various bureaucratic delays, no decision was made on her application until February 1991. Both her sick grandparents had died by the end of 1989.

The minister and his department quite reasonably thought that the grounds for Ms Surinakova remaining in Australia had disappeared on the death of her last grandparent. She appealed to the Federal Court, alleging that the decision makers had failed to take into account and give due weight to all the relevant humanitarian and compassionate considerations. The judge agreed with her, deciding that the decision makers should also have considered a romantic attachment that she had formed with an Australian citizen. She told the court, 'I have also developed a close relationship with an Australian man through my local Church. We see each other regularly. I would be very upset if we were separated.' Her friend gave evidence to the court:

> I have known Gabriela for a few months. My first contact with Gabriela was made in the Slovak Church at Lidcombe. I have the privilege to take her to church on Sundays, and wish to maintain it. I have been seeing Gabriela after my night lectures, during which time personal feelings and ideas were discussed over coffee. A certain fondness has crept into our relationship. However, that relationship has been unable to culminate considering Gabriela's current predicament. I solemnly believe that given time, a more genuine and lasting relationship would evolve. It would be very sad and an unpleasant feeling for me to bear, if we both were denied the opportunity.

The judge decided that this relationship was a relevant consideration which should have been taken into account by the decision makers and so he set aside the minister's decision and ordered that the decision be made again in the light of all the relevant evidence.[5] The public servants and politicians thought the judges had gone too far in appropriating to themselves the discretion in the administration of the onshore migration program. They were keen to get these decisions well away from the courts.

The major political parties in the parliament were agreed that the decision whether to allow someone to remain on humanitarian grounds when that person had failed to establish refugee status should be a matter for government and not the courts. In order to shield such decisions from any review by the courts, the politicians were convinced that the decision would have to be a personal, non-compellable, non-reviewable decision of the minister in each case. The decision would have to be made by the minister and not by one of his public servants. There would be no way that an applicant could have a court compel a public servant or tribunal to consider the application for humanitarian residence. There would be no appeal to the courts once the minister had made his decision. Ironically, it was the desire of the courts to extend the transparency of the government's decisions on humanitarian grounds that convinced the politicians that it was time to reduce the access to humanitarian considerations. Even though the minister does exercise this discretion hundreds of times a year, Australia now makes much less provision for onshore humanitarian cases than most other first-world countries. For example, in the United Kingdom in 2001 almost twice the number of persons granted asylum onshore were granted exceptional leave to remain, which is granted for strong humanitarian or compassionate reasons when an asylum claim is not warranted.

A systemic problem in the Australian law is how to decide to provide what is sometimes called 'subsidiary protection' for persons who are not refugees but who would face a dreadful situation if they were sent back home. Though a signatory to the UN Convention Against Torture and the International Covenant on Civil and Political Rights, Australia has no means other than the minister's personal discretion to decide whether to allow a person to remain in Australia. The Australian parliament has considered two cases that graphically highlight the problem. On 14 July 1997 Zhu Qing Ping was to be removed from Australia as a failed asylum seeker even though she was at least 35 weeks pregnant. The minister was overseas so the papers authorising her forced return were referred to the acting minister, Amanda Vanstone, who at no time was told of the woman's pregnancy. Less than a week after her forced return to China, her child was aborted. Back in May 1997 Ms Zhu had asked the deputy manager of the Port Hedland Detention Centre if she could stay at the centre until her child was born. The DIMIA manager was not able to give her any guarantee but reassured her by saying that she would not be able to travel in the late stages of pregnancy. None of her treating doctors were consulted before she was taken away. On the day she left, she met with the centre manager and the duty nurse who recorded, 'Patient visibly upset anxious and crying. Patient counselled by myself and centre manager for about one hour. Patient states that she wants to remain in Australia till she has her baby and that she is scared at the possibility of having a baby while flying to China and the possibility of losing her baby in China due to the fact that she has not obtained permission for a second child.' When the Senate Legal and Constitutional References Committee investigated the matter they concluded that it was 'more likely that the abortion was forced rather than voluntary' and that her removal from Australia and the subsequent abortion 'could put Australia in breach of our obligations under the Convention Against Torture'.[6] The Committee made recommendations as to how such a humanitarian tragedy could be avoided in the future, including:

> That pregnant women subject to removal should be given special consideration by the minister, or a senior delegate, to remain in Australia until after the birth to ensure that no woman is returned pregnant to a country in circumstances where there is a risk the woman will be coerced to undergo an abortion.

Eight months later the government replied, 'Existing measures to assess fitness to travel cover any physical problems likely to arise with pregnant women during removal. Any risk associated with returning a woman to her country of origin will have been assessed as part of the protection determination.'[7] The warm-hearted decent international citizen would have permitted Ms Zhu to remain the extra couple of weeks so she could give birth to her child, that being her expressed and recorded wish. Her continued presence in the Port Hedland Detention Centre was no threat to Australian security or to heightened sensitivities about national sovereignty.

In 1998 a failed Somali asylum seeker, Mr Sadiq Shek Elmi, complained to the UN Committee Against Torture that he would face a real risk of torture if forcibly returned to Somalia. The Australian government submitted that there was not sufficient evidence to establish the complaint and that in any event the threatened violence to him could not constitute torture because there was no established government in Somalia, only warring factions. The UN Committee begged to differ on the evidence and on the law, noting:

> The international community negotiates with the warring factions and ... some of the factions operating in Mogadishu have set up quasi-governmental institutions and are negotiating the establishment of a common administration. It follows then that, *de facto*, those factions exercise certain prerogatives that are comparable to those normally exercised by legitimate governments. Accordingly, the members of those factions can fall, for the purposes of the application of the Convention, within the phrase 'public officials or other persons acting in an official capacity' contained in article 1.[8]

Two years later the UN Committee provided general comments on Australia's regular report to the committee, expressing concern about 'the apparent lack of appropriate review mechanisms for ministerial decisions'.[9] The Senate Legal and Constitutional References Committee has expressed the same concern, but the government has blithely responded that the existing arrangement of the minister's personal non-compellable, non-reviewable, non-transparent discretion is adequate to ensure compliance with the Convention Against Torture and the International Covenant on Civil and Political Rights.

Adding more intrigue than light 18 months later, Alby Schulz, a government member, told parliament, 'When, under the natural justice provisions of application for protection in Australia, Mr Sadiq Elmi was shown that the Department knew he was not who he said he was and that, therefore, he was not entitled to refugee status, he withdrew his application and made arrangements to go elsewhere.'[10] It turned out that, as a result of inter-governmental investigations, the Australian government had discovered that Sadiq was in the United Kingdom and Italy making asylum claims at the very time he was supposed to have been back in Somalia suffering persecution. With little media attention, he decided to leave Australia voluntarily. Deciding the merits of a humanitarian claim to remain in the country can be a very difficult business. Understandably many citizens in a democracy say that it is not good enough simply to trust the minister about what may be life and death decisions when there is no guarantee that the minister has been properly apprised of the facts by his public servants. Because of privacy constraints, the public servants are unable to release further information about the plight and circumstances of those like Mr Sadiq.

There will always be people on our shores who are not refugees but who for good humanitarian reasons should not be forced home immediately. It is not satisfactory to leave the matter to the minister, who decides thousands of personal cases each year with no transparency of process either to the parliament or to the public. For more than a decade governments of both political persuasions in Australia have been prepared to prop up an inadequate procedure for the granting of humanitarian relief so as to exclude the judges. As the immigration officers informed parliament in 1991, humanitarian status 'is not an entitlement; it is a ministerial discretion; it is an act of grace on the part of the Minister'.[11] In 2001–2002 the minister was asked to administer this act of grace 5,005 times. He obliged on 372 occasions. One

Australian, 2 February 2002.
Reproduced with Peter Nicholson's permission.

hundred and ninety-nine of those cases related to persons who had been rejected for a protection visa by the Refugee Review Tribunal. However, the minister ordered the issue of a protection visa in only 25 of these cases. In the other matters, he would have ordered the issue of some other type of migration visa, avoiding the need to take another place from the refugee quota. Mr Ruddock has been more gracious than his predecessors. In fact, he claims that while in Opposition he convinced the government to retain some ministerial discretion.[12] The then minister, Robert Ray, was opposed to such a notion and he never exercised the discretion. Gerry Hand exercised the discretion four times a year, and Nick Bolkus exercised the discretion about 50 times a year. The minister, in the public interest, can exercise the discretion and he is required to table a statement of explanation in parliament each time.

The rigidity and complexity of Australia's onshore refugee determination process has worked great injustice in the case of the 1,800 Timorese whose protection applications had been put on hold for more than ten years. The government had gone to great lengths to assert that there were no East Timorese refugees onshore in Australia. At the same time that our government was in the International Court of Justice opposed to Portugal and claiming the validity of the Timor Gap Treaty negotiated with Indonesia, they were appearing in our domestic courts and tribunals claiming that the East Timorese could avail themselves of protection in Portugal. Whatever the correctness of the complex legal argument, the immorality of the government's position was plain for all to see. In one forum we were asserting that Indonesia had the right to control the oil resources of East Timor. In another forum we were claiming that the East Timorese were still under the mantle of Portugal. When in Opposition, our politicians seem to have a more ready understanding of these matters. The present Minister for Foreign Affairs, Mr Alexander Downer, when attacking Prime Minister Paul Keating on the plight of these Timorese, said that it was 'simply absurd and hypocritical' to claim that they had a Portuguese entitlement to protection. He said, 'Not one of these people is by any stretch of Mr Keating's vivid imagination a Portuguese citizen. Lying for domestic political gain is one thing but to lie internationally is downright damaging.'[13]

Except for the delaying tactics of the Hawke, Keating and Howard governments, these East Timorese would have had their refugee claims processed before 1999 and been granted permanent protection visas. For up to thirteen years these people have had to live with their lives on hold. If ever there was a case for the exercise of humanitarian discretion, this was it. With the change of regime in East Timor in 1999, their persecutors were no longer in government. Those who had fled persecution before 1999 were those least likely to be refugees now. They were more likely to be well connected to the new government in East Timor. East Timor desperately needs all the help it can get — especially from its own people who have the training and skills. Undoubtedly some of the 1,800 have a responsibility to the new emerging nation state. However, unemployment is very high and basic infrastructure including water and electricity is in increasingly short supply. At the time the Australian government was wanting to return them home, there was severe drought in the west of the country and severe food shortages were expected in the coming months. Should Australia force all these people home at such a time in the name of national self-determination and development? Would this actually help East Timor? Indonesia was not forcing home those still in camps in West Timor. Would those who did not want to return be contributing more to the development of East Timor by sending back money as they do and continuing to improve their work skills? If the Australian government decides on forced returns, advice should be sought from the political leadership in East Timor about the appropriate time for such a move. Untimely forced returns without the support of the East Timor government would be contrary to East Timor's national interest and inimical to good inter-governmental relations.

Of course Australia's national interest should be considered as well as East Timor's. Australia has contributed much to the liberation of East Timor. Australia has an interest in seeing East Timor succeed. Australia also has an interest in conducting an orderly migration program and in offering short-term safe haven to persons who might not be otherwise admitted to Australia. Australia also has a national interest in allowing local communities to decide that long-time residents are integral to the life of the community and should be permitted to remain. When five Melbourne mayors appear in Canberra pleading for the Timorese in their communities to be allowed to remain, our federal politicians should concede that they do not have the sole right to interpret the 'national interest'.

Some of the 1,800 Timorese had been in Australia up to 13 years. Some of them were still studying. Others had put down roots in Australia. Others were children who had no life experience of East Timor. If not all are permitted to remain, there is a need for a case-by-case assessment of the humanitarian needs of the applicants as against their likely capacity to contribute to the immediate development of East Timor.

The assessments must be made in a context where government for other reasons is unwilling to make broad humanitarian exceptions for people to stay permanently. One policy flow-on is that if all the East Timorese people stay, future governments will be less willing to allow temporary non-detained residence to future humanitarian cases. Presuming that any proven refugees will be allowed to remain permanently, a decision about forced returns should be taken only if that is judged by both governments to be in the national interest of both countries. If and when that joint decision is made, it would still be necessary to permit some to remain for substantive humanitarian reasons.

Government officers of good will accountable to politicians elected by the people have to make the difficult assessments in these cases. Every year there are instances where someone though not a refugee would face the risk of torture, degrading treatment or punishment if returned home. Basic human decency demands that persons not be returned in these circumstances. Signatories to the Convention Against Torture and the International Covenant on Civil and Political Rights have obligations. Honouring these obligations is not an interference with the right to decide who comes and who remains in the country. Rather it is a humanitarian exercise of the right by government in the name of the people to act decently in the international community.

Proposed EU grounds of subsidiary protection

The European Union's harmonisation process boldly envisages the drawing up of minimum standards for giving temporary protection to persons who are not refugees. These non-refugees will be displaced persons from third countries who cannot presently return to their country of origin, and any other persons who need international protection. The European Commission has proposed that this subsidiary protection be available to those persons who though not refugees have 'a well-founded fear of suffering serious and unjustified harm', having been forced to flee or to remain outside their country, and being unable or unwilling, owing to such fear, to avail themselves of the protection of their country.[14] Covering the relevant provisions of the European Convention on Human Rights, the Convention Against Torture and the International Covenant on Civil and Political Rights, the directive would give a broad reading to serious and unjustified harm, including:

(a) torture or inhuman or degrading treatment or punishment; or
(b) violation of a human right, sufficiently severe to engage the Member State's international obligations; or
(c) a threat to his or her life, safety or freedom as a result of indiscriminate violence arising in situations of armed conflict, or as a result of systematic or generalised violations of their human rights.

The draft directive proposes that refugees be given five-year residence permits which would be automatically renewable. Those with subsidiary protection would be guaranteed only a one-year residence permit renewable 'until such time as the granting authorities establish that such protection is no longer required'.[15] Refugees once determined to be so must be given immediate and equal access to employment and vocational training, but those on subsidiary protection could be denied the right to work for up to six months and be denied access to vocational training for up to a year. Given the watering down of the reception standards directive that occurred in the final phases of the consideration by the Council of Ministers, it is unlikely that a directive with an expansive brief for subsidiary protection would succeed.

The European Parliament's Committee on Citizens' Freedoms and Rights, Justice and Home Affairs has proposed even broader criteria for subsidiary protection, but this may simply be a negotiating strategy to counter further watering down in the final stages. There is not yet general agreement in the European Union that decision makers should consider whether there is a threat of persecution or other unjustified harm from non-state actors when the state is unable or unwilling to provide effective protection. The decision maker must make inquiry whether there is in place 'a system of domestic protection and machinery for the detection, prosecution and punishment of actions that constitute persecution or other serious and unjustified harm'.[16]

The proposed directive denies access to refugee status or subsidiary protection to any national of any member state of the European Union. This universal legal assertion that no one from a neighbouring EU state could ever be a refugee entitled to protection in another EU state may become problematic with the rapid expansion of the Union to include member states whose human rights record is more questionable. The proposed directive also envisages that protection could be provided to an asylum seeker 'by international organisations and stable quasi-State authorities who control a clearly defined territory of sufficient size and stability, and who are able to perform the functions of a government offering protection'.[17]

The Australian government and parliament have been anxious to confine the definition of 'particular social group' when it comes to determining whether someone has a well-founded fear of persecution for a Convention on Refugees reason. The European Commission is proposing a broad definition of 'social group' to include:

> a group which may be defined in terms of certain fundamental characteristics, such as sexual orientation, age or gender, as well as groups comprised of persons who share a common background or characteristic that is so fundamental to identity or conscience that those persons should not be forced to renounce their membership. The concept shall also include groups of individuals who are treated as 'inferior' in the eyes of the law.

Once again, there may be no real prospect of such a broad definition winning approval from the Council of Ministers, but these ideas set the parameters for the policy discussion in Europe. The European Parliament has proposed even wider definitions so that persons suffering persecution because they have AIDS would be guaranteed coverage by the directive.

Unlike Australia, the European Union accepts that there will always be a significant number of onshore persons seeking not just asylum as refugees but also other forms of international protection. Because of the European Convention for the Protection of Human Rights and Fundamental Freedoms (ECHR), member states in the European Union cannot send third-party nationals back home if there is a real prospect that they will face torture or inhuman or degrading treatment or punishment. They must provide applicants with access to the courts.

UK extended leave to remain

The UK government has been worried about the excessive willingness of decision makers to grant extended leave to remain (ELR) to those who are not strictly refugees. Over time, more applicants have been granted ELR than refugee status. In Australia, the minister exercises his humanitarian discretion for failed asylum seekers very rarely. Over the last three years he has exercised the discretion on average in 210 cases out of 2,890 applications a year. In the United Kingdom, ELR has been granted in 25 per cent of cases. ELR has been granted automatically to asylum speakers from countries such as Liberia, Libya and Somalia. The government is now putting a stop to this practice. Home Secretary David Blunkett has said, 'ELR should not be an alternative form of economic migration which acts as a pull factor to the UK.'[18] ELR has now been replaced by 'Humanitarian Protection', which will be granted initially for only three years and not the four years previously available to those with ELR. This new status is to be provided only to those who really need humanitarian protection. The Home Secretary also has the power to grant discretionary leave. For example, he might permit unaccompanied minors to remain until their eighteenth birthday if there were no adequate reception arrangements in place.

The provision of subsidiary protection to those who are not refugees but who are in need of humanitarian assistance has been a continuing problem for first-world countries that receive visitors from countries suffering natural or man-made disasters. Because these disasters are not discriminatory in the harm caused to particular groups, they do not produce refugees. When Labor came to power in the United Kingdom in 1997 after almost two decades in Opposition, it had a mandate for a more generous asylum policy. The then Home Secretary, Jack Straw, made it very clear in the 1998 White Paper *Fairer, Faster and Firmer — A Modern Approach to Immigration and Asylum* that the new Labor government did not want to be seen as a soft touch. Straw was in no doubt 'that large numbers of economic migrants are abusing the system by claiming asylum'.[19] Once the United Kingdom had incorporated the ECHR into its *Human Rights Act 1998*, which came into effect in 2000, people in the United Kingdom gained a legal right not to be returned to situations of torture or cruel, inhuman and degrading treatment. This right was of most relevance to those asylum seekers who could not prove that they were refugees. On 29 November 2002 the Home Office Minister, Beverley Hughes, announced:

> We will be introducing a further robust measure with the ending of ELR. I believe that our use of ELR has encouraged abuse and acted as a pull factor, encouraging economic migrants to apply for asylum in the UK in the belief that they will be given ELR when their asylum claim is rejected. We have already stopped the routine granting of ELR on a country basis and we are now significantly tightening the basis on which leave will be granted to all those who have been refused asylum. We are determined that protection should only be granted to those who really need it – our asylum system is not a short cut to work or settlement in the UK.[20]

In the United Kingdom, there would not have been any problem or question about allowing the East Timorese to remain. The Australian government insisted that most of the 1,800 Timorese would have to depart Australia even though it was the government and not the applicants who were responsible for putting the asylum claims on hold for over a decade. On 17 September 2002 the Home Office set out its policy on removal of long-time stayers to the Home Affairs Select Committee of Parliament:

> We will not normally seek to remove a family group where there are children who have spent in excess of seven years in the UK, or anyone who has been continuously resident here for more than 14 years. Similarly, marriage or a relationship akin to marriage may be a reason to allow someone who does not meet the strict conditions under the Immigration Rules to remain in the United Kingdom.[21]

On these criteria, very few of the East Timorese would be forced to leave Australia. Neither should they be. They would not need to prove that they were still refugees.

Germany's Duldung status

There are three different statuses available to those who succeed with their asylum claim in Germany. There is a small group who obtain the constitutional refugee status having established that they fled political persecution by the state. In 2001, 5.3 per cent of applicants received that status. Until 2003 they had the right to permanent residence, complete freedom of movement and the usual panoply of civil rights. There are then those who obtain Refugee Convention Status under the Aliens Law. In 2001, 15.9 per cent of applicants obtained this status. Prior to 2003 these refugees obtained only a two-year residence permit that was renewable if protection was still warranted. They had to wait eight years for permanent residence. A new migration law has been passed but it has been successfully challenged in the courts because the voting for the legislation was irregular. If the new law is enacted, both these classes of refugee are to receive a three-year residence permit that will be able to be converted to a permanent residence permit if the refugee status is still warranted at the end of the three years.

Then there is the Duldung status. This is almost a non-status. The person is tolerated to remain in Germany for the moment either because there is no practical way of removing this person or because there are humanitarian legal grounds for permitting the person to remain. A grant of Duldung status is a temporary suspension of the decision to deport the person. In 2001, 3.2 per cent of applicants received this tolerance status. There are 230,000 people in Germany with this status. In the past it was usually given when the authorities could not satisfy themselves that the applicant would be safe from torture or cruel and inhuman treatment if returned home. It has also been given when the authorities are unable to deport the person and there is no case for holding the person in detention.

In 2001, 24.4 per cent of the 107,000 cases processed resulted in the grant of some asylum status. If the new law receives approval, those who would have received Duldung status will receive a limited residence permit if they would face torture or inhumane treatment on their return. If they simply cannot be moved out of Germany at this time, they will receive a certificate stating that their deportation is presently suspended. They will receive basic welfare payments. They will not be able to work and some will have to stay in special new accommodation centres that will be like low-security removal centres.

US subsidiary protection

The domestic law of the United States incorporates Article 3 of the Convention Against Torture, which binds the government not to return people to their home country if there they face the risk of torture.

US migration law also makes provision for 'temporary protected status' (TPS), which is granted periodically to the nationals of various trouble spots in the world should they happen to be in the United States at the time. If a person is of a designated nationality, he or she may apply for TPS status. Whereas Mr Sadiq Elmi's only chance of remaining in Australia if he were not a refugee was the minister's gracious exercise of his personal discretion, he would have been entitled to TPS in the United States provided he had not committed any serious offence there. TPS for a country is pronounced by the attorney-general and is usually granted for an initial period of 12–18 months. In the case of Somalia, TPS has been granted since September 1991 and it is renewed each year. The Somalis in the United States have to register anually and seek an employment authorisation document. In July 2002 the attorney-general once again announced an extension of TPS for Somalis until September 2003. He published reasons for his decision:

> There is an ongoing armed conflict within Somalia and, due to such conflict, requiring the return of aliens who are nationals of Somalia (or aliens having no nationality who last habitually resided in Somalia) would pose a serious threat to their personal safety. Furthermore, there exist extraordinary and temporary conditions in Somalia that prevent nationals of Somalia (and aliens having no nationality who last habitually resided in Somalia) from returning home in safety. Finally, permitting nationals of Somalia to remain temporarily in the United States is not contrary to the national interest of the United States.[22]

There are presently ten countries that carry a TPS listing from the attorney-general. TPS can be granted if there is a situation of ongoing armed conflict, disruptive natural disaster, or extraordinary and temporary conditions that make it unsafe for persons to return. If a situation in a country becomes too protracted, the US president has the option of granting deferred enforced departure (DED) pursuant to his constitutional authority to conduct the foreign relations of the United States. DED is granted in the expectation that Congress will then legislate to grant the group permanent residence. DED has been used five times. Currently, nationals of Liberia are designated under DED.

Even if Somalia had not been on the attorney-general's TPS list, Mr Sadiq Elmi, had he been in the United States, would have been brought before an immigration judge for removal and he would have been able to claim protection under Article 3 of the Convention Against Torture. There would then have been a hearing to determine whether he could establish that it was more likely than not that he would be tortured on his removal to Somalia. In order to establish the risk of torture, the applicant must address five elements in the Convention's definition of torture:

- an act by which severe pain or suffering, whether physical or mental, is inflicted
- the act is intentionally inflicted
- for such purposes as obtaining from him or a third person information or a confession, punishing him for an act he or a third person has committed or is suspected of having committed, or intimidating or coercing him or a third person, or for any reason based on discrimination of any kind
- such pain or suffering is inflicted by or at the instigation of or with the consent or acquiescence of a public official or other person acting in an official capacity
- the act does not include pain or suffering arising only from, inherent in or incidental to lawful sanctions.

In March 2002 the US Board of Immigration Appeals had to consider whether open-ended detention of criminal deportees by Haitian authorities could constitute torture. By a majority of 13 to 7, the full panel noted that, though the United States had condemned the Haitian practice of indeterminate detention, such a detention policy 'in itself appears to be a lawful enforcement sanction designed by the Haitian Minister of Justice to protect the populace from criminal acts committed by Haitians who are forced to return to the country after having been convicted of crimes abroad'.[23] The panel conceded that there was evidence 'that isolated acts of torture occur in Haitian detention facilities. However, this evidence is insufficient to establish that it is more likely than not that the respondent will be subject to torture if he is removed to Haiti.'[24] Mr Sadiq Elmi would still have had a difficult time convincing the US Board of Immigration Appeals that he faced a real risk of torture, but he would have been assured of a more transparent, open process in the United States than in Australia.

Conclusions

Article 3 of the Convention Against Torture provides:

1. No State Party shall expel, return ('refouler') or extradite a person to another State where there are substantial grounds for believing that he would be in danger of being subjected to torture.
2. For the purpose of determining whether there are such grounds, the competent authorities shall take into account all relevant considerations including, where applicable, the existence in the State concerned of a consistent pattern of gross, flagrant or mass violations of human rights.

The Australian government continues to claim that it is able to honour the obligations under this Article despite the shortcomings highlighted in the cases of Zhu Qing Ping and Sadiq Elmi. In June 2000 the Senate Legal and Constitutional References Committee recommended that the government provide amendments to Australian migration law 'so as to explicitly incorporate the non-refoulement obligations of the Convention Against Torture and the International Covenant on Civil and Political Rights in domestic law'.[25] The UN Committee Against Torture also expressed its concerns in November 2000 about Australia's 'apparent lack of appropriate review mechanisms for ministerial decisions in respect of cases coming under Article 3 of the Convention'.[26] The Committee recommended that Australia provide 'a mechanism for independent review of ministerial decisions'. The government has remained unmoved, informing the Senate that the current provisions 'allowing for ministerial discretion on humanitarian grounds are adequate to ensure compliance with CAT and ICCPR'. They are not. The minister's personal, non-compellable, non-reviewable discretion is fallible and shrouded in secrecy. Given the government's concern to keep judges away from the process, they should at the very least set up a ministerial advisory group, including community representatives, who can screen cases for the minister. A parliamentary committee should also regularly review the minister's decisions.

The shortcoming in the Australian law and practice has been highlighted by the treatment of the 1,800 East Timorese. There has been no point in requesting most of them to submit to another interview and appeal to the RRT determining whether they are refugees, before the minister then decides to exercise his humanitarian discretion. When people have been kept in legal suspense for years by government delaying decisions, they should be allowed to remain on humanitarian grounds. If there are good humanitarian grounds for allowing a person who is not a refugee to remain in Australia, they should not need to go through the legal charade of applying for refugee status in order to access the minister's humanitarian discretion. When people come from countries that are besieged by humanitarian disaster, they should, as with the US model of Temporary Protected Status, routinely be allowed to remain in Australia until the crisis passes back home. In Australia, we must move beyond the presumption that those who have no refugee claim have no legal rights to remain but only an uncertain opportunity to invoke the minister's gracious discretion. If there were proof that someone would face torture or cruel, inhuman or degrading treatment on return home, that person should be guaranteed a fair and transparent hearing and the opportunity to remain in Australia until the threat has passed.

Though Australia maintains a generous offshore humanitarian program, we have very little opening for humanitarian cases onshore when the applicant is not proved to be a refugee. The only avenue is the minister's s. 417 discretion. The government claims that it is sufficiently attentive to any humanitarian demands. In spite of the department having prepared 9,422 assessments in 2001–2002 to assist the minister, he exercised his personal discretion in favour of an applicant granting a protection visa on only 25 occasions. Labor's Senator Barney Cooney has advocated that Australia should have an onshore humanitarian program. He is right to observe that:

> Section 417 does not constitute a program, a system, an ordered process for dealing with those who claim humanitarian relief from Australia. Nor in my view should it. It ought be used only for the purpose for which it was legislated into law. To have it do more is to put too great a strain on its

proper function and is to give a false response to Australia's obligation to afford humanitarian relief in appropriate circumstances.[27]

The European Union, United Kingdom, Germany and the United States all accept that there is a need to grant subsidiary protection through due process to those persons in great humanitarian need. Australia should do the same. Though each of these countries is getting stricter in setting time limits on residence in these humanitarian cases, they continue to accept that recognised refugees who are granted residence rights should ultimately be allowed to stay permanently. Australia should do the same. There is no need to create a permanent underclass of refugees restricted to a constantly renewed three-year visa with no rights to family reunion or travel simply because they arrived in the first instance without a visa or with a visa obtained using a fraudulent document. A perpetual TPV is punitive and counter-productive.

CHAPTER 8

A warm-hearted, decent international citizen once again

In 1949 the Opposition leader, Mr Robert Menzies, challenged the Chifley Labor government over its proposal to deport an Indonesian family whose mother had married an Australian citizen, Mr John William O'Keefe. The woman had remarried after the death of her first husband who was a Dutchman killed in an air crash while in the service of the Allies during the war. The plea for the children was on the basis that they were still receiving their schooling in Australia. Even the local parish priest, Fr Fitzpatrick, took up their cause from the pulpit. He had performed the nuptials for the mother and Mr O'Keefe and was anxious that her children should receive a Christian education before returning to Indonesia. Harold Holt and Robert Menzies enjoyed taunting immigration minister Arthur Calwell about the case. Calwell spoke in passionate defence of the White Australia policy, telling parliament, 'We can have a white Australia, we can have a black Australia, but a mongrel Australia is impossible and I shall not take the first step to establish precedents which will allow the floodgates to be opened.'[1]

Menzies conceded that there were international criticisms of Australia's migration policy at the time. He urged this advice on the Chifley government:

It is elementary that our immigration policy, firmly as we hold it and clear and absolute as it is, must be wisely and fairly presented to the people of the world so that it may be seen by them, as it should be seen by them if we are sensible people, as a sensible, legitimate national movement of the kind that they well understand themselves and not as a crude, provocative or unreasonable policy. It is our duty to ourselves to handle this policy so that it is presented to the rest of the world in its proper terms and in its true light. That means that it must not only be a sound policy but also that it must be applied by a sensible administration, neither rigid nor peremptory, but wise, exercising judgment on individual cases, always remembering the basic principle but always understanding that harsh administration never yet improved any law but only impaired it, and that notoriously harsh administration raises up to any law hostilities that may some day destroy it.[2]

Governments of first-world countries are under pressure from asylum seekers and from their own electors as they strive to find the balance between the protection of borders and the protection of the asylum seekers who, like the poor, are with us always. Though the boats have stopped coming, we Australians have not found the balance. In the long term, we will need a refugee policy that is workable, decent, affordable and efficient. We need to revise our system for processing onshore asylum applications. We need to be more neighbourly, generous and collaborative with other countries in assisting refugees in countries of first asylum. We need to pull our weight internationally, rather than exporting our problems or keeping them offshore out of sight and out of mind.

The European Union is now trying to formulate common standards and a unified approach to the processing of asylum applications. In Europe, they do not have the luxury of going it alone because methods that deter access to a national territory merely shift the burden from one country to another. It is very unneighbourly behaviour.

We Australians must address our own fears rationally and ensure that we act decently. Compared with the European numbers, ours is a small nut to crack. Is that any reason for us to use a large sledge hammer that would inflict untold damage if used in other places? Our present policy can be posited only on one of two options. Either we want to be so tough that no other country will dare to imitate us and so we will maintain the advantage that asylum seekers will want to try anywhere but here. Or we are happy to lead other countries to a new level of toughness, leaving bona fide asylum seekers more vulnerable in the non-existent queues.

If democracy is about honouring the will of the people and protecting the rights and dignity of all, it is essential that our political leaders respond responsibly to our fears rather than feeding those fears. They should still our fears with policies that are faithful to our values, respecting the integrity of our social institutions. Because of the electoral fervour and the talk-back radio lather about the issue, we have not taken sufficient stock of the damage and cost being inflicted by our present policy. Our policy presumes that we can isolate Australia from the population flows that affect the rest of the world. We think we can stop or control the flow by sending a harsh message. We should rather manage the flow by keeping step with other first-world countries and by maintaining a principled commitment to human rights.

A simple thought experiment highlights the immorality and inequity in world burden-sharing resulting from our policy. Imagine that every country signed the Convention on Refugees and then adopted the Australian policy. No refugee would be able to flee from their country of persecution without first joining the mythical queue to apply for a protection visa. If anyone dared to flee persecution, they would immediately be held in detention (probably for a year or so) awaiting a determination of their claim. All refugees in the world would be condemned to remain subject to persecution or to proceed straight to open-ended, judicially unreviewable detention. The purpose of the Convention on Refugees would be completely thwarted.

Australia has never seen itself as a country of first asylum. Australia has always presumed that it can pull its weight internationally while being free to choose who enters Australia, no matter what the scale of any humanitarian disaster anywhere on the globe. Australian governments have long viewed boat people as secondary movers who could have stopped elsewhere on their journey but who selfishly came on wanting a better economic future. In the 1980s Australian politicians skewed the asylum debate in part because they were caught by surprise when judges said they could review asylum decisions by ministers. The politicians then tried to codify migration law thinking strangely that a more detailed law would reduce the prospect of judges interfering. The asylum debate was skewed even more because our political leaders wanted to strut the world stage with a peace plan for Cambodia. They knew that the peace plan could come unstuck if courts started saying that Cambodians arriving in Australia could be refugees. Onshore detention was conceived. By 1990 the Evans Peace Plan was being hailed as a success, and indeed Cambodian refugees in camps at the Thai border were returned home in 1993, despite the fact that the essential requirement of disarmament had been quietly dropped from the Peace Plan and the civil war smouldered until the final Khmer Rouge surrender in late 1998. Then in 1999 Australia took the high moral ground, rightly castigating Indonesia for its activities in East Timor and wrongly appropriating the role of US deputy sheriff in the region. Once Afghanistan boiled over and Iraq kept ulcerating, it was no coincidence that the fourth wave of boat people from Indonesia was the largest ever. Many of the Afghans and Iraqis who came were among the millions of refugees who had been waiting without let-up in their adjoining countries, Pakistan and Iran. There they found no guaranteed protection. Some, admittedly those with great courage and initiative, took what opportunity they could to seek protection further afield. Others like the young Hazaras quoted in this book fled directly from their home villages seeking protection in the only place the smugglers could offer them at an affordable price. Being Muslim, they gained ready access to Malaysia, which under Dr Mahatir had no brief for maintaining Fortress Australia, and then to Indonesia. Some authorities in Jakarta had little interest in sparing Australia the inconvenience of an increased flow of boat people. The *Tampa* debacle was just waiting to happen.

The 8,000 boat arrivals in Australia in the two years before the *Tampa* steamed in to the migration debate demonstrated that the introduction of the temporary protection visa and the ongoing use of mandatory detention did not constitute a decent and sustainable firebreak. It simply resulted in the women and children more often joining their husbands and fathers on the perilous voyage. Upstream disruption in Indonesia, the tragic loss of life on the SIEV X, the brinkmanship of Operation Relex and the Pacific Solution added elements that constituted a real firebreak. But at what cost? Half of those held on Nauru and Manus have still been proved to be refugees. No one can blame Australian judges for that. The vast majority of those who make the perilous journey in leaky boats, having engaged a people smuggler, are refugees fleeing persecution and the uncertainty of any other protection offered en route. Other countries are not much interested in taking refugees from the Pacific Solution. They rightly regard this caseload as the primary responsibility of the Australian government and those governments that have chosen to benefit financially from this novel, unilateral arrangement. It is problematic for all governments involved when proven refugees are then held in ongoing detention simply because there is nowhere else for them to go. Despite the insistence of Prime Minister Howard that none of the Pacific Solution refugees would come to Australia, more than 300 of them have now settled in Australia because they already had family members here. There was no other humane option.

No boats have reached Australia since the *Tampa* incident. Boat people have been interdicted on the high seas and returned to Indonesia. In the three years to 31 October 2002, 3,830 people had been interdicted, of whom 910 were then classified by the UNHCR as

Reproduced with Bill Leak's permission.

refugees. Australia continues to fund much of the refugee-processing operation in Indonesia. Australia understandably is unwilling to take many of the refugees from Indonesia for resettlement lest their acceptance in Australia be an added incentive for people to come from far-away places to Indonesia seeking asylum with the hope of resettlement in Australia. In three years Australia has taken only 39. Why shouldn't those refugees who reach Indonesia then attempt to reach Australia for real and enduring protection?

It has been too easy for Australian politicians to salve the con-sciences of the nation by telling voters that we do our part by taking 12,000 offshore humanitarian applicants a year. We often overlook the fact that only 4,000 of these are refugees who do not need to have an Australian connection and who may be some of the refugees in greatest need. We have then decided that every successful onshore asylum seeker will take the place of one offshore refugee. This helps to culti-vate the spurious moral argument that we need to be tough on onshore applicants so we can keep places for those offshore in greatest need. The United States makes no such connection. Neither does Canada. Canada takes at least 12,000 offshore applicants a year. We have set our offshore quota at 12,000 for many years. In Canada it has gone as high as 35,000 back in 1989. Having emerged from our largest wave ever of boat people, we then granted 3,885 onshore protection visas in one year in 2001–2002, having processed 11,635 onshore asylum seekers. In 2001 Canada finalised 28,418 onshore asylum claims of whom 13,383 were found to be refugees. These onshore refugees did not take anyone's places. Despite Minister Ruddock's claim that the Australian onshore processing system is soft because of the judges, 47 per cent of Canada's onshore asylum seekers succeeded in 2001 but only 33 per cent succeeded in Australia. With an immigration program twice the size of Australia's, Canada on average has 439 people a day detained in immigration detention. Even putting to one side the man-datory detention of boat people at all stages of their processing, Austra-lia has 835 non-boat people a day in immigration detention. Any foreigner coming to Australia is four times more likely to end up in immigration detention than a foreigner coming to Canada.

Even those of us highly critical of the government's firebreak policy can hope that we can all now enjoy its benefits having endured its cal-

Sydney Morning Herald, 19 November, 2000.
Reproduced with Cathy Wilcox's permission.

lousness. We have the time and the space to design a policy which is
more humane and more consistent with international best practice before the fifth wave of boat people come. Make no mistake: there will be
a fifth wave at some stage. No matter how harsh and punitive our regime for the reception of boat people, it will never match the cruelty of
the regimes that these people are fleeing. When there are mass population flows out of countries gripped by humanitarian disaster, desperate
people will scatter to the four corners of the earth, including Australia.
As no boats are coming at the moment, we can correct those parts of the
firebreak which are unacceptable and unsustainable in the long term
and we can amend our laws and policies to ensure that our approach is
firm but fair. We should especially change those aspects that are highly
punitive without delivering any benefit to the national interest.

If Indonesia were a robust parliamentary democracy, there would be
no prospect of an upstream disruption regime being negotiated on a
wink and a nod with a cheque book and the assurance of silence. Given

the unexplained sinking of SIEV X, it is imperative that our government be more transparent with our parliament about the details of upstream disruption. During peacetime, there is no need for Australian Navy personnel to wait until a boat actually sinks before taking children on board. With no threat to border protection or national sovereignty, children can be safely taken on board a couple of hours before when it is known that the boat is only 'marginally seaworthy'.

No one seriously doubts the adverse effects of long-term detention on children. The government itself has now decided that unaccompanied minors will be released from detention at the earliest opportunity — either into the community on a bridging visa or to an alternative place of detention. The government is now open to alternative housing and detention arrangements for women and children in detention, provided that if there be any adult male in the family at least one adult male remain in detention as security.

Given that detention during the processing of claims has been shown not to be a deterrent to unlawful arrivals, and given that the government for constitutional reasons insists that detention is not punitive nor designed as a deterrent, why have it after the initial health, security and identity phase? The government continues to claim that it is needed so that those denied refugee status or humanitarian residence can be available for removal if they fail in their refugee claim. Detention is not imposed on those persons who apply for asylum in Australia once their short-term visitor visas have expired. Those in detention are far more likely to be found to be refugees because they are. The detention regime for unlawful entrants has impacted most on Afghans, Iraqis and Iranians during the time of the firebreak. Over 90 per cent of the Afghans and Iraqis have been proved to be refugees. Though detention is said to assist with the processing of their claims, we know from the annual statistics of the Refugee Review Tribunal that this is not true. There is no justification for the automatic detention of unlawful non-citizens arriving in Australia claiming asylum.

The existence of a comprehensive visa regime, carrier liability for the carriage of undocumented passengers, and airline liaison officers posted at major airports, together with Australia's geographic isolation, combine to guarantee that no bona fide asylum seeker can turn up in Australia legally and honestly primarily for the purpose of seeking asylum. A lawful asylum seeker has to come here for another purpose and then make the claim for asylum. If the applicant does not come with that other purpose, it will be necessary to fabricate some other purpose. There is only one conceivable case of the totally honest, legal asylum seeker — the person who comes to Australia with a visa for a lawful and bona fide purpose, with no intention of claiming asylum, but who while in Australia learns of a change in circumstances back home, necessitating the lodgment of an asylum claim. Putting this rare case to the side, we need to consider the morality or utility (and not just the political popularity) of treating so differently the two classes of asylum seeker — the unlawful non-citizen who comes transparently claiming that the motivation for travel was to seek asylum, and the lawful non-citizen who claims asylum having gained admission as a tourist, a student, or a business migrant.

Though mandatory detention of unlawful non-citizens had been on the statute books for a decade, it did not in fact deter the stream of boat people that came from Afghanistan and Iraq in 2001. Considering all the other push and pull factors, detention for the period of processing claims is not in fact a deterrent. For constitutional and legal reasons, the government continues to claim that detention is not punitive and not a deterrent. It is not a deterrent in fact, by design or by intention. Then why have detention at all stages of the process rather than simply on admission for security, character, health and identity reasons and on departure because of the likelihood of absconders?

The government used to claim that detention was helpful for the processing of claims. The discrepancies in the appeal rates before the RRT indicate that the primary decision maker is more likely to get the decision wrong if the applicant is in detention rather than living in the community. Also the decision maker is very likely to get the decision wrong if the applicant is an Afghan or Iraqi being held in detention. Detention in an Australian equivalent of Oakington (see Chapter 5) may assist with the processing of claims. Detention in a place like Woomera has been a disincentive rather than incentive to good decision making. Given that most unlawful non-citizens are now held inland in South Australia, it is no longer possible to claim, as did the parliamentary committee back in 1994, that there were benefits in 'placing detainees in a centre which is in reasonable proximity to where most of the boat arrivals first land, and where the remoteness of the location provides a disincentive to abscond from the centre'.[3] Since 1994 we have had the benefit of the research from the United States and the United Kingdom that demonstrates the self-evident proposition that asylum seekers are not very likely to abscond when their asylum claims are still being processed. They have an incentive for maintaining contact with the authorities for as long as there has been no determination of their case. What then is the rationale for such detention, especially when it is so expensive? The tabloid press has even taken to claiming 'Park Hyatt cheaper than Woomera for detainees'.[4] The only possible advantage is that this small cohort of unlawful non-citizens who are ultimately rejected as refugees are on hand for removal at the end of the process. With 60,000 overstayers in the country each year and only 177 removals of boat people in 2000–2001 and 308 removals in 2001–2002, you have to wonder about the cost and the proportionality of the government's response. There were 10,894 removals of persons who had no authority to remain in Australia in 2001–2002. If a handful of those 308 boat people had slipped through the net because they were not held in detention from go to woe on arrival in Australia, there would not have been any appreciable dint made in the government's removal program.

The lack of a coherent rationale for mandatory detention and the proven harm done by mandatory detention are starting to have some political effect in Canberra. Labor, which first instituted mandatory detention during all three phases of (1) health and security screening, (2) assessment of refugee claims, and (3) awaiting removal, has now formally abandoned a policy of mandatory detention for all unvisaed arrivals during the second phase while their claims to refugee status are assessed. Instead Labor will follow other countries such as the United Kingdom and set up supervised hostels in regional communities that will accommodate asylum seekers while their claims are being processed. This is very significant, because it is the second phase of detention that is the longest, doing the gravest harm to everyone, including those who are proved to be refugees.

The Coalition government has also moved slightly. By the end of 2002 there were no longer any women or children being held at Woomera. Minister Ruddock hopes to institute a residential housing project for women and children at Baxter. He has published an instruction stipulating that 'every effort should be made to enable the placement of women and children in a residential housing project as soon as possible. All decisions should be made as expeditiously as possible.'⁵ The minister says that residential housing projects are designed for detainees 'with special needs'. There is still no provision for men 'with special needs' in detention, either to join their families or else to be in separate arrangements. That should be possible in time if there are falling numbers and a utilisation of the spare housing stock at Whyalla.

If there is to be sexually discriminatory, ongoing detention of adult male asylum seekers during the processing phase, they should have access to the courts to apply for bail in the same way as persons charged with criminal offences may apply for bail before conviction. Labor's Senator Barney Cooney has long been an advocate of appropriate judicial review of migration detention. Back in 1994 he told the Joint Standing Committee on Migration:

> The judiciary should have the power to release people held in custody by the Executive, both on the ground that such detention is unlawful and on the ground that, though lawful, it is appropriate in all the circumstances that the person detained be released on reasonable terms.
>
> If the courts were denied the jurisdiction to release people detained under the *Migration Act* for other than a criminal offence it would appear, whatever the reality, that the Parliament lacked proper trust in the Judiciary. This would be an unhappy situation.⁶

Without such judicial discretion, Australian migration detention will continue to be rightly classified by the UN Working Group on Arbitrary Detention as 'mandatory, automatic and indeterminate'.⁷

The lack of coordination for basic service delivery between the Commonwealth and the states continues to cause great harm to detainees in immigration detention facilities. It is irresponsible of the Commonwealth to pursue a detention policy without the full cooperation of the states unless the Commonwealth is in a position to make right the shortfall in the basic government services that must be provided for the protection of those in the government's care. It is imperative that the Commonwealth reaches agreement with the states about the delivery of basic services, including police services.

Those detained during phases one and three should be provided with coordinated police, welfare and medical services. Most persons should be eligible for release from detention during phase two. The Justice for Asylum Seekers (JAS) Alliance has proposed a detailed and workable alternative. Their 'Reception and Transitional Processing System' model draws on the practices in the United Kingdom, the United States, Sweden and New Zealand.[8] They propose that each asylum seeker be allocated a case worker during their detention in phase one. After receiving a psycho-social risk assessment, the asylum seeker would then be presented to an assessment panel that would determine whether the applicant was an ongoing security risk or flight risk. If so, the applicant would be kept in detention during phase two. If not, the applicant would be permitted to live in the community under a Structured Release Program. Some applicants would be required to reside in an open hostel. Others would be under a 'community agency release', with a church or community group providing and supervising their accommodation. Others could be released into the care of a family member who would provide the accommodation. Some could even be released on their own undertaking. If there were a sharp increase in the number of onshore asylum seekers, there may be a case for insisting that applicants live in more remote locations rather than putting added pressure on the infrastructure of western Sydney, the preferred destination for many asylum seekers.

It is difficult to provide accurate cost comparisons between detention and community release. According to JAS, 'it cost approximately $150 million in 2001–2002 to detain 3,500 people in mainland detention centres'. In 2000–2001, the Commonwealth funded the Australian Red Cross to provide welfare assistance to asylum seekers living in the community. 'The scheme assisted 2,691 clients at a cost of $11.185 million.'[9] Detention of an asylum seeker costs $120 a day. Welfare payments (including administration costs) are less than $32 a day.

Despite some stereotypical presentations of the Howard government, Australia has not been alone in tampering with asylum. Australia operates under fewer constraints than many other countries, as it has neither a bill of rights nor any land borders. Though the EU harmonisation process is proceeding with a full-scale, rhetorical commitment to human rights, tampering with asylum by individual states still remains an option in Europe. Though the Europeans have been critical of Australia's excesses, they have been interested to watch the Australian developments, wondering if the excesses might even provide a key to new ways of containing the flow of unlawful entrants across borders. As a variant on the Pacific Solution, the UK Cabinet Office and Home Office circulated a proposal in February 2003 for a 'new global asylum system' which would see five EU countries, perhaps together with Australia or the United States, funding the establishment of regional protection areas where asylum seekers of certain nationalities could be sent for up to six months under UNHCR supervision. For example, Iraqis arriving at Dover could immediately be fingerprinted under the new EURODAC arrangement and then sent to a camp in Turkey. If persons were still in the centres after six months, the proposal was that they would then be processed and if eligible for asylum settled in one of the subscriber countries under a burden-sharing arrangement. The proposal argued that the immediate deportation of asylum seekers to these protection areas should 'rapidly reduce the number of economic immigrants using asylum applications as a migration route', as well as being a deterrent to 'potential terrorists'. Such proposals are posited on the presumption that most persons seeking asylum are not bona fide asylum seekers. Bona fide asylum seekers, being the minority, should then suffer under the same disincentive for settlement in a first-world country. They would be guaranteed basic protection only in some place so unappealing that no one would want to go there unless they really needed protection. If they do need protection, they should expect to put their life on hold until the economic migrants have been sifted from their midst. With asylum applications topping 100,000 in 2002 in the United Kingdom, the UK proposal was presented to the UNHCR as a workable suggestion, with the insistence that there was no desire to dump asylum seekers on poor countries. Except for Australia's unilateral experiments, it is very unlikely that the UK public servants would have dared to float such a proposal.

While we await next year's European reviews of law and policy, our politicians should consider these immediate corrections to our own law and policy:

• Those claiming to be asylum seekers inside our territorial waters, coming from Indonesia, should be escorted for processing by Navy personnel who place the highest importance on the safety of life at sea and who always respond to those in distress.

- Though the government is committed to building an immigration facility on Christmas Island, it should not be used to isolate asylum seekers from advice and assistance. Initial detention at Christmas Island should be limited to identity, health and security checks. There should be resident child protection officers at Christmas Island. No child should be treated as a security risk.
- Those who have passed these checks and not been screened out as bogus claimants should be moved to the mainland on a structured release program for processing of their refugee claim.
- Successful applicants should be given a visa that entitles them to family reunion and international travel as specifically provided in Article 28 of the Convention on Refugees (which Australia is unquestionably breaching). A temporary protection visa should be made permanent if our protection obligations are still invoked three years later.
- We should maintain a commitment to at least 12,000 offshore refugee and humanitarian places each year in our migration program regardless of the number of successful onshore applications for refugee status. There is no reason to think that our onshore caseload will increase exponentially given the improved regional arrangements, the virtual offshore border and the tighter controls within Australian territory.
- We should abolish the Pacific Solution.
- We should abolish the concept of a distinct Australian migration zone given that our processing and appeal system can be sufficiently streamlined to process all comers. Asylum seekers entering Australian territory should be processed by Australian officials and given protection in Australia.
- The government must accept that judicial review of tribunal decisions is essential to maintaining the integrity of an administrative system that operates in private and with persons appointed by the government on short-term contracts.

For too long we Australians have assumed and insisted that we would never be a country of first asylum. In recent years our political leaders have convinced us that anyone turning up on our shores is engaged in secondary movement and therefore not entitled to asylum without penalty for their unlawful entry. Until the *Tampa* incident, our political leaders did concede that there was a moral dilemma between making a humanitarian response to asylum seekers and protecting our borders. By demonising people smugglers and heightening our own security concerns since September 11, we have managed to resolve the dilemma to the satisfaction of most voters, pretending that absolute border security is a precondition to being able to help the real refugees in camps on the other side of the world. We have not resolved any moral dilemma. We have simply reverted to the splendid isolationism of the Australian mantra: being an island nation continent we think we have the luxury and the right to determine who comes here regardless of their immediate entitlement to asylum. Being one of the few western countries without a domestic bill of rights and without a binding international commitment to the protection of human rights, we have gone our own way, scorning those UN bodies and international human rights agencies that demand that we pull our weight. There is a moral dimension to setting limits on how far we might tamper with asylum in our own national interest. It is no answer to say that we close the door on the asylum seeker at our doorstep in order more readily to assist the refugee in the faraway camp.

It is time we once again faced the challenging dilemma of behaving like a humanitarian, decent country while making certain that we do not become just an easy touch for illegal immigrants. In 2001 John Howard and Philip Ruddock found advantage in pretending there was no dilemma, proposing tough new measures against unlawful non-citizens and dressing them up as the response of a thoroughly modern, post-September 11, humanitarian and decent country.

In 2002 the UNHCR presented the prestigious Nansen Refugee Award[10] to Captain Arne Rinnan and the crew of the *Tampa*. At the presentation, Ruud Lubbers, the United Nations High Commissioner for Refugees, expressed deep appreciation of 'the team's noble and principled humanitarian action, and its adherence to the time-honoured code of chivalry at sea'. He acknowledged 'that the manner in which the team fulfilled its international obligations towards people in distress reflected the true spirit and commitment of Fridtjof Nansen'.[11]

When asked about the appropriateness of the award, John Howard saw no need to revise his government's treatment of the *Tampa* and its human cargo. The prime minister said:

> Our quarrel with the *Tampa* was not that they rescued the asylum seekers. Our quarrel was that there should have been a different pattern of conduct after that. So I think the two things are quite consistent. Our position is correct and their humanitarian gesture should be appropriately recognised and I congratulate them.[12]

Except for the intractable stand of the Howard government, the UNHCR would not have been honouring the crew of the *Tampa* with its highest award for assistance to refugees. Insofar as the award was deserved, the actions of the Australian government commensurately fell short of 'noble and principled action'. Captain Rinnan's internationally acknowledged chivalry was demonstrated from the moment he diverted his ship to pick up the asylum seekers, during the stand-off as he approached Christmas Island, and until he discharged the asylum seekers under the supervision of the Australian SAS. Captain Rinnan said, 'I'd do it again. I hope all my seafaring colleagues would do the same thing.'[13] John Howard might do the same again. But if all governments were to deny the *Tampa* permission to land, there would be no grounds for hope. Despite the prime minister's spin on the Nansen Award, there is no reading of the stand-off on the high seas that permits both Rinnan and Howard to sail away with honour.

Fear and isolationism need not defeat us. We can both secure our borders and honour our international humanitarian obligations without terrorising asylum seekers on the high seas, detaining them in the desert, transporting them to Pacific islands, and putting on hold their reunion with family and their new life among us. We must prepare for the fifth and subsequent waves of boat people confident that we can join again those nations who wrestle daily with the dilemma. The *Tampa* has come and gone, and so has the time for tampering with asylum, building non-durable, indecent firebreaks. Many of us would like to return collectively to being 'a warm-hearted, decent international citizen', at home and abroad.

Notes

Introduction

1. Martin Gilbert, *The Holocaust*, Collins, London, 1986, p. 64.
2. Quoted in Annemarie Devereux, *Australia and the Negotiations of the International Bill of Rights (1946–1966)*, PhD thesis, Australian National University, 2001, p. 76.
3. Cablegram 2237, A. Calwell to J. B. Chifley, 30 June 1947, in *Australia and the Postwar World, Documents 1947*, Department of Foreign Affairs and Trade, Canberra, 1995, p. 489.
4. Notes of Discussion in the Office of the Secretary of State for Dominion Affairs, 2 July 1947, in *Australia and the Postwar World, Documents 1947*, Department of Foreign Affairs and Trade, Canberra, 1995, pp. 489–90.
5. Ann-Mari Jordens, *Alien to Citizen*, Allen & Unwin, Sydney, 1997, p. 10.
6. P. Ruddock, 'Ensuring a Fair Go for Those Most in Need', Address to Anglican Synod, 27 July 2001, DIMIA, 2001, p. 10.
7. UNHCR, *Statistical Year Book 2001*, October 2002, p. 64, Table IV.2, 'Asylum Applications, Admission and Pending Cases, 2000–1'.

1 The 1951 Convention on Refugees and the moral complexities of today

1. Article 1 (2), Convention Relating to the Status of Refugees.
2. Article 33 (1).
3. Article 31 (1).

4. In a communication received on 1 December 1967, the Government of Australia notified the Secretary-General of the withdrawal of the reservations to Articles 17 (wage-earning employment), 18 (self-employment), 19 (liberal professions), 26 (freedom of movement) and 32 (expulsion), and, in a communication received by the Secretary-General on 11 March 1971, of the withdrawal of the reservation to paragraph 1 of Article 28 (travel documents) of the Convention.

5. (1962) CPD 752 (HofR), 23 August 1962.

6. Quoted in Neumann, K., 'Asylum Seekers and "Non-Political Native Refugees" in Papua and New Guinea', *Australian Historical Studies*, No. 120, October 2002, p. 364.

7. ibid.

8. Charles A. Price, 'Australia and Refugees 1921–1976', May 1990, pp. 45–46 (unpublished manuscript).

9. N. Viviani, *The Indochinese in Australia 1975–1995: From Boats to Barbecues*, Oxford University Press, Sydney, 1996, p. 6.

10. *Al Masri v. Minister for Immigration & Multicultural & Indigenous Affairs* [2002] FCA 1009 (15 August 2002) para 61.

2 Four waves, *Tampa* and a firebreak

1. Quoted in C. Cameron, *China Communism and Coca-Cola*, Hill of Content, Melbourne, 1980, p. 230.

2. *Sun-News Pictorial*, 22 December 1976, quoted in Nancy Viviani, *The Long Journey*, Melbourne University Press, 1984, p. 70.

3. *Minister for Immigration and Ethnic Affairs v. Mayer* (1985) 157 CLR 290.

4. M. Fraser, 'Address at the Conferral of the Degree of Doctor of Laws', University of Technology Sydney, 29 April 2002, p. 9.

5. *Chan Yee Kin v. Minister for Immigration and Ethnic Affairs* (1989) 169 CLR 379.

6. ibid., p. 389 (Mason CJ).

7. ibid., p. 392.

8. E. Arthur, Director, Asylum Policy Branch, Department of Immigration, 1991, quoted by M Crock, *Immigration and Refugee Law in Australia*, Federation Press, 1998, p. 134.

9. *Weekend Australian*, 21–22 July 1990.

10. European Convention for the Protection of Human Rights and Fundamental Freedoms, Article 5 (1)(f).

11. *Chu Kheng Lim v. Minister for Immigration, Local Government and Ethnic Affairs* (1992) 176 CLR 1 at p. 33 (Brennan, Deane and Dawson JJ).

12. P. Ruddock, Letter to the Editor, *Medical Journal of Australia*, Vol. 176, No. 2, p. 85, 21 January 2002.

13. Quoted in M. Kingston's 'Government on Trial over Persecution', *Canberra Times*, 29 April 1993.

14. ibid.

15. Department of Immigration and Ethnic Affairs, 'Submission to the Joint Standing Committee on Migration Inquiry into Detention Practices', 13 August 1993, p. 16, reported at *Submissions*, Volume 3, S655.

16. N. Viviani, *The Indochinese in Australia 1975–1995: From Boats to Barbecues*, Oxford University Press, 1996, p. 27.

17. Quoted in P. Mares, *Borderline*, 2nd edition, 2002, University of New South Wales Press, Sydney, p. 122.

18. (2001) CPD 30235 (HofR), 27 August 2001.

19. 'Note Verbale to the Royal Norwegian Embassy', Canberra, Department of Foreign Affairs and Trade, Canberra, 28 August 2001.

20. J. Howard, (2001) CPD (HofR) 30517, 29 August 2001.

21. 'MS *Tampa* — Refugees at Sea', SBS Television, 4 March 2003.

22. ibid.

23. J. Howard, (2001) CPD (HofR), 30235, 29 August 2001.

24. Interview with Camilla Cowley, 24 January 2003.

25. 'The Hazara People of Afghanistan — A Century of Persecution', compiled by Hussain Razai & Fr Tony Pearson, Otherway Centre, Adelaide, 2002, p. 12.

26. W. Maley, 'Security, People-Smuggling, and Australia's New Afghan Refugees', *Australian Journal of International Affairs*, (2001) Vol. 55, p. 357.

27. Sha Hussain Hassani's interview with Camilla Cowley, 23 January 2003.

28. Atiq Hashemi's interview with Camilla Cowley, 23 January 2003.

29. Mortaza Ali Askary's interview with Camilla Cowley, 25 January 2003.

30. Mohammed Reza Jaffari's interview with Camilla Cowley, 23 January 2003.

31. Interview with Camilla Cowley, 25 January 2003.

32. Interview with Camilla Cowley, 23 January 2003.

33. Radio 2GB, Sydney, 5 February 2003.

34. Letter to author, 22 August 2002.

35. *Hansard*, Joint Standing Committee on Migration Regulations, 10 March 1992, p. 1629.

36. UNHCR, *Guidelines on Applicable Criteria and Standards Relating to the Detention of Asylum Seekers*, para. 4.

3 Border control

1. J. Howard, 'Radio interview with Neil Mitchell', 3AW, 17 August 2001.
2. Rear Admiral Smith, Transcript of Evidence, Select Committee on a Certain Maritime Incident, p. 504, quoted in *Report*, Select Committee on a Certain Maritime Incident, Senate, Canberra, October 2002, p. 26.
3. Transcript of Evidence, Select Committee on a Certain Maritime Incident, p. 457.
4. Quoted in the *Australian*, 8 October 2001.
5. G. F. Smith, Letter to the Editor, *Sydney Morning Herald*, 15 July 2002.
6. This suspected illegal entry vessel had not been allocated a number. That is why it is referred to as SIEV X.
7. *R v. Uxbridge Magistrates Court, Ex Parte Adimi* CO/2533, 3007; 29 July 1999.
8. House of Lords, *Hansard*, 23 January 2002, column 1462.
9. House of Commons, *Hansard*, 2 December 2002, column 614.
10. House of Commons, *Hansard*, 24 April 2002, column 341–42.
11. A. Schoenholtz, 'Aiding and Abetting Persecutors', *Georgetown Immigration Law Journal* (1993), Vol. 7, p. 71.
12. US Newswire, 29 July 1992.
13. *Washington Post*, 13 November 1992.
14. *Sale v. Haitian Centers Council* (1993) 509 US 155 at p. 165; 113 S. Ct. 2549.
15. ibid., pp. 207–8.
16. 'Safety Zones: Executive Summary', UNHCR RefWorld Database, Legal Information Section (1998), p. 2.
17. 'Summary Record of the 20th Meeting of the Ad Hoc Committee on Statelessness and Related Problems', 1 February 1950, 1st Session at 11–12, UN Doc. E/AC.32/SR.20 (1950).
18. *Sale v. Haitian Centers Council* (1993) 509 US 155 at p. 183; 113 S. Ct. 2549.
19. A. C. Helton, *The Price of Indifference*, Oxford University Press, Oxford, 2002, p. 300.

4 Reception and detention of unauthorised asylum seekers in Australia

1. Regulation 2.20 (9)(c), Migration Regulations 1994.
2. Guideline 3, UNHCR, Revised Guidelines on Applicable Criteria and Standards Relating to the Detention of Asylum Seekers, February 1999.
3. (1992) CPD (HofR) 2372, 5 May 1992.
4. Department of Immigration and Ethnic Affairs, 'Submission to the Joint

Standing Committee on Migration Inquiry into Detention Practices', 13 August 1993, p. 16, reported at *Submissions*, Volume 3, S655.

5. Joint Standing Committee on Migration, *Hansard*, 13 October 1993, p. 969.

6. ibid., p. 19 at S658.

7. ibid., p. 22 at S661.

8. ibid. p. 27 at S666.

9. M. Sullivan, Joint Standing Committee on Migration, *Hansard*, 13 October 1993, p. 1008.

10. Joint Standing Committee on Migration, *Hansard*, 13 October 1993, p. 965.

11. ibid., p. 965.

12. M. Sullivan, Joint Standing Committee on Migration, *Hansard*, 13 October 1993, pp. 995–96.

13. ibid., p. 994.

14. ibid., p. 995.

15. ibid., p. 1000.

16. Advice from Henry Burmester, 25 August 1993, 'Detention and Human Rights', attached to Submission 97 to Joint Standing Committee on Migration Inquiry into Detention Practices, S997.

17. ibid., S998.

18. Joint Standing Committee on Migration Inquiry Into Detention Practices, *Hansard*, 12 October 1993, pp. 783–84.

19. ibid., p. 785.

20. This statement was quoted with approval by Minister Ruddock in Parliament, (2002) CPD (HofR) pp. 293–94, 19 February 2002.

21. UNHCR, Conclusions of the Executive Committee, No. 44, 1986, and reiterated in Conclusion 55 of 1989, and reaffirmed in Conclusion 85 of 1998.

22. Commission on Human Rights, 'Situation Regarding Immigrants and Asylum-Seekers', Principles 3 & 7, Annex II, Deliberation No. 5, E/CN.4/2000/4, 28 December 1999.

23. Joint Standing Committee on Migration, *Asylum, Border Control and Detention*, 1994, p. 147.

24. ibid., p. 154.

25. *A v. Australia*, Communication No. 560/1993, Human Rights Committee, CCPR/c/59/D/560/1993, 30 April 1997.

26. Joint Standing Committee on Migration, *Asylum, Border Control and Detention*, 1994, p. 192.

27. Department of Immigration and Multicultural and Indigenous Affairs,

Interpreting the Refugees Convention — an Australian Contribution, 2002, p. 135.

28. Senate Legal and Constitutional Committee, 17 September 2002, p. 253.

29. Human Rights Watch, *By Invitation Only: Australian Asylum Policy*, Vol. 14, No. 10 (c), December 2002, p. 36.

30. Statement by R. Lubbers to the European Union Justice and Home Affairs Council, Copenhagen, 13 September 2002.

31. ibid.

32. 'False Refugees and Misplaced Compassion', *Quadrant*, October 2002, p. 2.

33. The MOU on child protection with the South Australian Department of Human Services (Family and Youth Services) was not signed until 6 December 2002. The MOU on education was not signed until 17 December 2002.

34. The names of the mother and son are omitted.

35. Letter to author, 22 August 2002.

36. Letter to author, 17 February 2003.

37. This budget item covers the provision of services on Nauru, Manus Island, Christmas Island and Cocos (Keeling) Island.

38. Email of Ann Duffield to author, 20 March 2002.

39. Select Committee on a Certain Maritime Incident, *Hansard*, 1 May 2002, p. 1411.

40. Guideline 1, UNHCR, Revised Guidelines on Applicable Criteria and Standards Relating to the Detention of Asylum Seekers, February 1999.

41. Letter to author, 22 August 2002.

42. Response of the Office of the United Nations High Commissioner for Refugees to the Senate, Legal and Constitutional Committee request for comments on the Migration Legislation Amendment (Further Border Protection) Bill 2002, paras 26–27.

43. Recommendation B, Final Act of the United Nations Conference of Plenipotentiaries on the Status of Refugees and Stateless Persons, 28 July 1951.

44. Letter to author, 22 August 2002.

45. E/CN.4/2003/8/Add.2, page 7, para 15.

46. (2002) CPD 3349 (HofR), 6 June 2002.

47. Australian Government Comments on the Advance Copy of the Report of the Working Group on Arbitrary Detention, October 2002, p. 7.

48. Lord Steyn, *Ex parte Daly* [2001] UKHL 26 at para. 27, adopting the test set down by Lord Clyde in the Privy Council in *de Freitas v. Permanent*

Secretary of Ministry of Agriculture, Fisheries, Lands and Housing [1999] 1 AC 69 at p. 80.

49. DIMIA, 'Australia Not Alone in Detention Stance', in *UNHCR Discussion Paper* No. 2, 2002, UNHCR Regional Office for Australia, New Zealand, Papua New Guinea and the South Pacific, p. 7.

50. Question on Notice, (2002) CPD P4858 (HofR), 19 August 2002.

51. *Age*, 18 February 2003.

52. Letter to the editor, Marion Le, *Canberra Times*, 22 February 2003.

5 Reception and detention in Europe and the United States

1. K. Kopp, 'Europe — Quo Vadis? The Status Quo of the European Policies on Asylum and Migration', International Conference: The Baltic Sea as an Escape Route, 2002, pp. 12–13.

2. Article 7.2, Draft Directive Laying Down Minimum Standards on the Reception of Applicants, proposal for a Council Directive submitted by the Commission of European Communities, 3 April 2001, COM (2001) 181 final.

3. Article 7.2., Council Directive 2003/9/EC Laying Down Minimum Standards for the Reception of Asylum Seekers, Official Journal of the European Union L 31/20, 6 February 2003.

4. Article 13(2).

5. Article 16(2).

6. *EU Institutions Press Release*, Brussels, Memo/02/300, 19 December 2002.

7. UK Parliament, Select Committee on Home Affairs, *Minutes of Evidence*, 18 September 2002, Question 59.

8. UK Parliament, Select Committee on Home Affairs, *Uncorrected Evidence*, 17 September 2002, para. 88.

9. ibid.

10. European Council on Refugees and Exiles (ECRE), 'Taking Stock of the Harmonisation Process at the End of the Danish Presidency', 19 December 2002, p. 3.

11. Section 55(5) of the *Nationality, Immigration and Asylum Act 2002*.

12. *The Guardian*, 19 February 2003.

13. ibid.

14. *The Queen on the Application of Q & others v. Secretary of State for the Home Department* [2003] EWCA Civ 364.

15. Quoted in Bail for Immigration Detainees (BID), *Immigration Detention in the UK*, September 2002, p. 22.

16. Tina Heath & Rachel Hill, *Asylum Statistics United Kingdom 2001*,

Home Office, Research Development and Statistics Directorate, 31 July 2002, p. 1.

17. Bail for Immigration Detainees (BID), *Immigration Detention in the UK*, September 2002, p. 18.

18. *R v. Secretary of State for the Home Department Ex Parte Saadi and Others* [2002] UKHL 41 at para. 21 (Lord Slynn of Hadley).

19. ibid., paras 45, 47.

20. Quoted in Bail for Immigration Detainees (BID), *Immigration Detention in the UK*, September 2002, p. 41.

21. Letter of Lord Filkin, Parliamentary Under Secretary of State for the Home Office to the Parliamentary Joint Committee on Human Rights, 2 July 2002.

22. House of Commons, *Hansard*, 24 April 2002, column 359.

23. UK Parliament, Select Committee on Home Affairs, *Minutes of Evidence*, 18 September 2002, Question 57.

24. Mr Oliver Letwin, House of Commons, Hansard, 2 December 2002, column 613.

25. Vera Institute of Justice, 'Testing Community Supervision for the INS: An Evaluation of the Appearance Assistance Program', Volume 1, 2000, pp. 32–3.

26. World News USA, ' Hope for Speedy Release of Haitian Refugees Fades', 16 December 2002.

27. INS Statement, 'INS Announces Notice Concerning Expedited Removal', 8 November 2002.

28. DIMIA, 'Australia Not Alone in Detention Stance', UNHCR Discussion Paper, No. 2, 2002, Canberra, p. 7.

29. 'Agenda for Protection', A/AC.96/965/Add.1, p. 8.

30. 'Draft Conclusion on Reception of Asylum Seekers in the Context of Individual Asylum Systems', Conc.2/Rev.1, 23 August 2002, p. 2.

6 Courts and the adjudication of asylum claims

1. UNHCR, *Handbook on Procedures and Criteria for Determining Refugee Status*, HCR/IP/4/Eng.Rev.1, Geneva, 1988, p. 46.

2. (1989) CPD 922 (S), 5 April 1989.

3. Joint Committee on Migration Regulations, *Hansard*, 10 March 1992, pp. 1601–2.

4. ibid., p. 1612.

5. 'Text of Statement Made by Chief Justice Black of the Federal Court of Australia', NAAV of 2001 v. MIMIA (N265 of 2002), NABE of 2001 v.

MIMIA (N282 of 2002), Ratumaiwai v. MIMIA (N399 of 2002), Turcan v. MIMIA (V225 of 2002), MIMIA v. Wang (S84 of 2002), 3 June 2002.

6. Sir Gerard Brennan, 'The Rule of Law and the Separation of Powers in Australia', Australian Studies Centre, University of Indonesia, 2 July 2002, p. 20.

7. *Plaintiff S157/2002 v. Commonwealth of Australia* [2003] HCA 2, 4 February 2003.

8. ibid., para 26.

9. ibid. para. 37.

10. ibid., para. 67.

11. *Re Minister for Immigration and Multicultural and Indigenous Affairs; Ex parte Applicants S134/2002*, [2003] HCA 1 at paras 82–85, 4 February 2003.

12. *Plaintiff S157/2002 v. Commonwealth of Australia* [2003] HCA 2 at para. 98, 4 February 2003.

13. ibid., para. 174.

14. Martin Ferguson (1997) CPD (HofR) 8278, 24 September 1997.

15. Philip Ruddock told Parliament, 'The privative clause is one that we believe will work. We have had opinions from very eminent counsel, admittedly — two distinguished former Attorneys-General, Tom Hughes and Bob Ellicott, from Richard Tracey, David Bennett and Dennis Rose. They tell me that it is constitutional and they tell me that it is legal.' (1997) CPD (HofR) 8304–5, 24 September 1997.

16. Legal and Constitutional Legislation Committee, Senate, *Hansard*, 29 January 1999, L&C 50.

17. (1998) CPD (HofR) 1135, 2 December 1998. Sir Gerard Brennan is the author's father.

18. DIMIA Fact Sheet 68, 'Temporary Protection Visa Holders Applying for Further Protection', 13 February 2003.

19. Legal and Constitutional Legislation Committee, Senate, *Hansard*, 29 January 1999, L&C 64.

20. (1997) CPD (HofR) 8304, 24 September 1997.

21. Department of Human Services, Family and Youth Services, *Social Work Assessment Report on the Bakhtyari Family*, 9 August 2002, p. 3.

22. *Canberra Times*, 2 August 2002. Ellis later wrote to the lawyers apologising for his publishing activity. His letter of apology was quoted at length in Piers Akerman's column in the *Daily Telegraph*, 17 December 2002: 'My going into Woomera may have harmed your cause and I am sorry. I quickly became a devious undercover journalist, sniffing about for scandals in the usual way. Members of your team were very upset, I know, and

conveyed to me in some distress and rage that my breach of trust might wreck your efforts to help the Bakhtyaris to their freedom. I said I believed, but I wasn't sure, the publicity would hasten their release. I emphasised that I wasn't sure, but made what I called "a political judgment" in acting as I did, illegally and sensationally.' The lawyers presume that DIMIA officers leaked the letter to the media.

23. Usually RRT decisions are not published in a form that permits identification of the applicant. But in this case, the High Court reproduced part of the decision in its judgment, *Re Minister for Immigration and Multicultural and Indigenous Affairs; Ex parte Applicants S134/2002* [2003] HCA 1 at para. 6, 4 February 2003.

24. Joint Standing Committee on Migration, *Hansard*, 13 October 1993, p. 1017.

25. Legal and Constitutional Legislation Committee, Senate, *Hansard*, 29 January 1999, L&C 49.

26. M. McHugh, 'Tensions Between the Executive and the Judiciary', Australian Bar Association Conference, Paris, 10 July 2002, p. 7.

27. Letter to author, 3 February 2003.

28. Addendum by Senator Barney Cooney, *Asylum, Border Control and Detention*, Joint Standing Committee on Migration, February 1994, p. 197.

29. *SBBK v. Minister for Immigration & Multicultural & Indigenous Affairs* [2002] FCA 565 (10 May 2002), paras 29–30.

30. *Minister for Immigration and Multicultural Affairs v. Khawar* (2002) ALR 574.

31. ibid., p. 582.

32. Medical Report, 28 June 2002, provided to author by applicant and quoted in letter to Mr Ruddock, 31 July 2002.

33. Article 17.1, COM (2002) 326 final/2, 3 July 2002.

34. Section 94(7) of the *Nationality, Immigration and Asylum Act 2002*.

35. *Zadvydas v. Davis* No. 99–7791, 28 June 2001, (2001) 533 US 701.

36. *Jackson v. Indiana* (1972) 406 US 715 at p. 738.

37. Breyer J, *Zadvydas v. Davis* No. 99–7791, 28 June 2001, Section IIIA.

38. Merkel J, *Al Masri v. Minister for Immigration and Multicultural and Indigenous Affairs* [2002] FCA 1009 at para. 38.

39. Bidoons are stateless persons from Kuwait.

40. *Minister for Immigration & Multicultural & Indigenous Affairs v. Al Masri* [2003] FCAFC 70 (15 April 2003), para. 136.

41. ibid., para. 155.

7 Refugee and humanitarian status

1. Special Benefit (paid at Newstart rates but subject to a strict means test), Rent Assistance, Maternity and Family Allowance, Family Tax Payment.
2. Para 13.1.
3. *Age*, 7 February 2003.
4. P. Ruddock, Migration Series Instruction, MSI 225, 31 March 1999.
5. *Surinakova v. Minister for Immigration, Local Government and Ethnic Affairs* (1991) 26 ALD 203 at p. 205 (Lee J).
6. Senate Legal and Constitutional References Committee, *A Sanctuary Under Review*, June 2000, p. 296.
7. 'Government Response to the Senate Legal and Constitutional References Committee Report: A Sanctuary Under Review', 8 February 2001.
8. Para 6.5, Communication No. 120/1998, 17 November 1998.
9. Committee Against Torture, 25th Session, 13–24 November 2000.
10. (2002) CPD 4231 (HofR), 24 June 2002.
11. W Gibbons, Evidence to Joint Standing Committee on Migration Regulations, 3 July 1991, p. 1344.
12. (1998) CPD P890 (HofR), 2 December 1998.
13. Quoted in P. Mares, *Borderline*, 2nd edition, University of New South Wales Press, Sydney, 2002, p. 217.
14. Commission of the European Communities, *Proposal for a Council Directive on Minimum Standards for the Qualification and Status of Third Country Nationals and Stateless Persons as Refugees or as Persons Who Otherwise Need International Protection*, COM (2001) 510 Final, Article 5.2.
15. ibid., Article 21.2.
16. ibid., Article 9.2.
17. ibid., Article 9.3.
18. D. Blunkett, 'We are a haven for the persecuted, but not a home to liars and cheats', *The Times*, 7 October 2002, Comment, p. 18.
19. Preface, *Fairer, Faster and Firmer — A Modern Approach to Immigration and Asylum*, UK Parliament, Cm 4018, 27 July 1998, p. i.
20. Home Office Press Release, 'Home Office Publishes Latest Asylum Statistics — Robust New Measure to Tackle Asylum Abuse Announced', 332/2002, 29 November 2002.
21. Home Office, Memorandum Submitted to Home Affairs Select Committee Inquiry into Asylum and Immigration, 17 September 2002, para. 31.
22. Department of Justice, Immigration and Naturalization Service, Federal Register: 26 July 2002 (Vol. 67, No. 144) pp. 48950–52.
23. *In re J-E*, 23 I&N Dec. 291 at p. 300 (BIA 2002).

24. ibid., p. 303.
25. Senate Legal and Constitutional References Committee, *A Sanctuary Under Review*, June 2000, p. 60.
26. 'Concluding Observations of the Committee Against Torture: Australia', 21 November 2000, A/56/44, para. 52.
27. Senate Legal and Constitutional References Committee, *A Sanctuary Under Review*, June 2000, p. 347.

8 A warm-hearted, decent international citizen once again

1. (1949) 201 (pt 1) CPD 66 (HofR), 9 February 1949.
2. ibid. pp. 67–68.
3. Joint Standing Committee on Migration, *Asylum, Border Control and Detention*, AGPS, Canberra, February 1994, p. 192.
4. *Sun-Herald*, 22 December 2002, p. 24.
5. Migration Series Instruction 371.
6. Joint Standing Committee on Migration, Asylum, Border Control and Detention, February 1994, pp. 195–96.
7. Report of the Working Group on Arbitrary Detention, Visit to Australia, E/CN.4/2003/8/Add.2, p. 19.
8. Justice for Asylum Seekers (JAS) Alliance, *Detention Reform Working Group, Alternative Approaches to Asylum Seekers: Reception and Transitional Processing System*, June 2002.
9. ibid., p. 12.
10. In 1954 the UNHCR established the Nansen Refugee Award to promote global interest in refugees, and to keep alive the spirit of Fridtjof Nansen, the first high commissioner for refugees in the League of Nations period. The award was instituted in the belief that an honour named after Nansen, and given for outstanding service to refugees, would help to focus attention on their suffering and increase international support for efforts to meet their needs. Sir Tasman Heyes who was head of the Australian Department of Immigration from 1946 until 1961 was presented with the Nansen Award in 1962. Nansen once wrote: 'Never stop because you are afraid — you are never so likely to be wrong. Never keep a line of retreat: it is a wretched invention. The difficult is what takes a little time; the impossible is what takes a little longer.' (*The Listener*, 14 December 1939)
11. Statement by Mr Ruud Lubbers, United Nations High Commissioner for Refugees, at the Nansen Refugee Award Ceremony, Oslo, 20 June 2002.
12. J. Howard, *AM*, ABC Radio, 20 March 2002.
13. 'MS *Tampa* — Refugees at Sea', SBS Television, 4 March 2003.

Index